Multi-Dimensional
EDUCATION

We would like to thank our wives, children, and many colleagues for all of their support and inspiration on this project. We would also like to thank the educational agencies, school systems, and educators that have allowed us the opportunity to work with them.

Multi-Dimensional
EDUCATION

A Common Sense Approach
to Data-Driven Thinking

**Michael W.
Corrigan** | **Doug
Grove** | **Philip F.
Vincent**

CORWIN
A SAGE Company

CORWIN
A SAGE Company

FOR INFORMATION:

Corwin
A SAGE Company
2455 Teller Road
Thousand Oaks, California 91320
(800) 233-9936
Fax: (800) 417-2466
www.corwin.com

SAGE Ltd.
1 Oliver's Yard
55 City Road
London EC1Y 1SP
United Kingdom

SAGE India Pvt. Ltd.
B 1/I 1 Mohan Cooperative Industrial Area
Mathura Road, New Delhi 110 044
India

SAGE Asia-Pacific Pte. Ltd.
33 Pekin Street #02-01
Far East Square
Singapore 048763

Acquisitions Editor: Arnis Burvikovs
Associate Editor: Desirée A. Bartlett
Editorial Assistant: Kimberly Greenberg
Production Editor: Cassandra Margaret Seibel
Copy Editor: Alan Cook
Typesetter: C&M Digitals (P) Ltd.
Proofreader: Susan Schon
Indexer: Maria Sosnowski
Cover Designer: Rose Storey
Permissions Editor: Karen Ehrmann

Printed in the United States of America.

Library of Congress Cataloging-in-Publication Data

A catalog record of this book is available from the Library of Congress.

978-1-4129-9259-6

This book is printed on acid-free paper.

11 12 13 14 15 10 9 8 7 6 5 4 3 2 1

Contents

Preface

There is not another set of professionals that we respect and appreciate more than educators. Beyond a few other civil servants such as police officers and our military, there are few professionals who work as hard as educators, provide such an essential service to society, and receive so little in compensation and gratitude. It takes an amazing individual to become and remain an outstanding educator. It takes even more sacrifice and commitment to become and remain an educational and instructional leader. Thank you for all that you do! We hope the information we provide in this book can help you in many ways to support your efforts and increase your effectiveness.

We (the authors) are former K–12 educators and administrators. We are now professors of educational psychology, research, and leadership, and we know through practice and research that many factors impact and embody a student's ability to achieve academically as well as socially and ethically. The current education system, however, relies heavily on a few numbers (e.g., standardized achievement scores) to measure academic achievement. Research and common sense suggest that these numbers rarely ever accurately highlight the array of admirable efforts put forth by educators that benefit students. We believe that looking at isolated test scores can only provide a minimal understanding of the many possible reasons for the students' levels of achievement. *High achievement is a worthy goal, but knowing how best to improve achievement is even better.* Schools are complex organizations, and to understand them more completely, meaningful and useful data must be captured and connected from more than one source and on more than one variable. This is the basic logic behind Multi-Dimensional Education.

We see the education provided within schools as a system that has many parts. It is the sum of these parts that create the synergy needed to help students and teachers succeed. Some of these parts you have more control over than others. Some of these parts (e.g., finance) you might have no control over. But remember, it is the sum of the parts that create the synergy needed to generate the energy to improve. And if we can more accurately monitor the functionality of the more meaningful parts and more closely assess the impact they are having, the better chance we have to offset the possible negative impact. We do this by having you focus on seven dimensions of education that have been linked to highly effective schools by more than 40 years of research. The Multi-Dimensional Education approach provides you with a more comprehensive understanding of the *systemic* efforts of your school. By adapting your school improvement efforts to use these seven dimensions of data to address and improve your school's curriculum, community, climate, and character (what we refer to as the 4Cs), your efforts can result in greater academic success for students and career satisfaction for educators.

A Framework for Data-Informed Success

If you believe that accountability and data-driven decision making need to be based upon much more than student achievement test scores, then you will find this book of interest. If you want to collect a body of evidence in your school that can help you actually identify what needs to be addressed in order to increase both achievement test scores and other measures of success such as graduation rates and retention of highly effective teachers, then the Multi-Dimensional Education process this book explains will be of even more interest. This book provides educational leaders at the school level with a framework for collecting, organizing, and utilizing seven dimensions of *data* to truly *drive* improvement efforts in the right direction. As the research, practices, and strategies we will share with you show, there are seven dimensions of data that can help you become more successful at using data to drive school improvement and turn around persistently low-performing schools.

As you will see, these dimensions are not new. You have thought about them and discussed them before. Many of you, however, may not have considered assessing the seven dimensions or organizing existing data under them. And despite decades of research showing how success is reliant upon these seven dimensions, most educators have not connected the evidence from each dimension to guide achievement. As we emphasize throughout the book, it is not about measuring whether you are the best or most proficient school. It is not about measuring how far you are from becoming the best. *It is about measuring what you need to know and fix in order to be the best.*

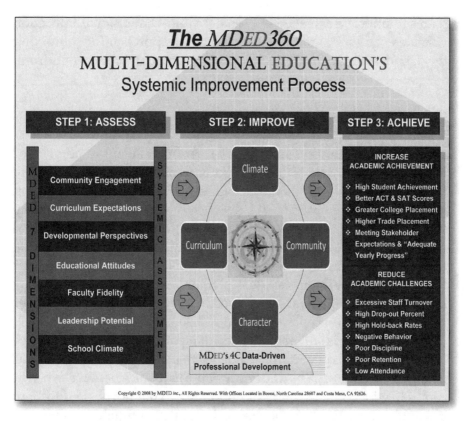

Whether you like the term or not, the bottom line is that educators are now expected to be *data-driven*. Regardless of whether you would rather call it *data-aware* or *data-informed*, unfortunately for many this expectation for using data often does not come with an adequate amount of meaningful data to consider and the guidance needed to actually use such data to steer school improvement efforts. In order to bring about successful and, more importantly, long-lasting improvements in academic achievement, decreases in academic challenges, and higher levels of teacher effectiveness, educators need greater support in developing a framework to make data-driven decisions. This book will provide you with the support, examples, and framework needed to do it right.

By organizing your school's data under the seven dimensions most often associated with highly effective schools and applying this data to improve the 4Cs of education, Multi-Dimensional Education (MDed) can help you develop a more robust and fair growth model that your educators can use to assess, improve, and achieve. Instead of focusing on a *systematic* approach to education like other books that have you focus on improving a certain area or using achievement scores to improve achievement scores, Multi-Dimensional Education provides you with a more holistic systemic approach for connecting the data-driven pieces needed to solve the accountability conundrum.

Why Did We Write This Book?

To answer this question simply: Whether others want to admit it or not, we believe that a number of parts of our education system are broken. The way we assess our success and base such success on achievement score proficiency is short-sighted, to say the least. Many schools are not reaching their full potential; we must develop a better system to fix the flaws. If a strict focus on improving the curriculum, raising the standards, and fixing the achievement tests has not helped to significantly raise our test scores, improve our international rankings, recruit and retain more qualified teachers, and graduate a higher percentage of well-prepared students, then common sense would tell us that the *system* is still in great need of repair. There is an abundance of qualitative and quantitative evidence that needs to be added to our data-driven efforts. Why did we write this book? Because when it comes to education, and more importantly to data-driven education, it would appear that common sense is not that common anymore.

In the United States, more than a third of new teachers leave the profession within 3 years of entering it. Every 5 years, half of them must be replaced (National Commission on Teaching and America's Future, 2008). Canada is experiencing a similar problem, with 27% of new teachers leaving within 3 years (Government of Ontario, 2005). Additionally, a great number of our most experienced teachers are taking early retirement or leaving to pursue work in another field. Many of these once-inspired educators are leaving because they feel under-supported, unappreciated, and underpaid. They also report concern with student behavior problems. A 2008 study showed that the cost of per teacher turnover ranges from $4,000 in rural districts to $17,000 in large urban districts (National Commission on Teaching and America's Future, 2008). This trend of losing educators is unfortunate; to correct it we must get beyond a strict focus on using student achievement scores as our indicator of success. We must also focus on better assessing how to support and better prepare our teachers.

Meanwhile, as the exodus of educators progresses, every 9 seconds in America a student becomes a dropout (Lehr, Johnson, Bremer, Cosio, & Thompson, 2004). It's sad but true that only about two thirds of all students nationally who enter ninth grade will graduate with regular high school diplomas four years later (Orfield, 2004; Swanson, 2004). Our education system is producing millions of young people who are degreeless and ill-equipped to compete in today's workforce and economy. In the 2006 High School Survey of Student Engagement, 24% of students who have considered dropping out of high school reported that "No adults in the school care about me" (Yazzie-Mintz, 2007, p. 5). That means that in a class of 20 students about 5 feel this way. Additionally, 73% didn't like school, 61% didn't like the teachers, and 60% did not see value in the work they were being asked to do. One significant reason students drop out of school is that they lose interest and motivation because the curriculum does not seem to have a real-world application. A 2006 poll by Peter D. Hart Research Associates, Inc., of California ninth and tenth graders considered at risk found that 6 in 10 respondents were not motivated to succeed in school (Bridgeland, DiIulio, & Burke Morison, 2006). Of those students, more than 90% said they would be more engaged in their education if classes helped them acquire skills and knowledge relevant to future careers. But it is not just the potential dropouts that are expressing concern. According to the Survey of Student Engagement, 50% of all students report being bored every day, while 58% report that the reason they come to school is because it is the law (Yazzie-Mintz, 2007).

These are not good signs for the future success of education. Common sense would suggest that a broader focus on developing the whole child, a focus that gets beyond preparing for a test that students see as somewhat meaningless to graduating or preparing for adult life might result in increasing motivation and positive feelings toward school. If research shows that motivation and feelings toward school consistently account for 20% of the reason a student does well or does not do well, then common sense would tell us that if we increase motivation and positive feelings toward school we increase achievement. It's not just about increasing a student's content knowledge or ability to think critically. We must find better ways to energize our students, educators, and parents to become a part of something different and more positive. The fact is that achievement scores do not help us measure the true success or failure of teachers or school leadership (Baker et al., 2010). We would also venture to say that achievement scores rarely measure all that a student has gained from teachers. As many learned in their classroom assessment courses, the way teachers assess students' learning influences what and how the students actually learn in the classroom. This same concept applies to how we assess schools. The way we assess school performance influences performance. Because an abundance of data supports these facts, it is rarely argued that we can't do a better job of educating our future citizens and workforce or developing and retaining more highly qualified teachers. The Multi-Dimensional Education system this book will share with you holds great promise for educators to accomplish such redirection in schools. *We write this book to help you use a Multi-Dimensional Education focus to assess and identify how you can better support and nurture better students and educators.*

Who Did We Write This Book For?

If you are still reading this preface, there is a good chance that this book will be of interest to you. If the title was of interest, then the contents will provide many moments of reflection and strategies for change. But mainly, we write this book for individuals who share the responsibility for the leadership of a school. To us, leadership is paramount to success in schools. Leadership can either kindle or kill innovation and improvement. Leadership can support or sink success and achievement of all educational stakeholders.

To us, leadership extends from the classroom to the district administrators. We state it this way because too often leadership flows mainly in one direction: from the district office down to the classroom. When it comes to the data-driven side of education, too often school-level administrators and teachers are told what scores or statistics they will be responsible for rather than being provided with the scores and statistics they need to improve the areas they are responsible for. If you have ever tried to lose weight, you know that getting on the scale every morning and staring at the number will not help that number improve. No matter how much we wish we might lose weight, it does not happen until we actually do something. We could just adjust the scale so that it appears we lost weight, but that would not accomplish the goal. You could also change your diet. And for some this will help. But though it might help you drop your weight, it might not help improve your health, cardiovascular fitness, or muscular definition. Most of us who are trying to become healthier have to change our diets and our daily routines. We often have to add different activities and exercise to our schedules. We often need to eliminate unhealthy practices, because a change in our *being* is frequently dependent upon changing what we are *doing.*

We write this book for the shared leadership teams in schools who are growing frustrated with focusing on achievement and proficiency scores. We write this book for the educators who continue to wish (and pray) that their scores improve. We write this book for the educational leaders who have embraced a new curriculum "diet" that helped to improve things a little but did not get them to where they want to be. We write this book to provide educators with an exercise regimen that forces them to focus on improving four areas (*curriculum, community, climate,* and *character*) essential to healthy schools. And to help you improve in the 4Cs, we encourage you to focus on seven dimensions that historically have been associated with highly effective and excellent schools. *We write this book for shared leadership teams that are looking for guidance on identifying data they need to improve the success and satisfaction of students, parents, and educators.*

What Makes This Book Special?

While other books might try to get you to focus systematically on one thing or the other, this book is intended to help you look at the big picture and embrace a systemic approach to school improvement. This text provides you with a new lens for seeing how school-level and stakeholder data can be collected to help you reach your true potential for increasing achievement by directing your data-driven thinking toward qualitative and quantitative assessment of dimensions such as Leadership Potential, Faculty Fidelity, and School Climate. These are just three of the dimensions of the Multi-Dimensional Education *system* we will share. The strategies and tools this book provides are meant to help you be successful in an outcome based accountability system by using a more comprehensive collection of process and formative data to guide your way. Seeing how a wide variety of data types fall into the seven dimensions can concentrate your focus and complement and guide what you do. This text challenges you as an educational or instructional leader to further apply educational research, theory, and measurement to educational practice, and helps you to better handle the school leadership and differentiated instructional challenges that arise in today's schools and classrooms.

What Is This Book's Purpose?

The purpose of this book is to give you the framework you need to make meaningful and lasting systemic change. Too many books and professional development efforts take what we refer to as the "triage approach." They urge you to focus on one area, one subject, or one problem in hopes that by fixing this one thing everything else will improve. And though such approaches might provide temporary relief, they rarely if ever bring about lasting change or significant gains. No matter how well teachers teach in a school and make their classrooms wonderful learning environments, if the school climate is leaving the students, parents, and educators feeling unsafe, unsupported, and unwanted, it will negate much of the teachers' efforts. No matter how hard school leaders try to get parents more involved with the school or their child's academics, if the teachers are not willing to buy in to the effort, it will rarely if ever make a significant sustained impact. The purpose of this book is to provide you with research, success stories, practices, and strategies showing why we must get all parts of the seven-dimensional system working together and utilize the 4Cs to increase achievement, and how to do so.

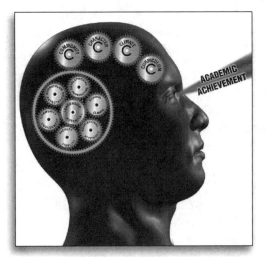

We do this by focusing in Part I on providing the research supportive of a seven-dimensional *assessment* approach (the rationale) and explaining the framework you need to put these seven dimensions to work in your school. In Part II, we turn the focus to *improvement* and explain how the seven dimensions of data can lead to improvement in curriculum (delivery), community, climate, and character. In Part III, we come back to how the Multi-Dimensional Education process can help you increase *achievement*. We show how seven dimensions of data applied to improving the 4Cs of practice can help you better focus on achievement while also improving many other indicators of your success and satisfaction when you adopt a multi-dimensional common sense approach to data-driven thinking.

Acknowledgments

Corwin would like to thank the following individuals for their editorial insight:

Jacie Bejster, Principal
Crafton Elementary School
Pittsburgh, PA

M. Susan Bolte, Principal
Providence Elementary
Aubrey, TX

Virginia Drouin, Principal
Alfred Elementary School
Alfred, ME

Addie Gaines, Principal
Kirbyville Elementary School
Kirbyville, MO

Kerry E. Williams, Learning Community Facilitator
Wayne State College
Wayne, NE

Jennifer Williams, Art Educator
Boise State University/Office of Teacher Education
Adjunct Professor/Supervisor
Boise, ID

About the Authors

The three authors are internationally recognized for their unique expertise in education and assessment. Together they have evaluated a number of large longitudinal U.S. Department of Education and other state departments of education grants. They also have managed research efforts funded through the National Science Foundation as well as the U.S. Department of Justice. They are respected professors at the college level (in education leadership, research methods, child development, and educational psychology), former teachers and administrators at primary and secondary levels, public speakers, researchers, community activists, and successful authors of manuscripts and numerous books.

 **Michael W. Corrigan** is a well-published Associate Professor and Director of Research at Marshall University in Huntington, West Virginia. He teaches Educational Psychology, Human Development, and Research Methods. Dr. Corrigan's more recent large scale research projects include five U.S. Department of Education grants studying character development and academic achievement in Florida, Ohio, North Carolina, Tennessee, and West Virginia; as well as a National Science Foundation grant collaborating with NASA that studies the impact of science-based inquiry on academic achievement in at-risk youth. Corrigan's earlier research into the deviant behavior of youth in relation to community engagement was funded through the Department of Justice. Dr. Corrigan has taught within a juvenile detention system and is also the founder of the nonprofit Neighbor's Day Initiative Group that seeks to build safer communities for youth. Corrigan's community work has been featured in the *Christian Science Monitor* and other national publications.

Doug Grove is well respected from coast to coast for providing outcome and process evaluation services to local and state education agencies. Grove is an Associate Professor at Vanguard University of Southern California where he serves as Director of Graduate Programs in the School of Education. Grove has an extensive background in Educational Leadership, Research Design, and Methodology. Dr. Grove's broad experience in educational evaluation includes the management of numerous state and federal grants, as well as many other local education agency-based initiatives on the west coast. As a respected professor, Grove has taught courses on classroom assessment, statistics, research design, and accountability in education. Dr. Grove has taught English, business, and physical education in public and private school settings. He has worked as a high school vice principal, the coordinator of a county office assessment unit, and school board member.

Philip F. Vincent, known to many as the voice of character education, and to others as the Poor Dr. Phil, brings more than 25 successful years of experience as an educator and an administrator to his consulting, grant project management, presentations, workshops, and many books. Dr. Vincent received his Master's degree in education from Appalachian State University in 1979 and his doctor of education degree in curriculum and instruction from North Carolina State University in 1991. Dr. Vincent has taught Grades K–12 as well as being a site and central office administrator. Dr. Vincent has done more than a thousand presentations and keynotes related to character education and moral development in more than 40 states and Canada. In November of 2007 he received the Sandy McDonald Award for Lifetime Achievement in the field of character education from the Character Education Partnership in Washington, DC. He was also given the Canadian Achievement Award in Character Education for his work in Ontario.

Introduction: A New Lens

Michael W. Corrigan

"He uses statistics as a drunken man uses lampposts—for support rather than illumination."

Andrew Lang

There's a Fly in the Ointment

For some strange reason that a Freudian therapist would probably diagnose as a sort of crazy, subconscious, maternally based psychological disorder, one of my most vivid childhood memories involves a trip to the eye doctor with my mother. I was a small child when she took me to see an optometric specialist on The Ohio State University campus. One of my older brothers suffered from cataracts that threatened his eyesight, and as a result my mother practiced extreme caution concerning matters related to the vision of any of her children. As she sat beside me that day, the doctor in the white coat asked me to look through a large binocular-like machine. As he began the eye test, he asked me to tell him when I saw something appear.

"Click," I heard the first lens engage.

"Do you see anything?" he asked softly.

"Nope." I replied proudly.

"Click, Click," echoed off of the walls while he switched the lens again.

"Anything yet?"

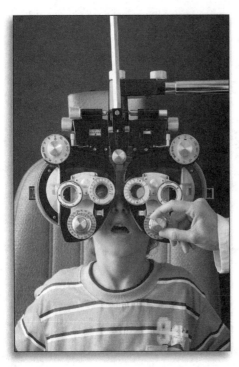

"Nope." I said again.

Click, click, click . . . "How about now?"

I looked again, and this time I stretched my peripheral vision to search the far sides of the piece of paper that hovered just past the lens.

"Still nothing. There's still *nothing* there!" I stated with a touch of that frustrated sarcastic tone you hear from children that implies they think they are smarter than the adult asking such obviously stupid questions.

And then, with one more click, something suddenly appeared on the paper in full three-dimensional splendor.

"A fly! I see a fly!" I exclaimed with great exuberance. "Mom, look! Mom, a *huge* fly!"

My mother leaned over and looked hesitantly through the lens, and with a hint of relief mixed with disbelief turned to me with her sweet smile to say she didn't see a fly.

Smashing my face anxiously into the lens, I looked again. And with a level of excitement that would surely get me labeled as ADHD today, I elaborated, "What are you talking about Mom? It's right there! It's a big green hairy fly! It's fuzzy! Look at its wings! It's a fuzzy fly!"

It seemed so real that I remember even reaching for it, but was unable to touch it.

I remember the doctor chuckling and telling my mom that her eyesight was different than mine and not to worry. I wasn't crazy. There was a fly on the paper, it was fuzzy, it was green, and my eyesight was (and, thankfully, still is) actually better than 20/20. And on that day, I left the doctor's office wondering if I might someday wear a white lab coat—not as an optometrist, but as an entomologist—and perform such impressive magic tricks with flies and maybe other, hairier insects when I grew up.

For some strange reason, some 40 years later, this memory is still vivid. And I am glad it is. My mom passed away of cancer about 18 years ago and it certainly is nice to remember random moments spent with her growing up.

Yet this memory also reminds me of something very important, and quite relevant to the main goals of this book: *It can't hurt to have our vision checked.* To make education more meaningful and beneficial for students, parents, and educators, many of us could probably use a new lens that would allow us to focus more clearly on what we are or are not seeing that is right in front of us, and what our educational efforts might encounter in the not so distant future. A new lens can help us focus on what is truly important to our success.

The truth be told, this incident was not the first nor would it be the last time that my mom and I did not see things the same way. Because, let's face it, parents (and adults in general) often do not see things the way kids do. Sometimes adults do not even see what kids see at all, and vice versa. And while we are being honest, let's admit that we adults often see things quite differently than other adults. As a result, from meetings on Capitol Hill to the governor's office to school board and faculty meetings, our discussions related to education are often fraught with heated debate and disagreement rooted in the differing policy interpretations, perceptions, and expectations we hold about education.

Normally, those of us who are willing to debate and voice dissent are educators or concerned citizens who care deeply about the success of our educational system. No matter which side of the debate we take, we voice our concerns because we care and want our education efforts to be successful. This is normally what we hold in common. We disagree, however, because we do not always see eye to eye on the role that education should play in our society to achieve such success. We disagree because we do not all see the same path that should be taken to achieving success. We have differing opinions about what constitutes success. We disagree because there are probably a great number of flies in the ointment. And one of those flies is that we have yet to identify a comprehensive way to assess educational success. We have yet to agree on the measures that represent a fair and accurate documentation of success. But we don't have to disagree, because just as there are a number of alternative paths to the top of a mountain, there also are many ways to measure and guide educational success along the way.

If you have ever hiked to the top of a mountain, you know when you're there. The view is great, the air is fresh, the breeze feels good, and you can look back down to where you came from and identify the right and wrong choices you made on your way to the top. You do not have to measure to see if you are at the highest point or compare your elevation with that of others who hiked that same mountain. You can see where you started and you can point to the progress you have made to get to where you are. And that is what

Multi-Dimensional Education is intended to do. We want to help you document the path you are taking. Multi-Dimensional Education is intended to provide you with a unique data-driven thinking framework for conceptualizing, guiding, and assessing your educational progress and success.

To some extent my dream of becoming an entomologist came true. Although as an educational psychologist I do not get to study bugs (except on those lucky days when my daughter and son choose to build their utopian insect sanctuaries in the back yard), I do get to focus on what bugs me. And what bugs me and my coauthors is that despite all the research and knowledge available as to what can make education and learning flourish for all stakeholders, our best educators are too often handcuffed by policy and accountability demands that are unfortunately often reactionary in nature and lack vision, however well-intended they may be. This is why we want to share with you in this book a proactive data-driven thinking process.

Running With Binoculars

This childhood memory actually helps in illustrating two of the main points this book seeks to communicate. The first, as mentioned above, is that no matter whether we think we are seeing well enough or not, *it can't hurt to have our vision checked.* It can't hurt to see if putting on someone else's reading glasses or borrowing someone's binoculars might allow us to focus more clearly on what we are trying to see. We all know people who are farsighted or nearsighted. In our experience working in education, we have met people and even school systems that suffer from these same conditions when it comes to their educational vision. We see educational leaders who have great long-range vision, but are unable to see the challenges that lay just one step ahead, as well as those who are so focused on tomorrow that they have no vision for the future. While some are running with binoculars, others are hunched over a microscope studying the minutia. Nearly everyone has limitations when it comes to vision, and those limitations affect our ability to do our jobs. This is why many of us need to try a new lens. *And the new lens we want to introduce to you does not focus on measuring whether you are at the top or how far you are from the top. Instead it focuses on measuring what you need to get to the top.*

Not only do we need to have our vision checked to develop clarity regarding how to improve and enhance education, *we also need a shared vision free of the blinders* that so often force us to overlook the obvious artifacts and evidence, or not-so-obvious anomalies and out-liers, that hold so much potential for positive change. Though your school's achievement test scores might lead you to regard it as successful or unsuccessful, there may be many among your ranks who think that such perceptions are looking in the wrong direction. You might even be one of these folks. Beyond what our local, state, and federal departments believe represents effective education, our research shows that often the opinions of students, parents, and educators differ greatly as to how effective our education system is and what constitutes high achievement. As a society, we still have not come to a consensus as to what role our education system is meant to play or how best to accomplish and measure its success.

This is the second main point of this text: *Educational success is best achieved when there is a shared vision among politicians, community members, educators, parents, and students.* Educational stakeholders (lawmakers, taxpayers, employees, and recipients of education services) should, ideally, have some sort of say in what our education system is trying to accomplish and how best to go about it, and be satisfied with both the process and the results.

Developing such a shared vision presents a real challenge. Getting politicians, community members, educators, parents, and students to agree on anything would seem to require the mythical abilities of Rumplestiltskin. Yet it might be easier to turn straw into gold than to get these parties to agree with each other on anything at a national level or even to work harmoniously together at a local level, where the probability of directly influencing outcomes is higher. Lawmakers and policy developers focus much attention on how to word policy or legislation, label new initiatives, or market educational efforts. They reason that if it sounds good, then there is a better chance of selling it to the masses. If they successfully communicate their intentions, then there is a better chance of getting people on board.

For instance, No Child Left Behind (NCLB) at first sounded to some like a dream come true. It was worded in such a way as to help concerned parents and lawmakers feel good about the mission of education, because no child would be left behind, the gap between minorities would disappear, and every child would be 100% proficient by 2014. If NCLB was achieving these lofty goals, the lawmakers who supported it would now look wonderful to their voting constituents. If it had worked, school administrators and teachers would have been showered with flowers and cheers each morning as they pulled into the school parking lot: "Mrs. Rumplestiltskin, you are the greatest! We love you! Thank you for not leaving my child behind!" If it had worked, we wouldn't see so many teachers leaving for careers in different fields. If it had worked, we wouldn't see so many parents clamoring to enroll their children in charter schools. If it had worked, our students would be achieving more, more of them would be graduating, and they would be better prepared for college or careers. Unfortunately, such grandiose dreams have not yet come to fruition. A consistent shared vision has not been embraced by stakeholders. As a result, it would appear we still need a new lens.

20/20 Vision

This book explores how approaching education assessment multi-dimensionally provides a promising educational foundation that relates to higher and broader academic achievement, student development, educator satisfaction, and many other dimensions essential to success in your schools. However, this is not a book on statistical analysis. There are plenty of other resources that can help you analyze data and evidence. This is a book on how to gather data that can help you better assess and guide education. The data we suggest collecting can be easily organized; it is meaningful to and can be understood by school-level personnel.

Just as medical doctors have an assortment of approaches and techniques for diagnosing and quantifying their patient's differing ailments and health risks, educators need assessment tools to document the vital signs to help every child reach his or her full potential. And school leaders need access to tools that will help all educators reach their fullest potential. Multidimensional data has been shown valuable in diagnosing what changes are needed to improve educational achievement and educator effectiveness and in making those changes. This is why we refer to Multi-Dimensional Education as MDed (pronounced like a doctor named Ed: *M.D. Ed*). This book provides you with such tools that can produce such vital signs. Our goal is to share with you a new vision for meeting the educational needs of today and tomorrow, a vision that benefits from data-driven thinking and data-driven decision making.

When data-driven thinking succeeds and the numbers begin to reflect progress, the stress level for educators goes down, and teaching and leading a school become more fulfilling once again. At the end of the day, if you and the majority of your colleagues enjoy your job and the students enjoy or more deeply appreciate you and your efforts, then suddenly the disruptions and challenges to educating our youth will seem to fade away as well. When disruptions and challenges to educating our youth fade away, educational attitudes such as motivation to learn increase positively, school climate improves, and higher academic achievement can soon follow. Our goal is to help you be an outstanding leader in education that can focus on and utilize the right data to make informed decisions. And from the success we have experienced working in school systems from the Carolinas to California, we believe that looking at education *multi-dimensionally* is a new lens that can help many educators.

As experienced K–12 administrators, educators, evaluators, and consultants on dozens of federal and state education grants, and college professors who teach research methods, leadership, advanced instructional strategies, learning theory, and child development, we (the authors) know that the very mention of words like *data* or *statistics* (sometimes referred to by our qualitative colleagues as "sadistics") can induce a coma-like state or a fight or flight response. And so, in order to reduce this unfortunate anxiety associated with a promising data-driven practice, we will approach using data with humor, a bit of sarcasm and irony, and most of all a common sense perspective.

Before we begin, however, we would like to share a few disclaimers.

1. *This book is not for everyone.* Our system or process only works for educators who are dedicated to making change, and who are willing to use data to accomplish such change. We have worked with many districts and schools that have used our Multi-Dimensional Education process wisely, and there are an equal number of schools (or educational leaders) that have put our data on a shelf. To use an example from Chapter 7, *weather* is what the atmosphere is today, but *climate* is what the atmosphere was yesterday and will be today, tomorrow, and into the future. Our data are no different than the information a weatherperson gives you. They use indicators and patterns to determine or predict what is coming. Sometimes they are right; sometimes when the winds of change appear out of nowhere they are wrong. But the data they use provides for more accurate forecasts. The other option is to wake up and go outside holding your weather predicting finger up toward the sky and hope that the weather this morning will be the same all day and all week. This is the difference between being intuitive and being data-driven. You can choose to turn on the weather report and listen to the weatherperson's predictions based on the data, or you can ignore them and find yourself stuck in a snowstorm. Although some of the best educational

administrators we have worked with have an uncanny, innate ability to use intuition to pick the right path, we also know you need data to support and verify successful implementation, assessment, and documentation of strategic school reform. With Multi-Dimensional Education data, you can better assess what others are thinking, seeing, and doing, and you can use the data to complement your intuition and to forecast and make informed decisions that you can document.

2. *The stories in this book are real.* Having worked as educators in public, private, and correctional schools, and for the past 15 years having studied schools and consulted for thousands of educators, we have seen the good, the bad, and the ugly. So all of the stories we share about schools in this book are from experiences we have had in our travels or teaching careers. Just like on the old TV crime series *Dragnet,* however, some of the names have been changed to protect the innocent (and, in a few instances, the guilty). But also to illustrate a few points pertinent to this book or the specific example we wish to make within the chapters, we have augmented or added a few minor details. This should better illustrate what we hope you take from the story.

So if you're ready, let's try a new lens. Maybe put on one of those fancy white lab coats. And together let's start identifying and studying the bugs in your system: your backyard.

PART I

Assessment

The first three chapters in Part I of this book are intended to provide you with a comprehensive blueprint or schema to build and embrace a higher-level understanding of what we call Multi-Dimensional Education. Although this book presents a common sense approach to data-driven thinking, we want to make sure you have a comprehensive understanding of what it will take to accomplish this goal. We want you to not only understand the parts of our system and process of gathering and using multi-dimensional data, but also to be able to explain to others why this is important and promises to lead to success. We want to give you the knowledge base and the supporting research you need to convince others to try this approach with you.

As the subheading for each part of the book explains, we want to first address the assessment, next explain to you in Part II how to use the assessment to increase improvement, and then discuss in Part III a more systemic approach to using the seven dimensions and 4Cs to increasing achievement. From our experience in the training we have provided to educators, it doesn't work that well to just jump into the deep end of the pool when statistics or data are involved. We feel it is important first to discuss the current model of assessment and then explain how our Multi-Dimensional Education approach can complement and strengthen your efforts.

Part I of this book will help you understand the rationale behind why we use seven dimensions to assess schools. It will help you understand the research behind these specific seven dimensions and how these seven dimensions can provide the answers to your current accountability expectations and data-driven challenges. Part I will show you how to collect and organize data in your school under these seven dimensions. It will also present the ways in which these seven dimensions of data are what you need to improve the 4Cs of education. As a teacher we work with stated, "Finally, someone has explained how to actually do this thing called data-driven education." This section will provide the first part of a commonsense approach to data-driven thinking.

1

The Paradoxes, Oxymorons, and Myths of Education

In the summer of 2007, Johncarlos Miller was appointed principal of Northeast Middle School near Greensboro, North Carolina. At that time, the authors of this book had been conducting federally funded research at the school. Our research indicated that there were some severe problems at Northeast Middle School. It had been wracked by high faculty turnover, poor teacher morale, and serious behavior issues for the preceding few years. A retirement opened up the principal position, and Johncarlos received the nod.

During the summer of 2007, Principal Miller tried to meet with all the returning teachers. Their dialogue focused on what they perceived as problems within the school, the strengths of the school, and what they were willing to do to try to support efforts to improve the school. He also had numerous faculty positions to fill. Johncarlos was very careful in who he hired. He was looking for teachers who had a passion for teaching students, but who could also set and model high standards in all aspects of school life. And perhaps most importantly, Johncarlos was looking for teachers who loved students (in the best sense of that word) and truly believed they could help students achieve regardless of societal factors such as low socioeconomic status (SES). During the meetings with returning

(Continued)

(Continued)

teachers and hiring interviews, Johncarlos was also sharing data on the school. He discussed the student achievement data, noting that the school was failing to meet expected growth based on the North Carolina Assessment Model and the standards of No Child Left Behind (NCLB). Together they also looked at attendance, suspension, and office referral data from school and district reports. They discussed parental support or lack thereof. Finally they looked at the multi-dimensional data that was being provided via the research study.

The study utilized the Multi-Dimensional Assessment that examined seven dimensions of education from the perspective of educators, parents, and students. The surveys garnered data from all stakeholder groups; the data was compiled into an easily understandable narrative and visual report (Figure 1.1). It was clear from all stakeholders that there were some concerns but there were also some solid areas to build on. Based on this comprehensive collection of data, the school leadership team, working with the faculty and students, began to develop a comprehensive plan for school improvement. In order to improve they would build on their strengths while also addressing concerns with all stakeholders involved in their efforts. What was interesting in their approach was that they were not just going to focus on improving curricular outcomes, but wanted

Figure 1.1   N.E. Middle School's Overall Multi-Dimensional Mean Scores

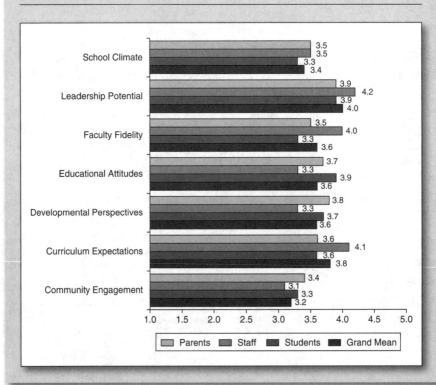

student learning to improve and would work diligently to make this happen. However, they understood that School Climate, Developmental Perspectives, Faculty Fidelity, Community Engagement, and Leadership Potential would also play important roles in improving academic outcomes. Drilling for the test would not be enough. Students and adults had to work together in all aspects of school life in order for the effort to succeed. They would be data-driven, but their data would be robust and comprehensive. It was understood that each aspect of the school influenced some other aspect of the school. It was expected that, as School Climate improved, Educational Attitudes of all stakeholders would improve as well. As academic support for students improved, academic outcomes would improve. Did they succeed?

In the accountability year 2007–2008, behavior incidents dropped dramatically and suspensions decreased by 60%. Also, the school achievement data improved. Please note that the state reading test was "renormed" for 2007–2008, and the reading scores for 2007–2008 cannot be compared with the prior year. However, the following table represents the results for 2007–2008 Reading in all Northeast Middle School (NEMS) subgroups as well as the results for Math 2006–2007 and Math 2007–2008. The table below shows how NEMS accomplished one of the strongest achievement increases in math for the district.

N.E. Middle School SUBGROUPS	READING 2007–2008	MATH 2006–2007	MATH 2007–2008
ALL	50.1%	54.5%	67.6%
AFRICAN AMERICAN	41.5%	43.2%	60.4%
HISPANIC	44.6%	40.9%	69.6%
WHITE	60.7%	67.0%	74.8%
FREE REDUCED LUNCH	41.7%	42.7%	64.0%
LIMITED ENGLISH PROFICIENT	23.6%	24.4%	50.9%
STUDENTS WITH DISABILITIES	16.2%	26.0%	46.2%

Often, an increase in one year is hard to sustain during the second year. However, this was not a typical middle school. All stakeholders were determined that they could do better. They reexamined their comprehensive data reports. They celebrated their strengths and developed strategies to address the concerns with greater intensity. Interestingly, the data from the research study were showing improvement within the seven dimensions. Some growth was significant, but much was pointing to a more gradual growth model. Meanwhile, as the dimensions developed, the 2008–2009 school year resulted in the following achievement growth.

(Continued)

(Continued)

N.E. Middle School SUBGROUPS	READING 2007–2008	READING 2008–2009	MATH 2007–2008	MATH 2008–2009
ALL	50.1%	62.3%	67.6%	80.6%
AFRICAN AMERICAN	41.5%	54.8%	60.4%	74.8%
HISPANIC	44.6%	55.6%	69.6%	84.0%
WHITE	60.7%	75.7%	74.8%	88.0%
FREE REDUCED LUNCH	41.7%	55.0%	64.0%	74.9%
LIMITED ENGLISH PROFICIENT	23.6%	35.8%	50.9%	79.2%
STUDENTS WITH DISABILITIES	16.2%	32.7%	46.2%	53.5%

As this book is being written, we are waiting for the third year of data. There were some obstacles, however, to overcome. The homeless population of students in the school was increasing. There had been a reduction of four teachers due to budget constraints while there was a slight increase in the number of students in the school. Yet all stakeholders in the building felt they could do better. No longer was economic difficulty seen as a deterrent to academic, social, ethical, artistic, or athletic growth. They were and are a data-driven school seeing their students thrive. This is a happy place to be, with teachers now trying to transfer to this school. What separates this school from many other schools is that they truly utilize comprehensive data, study the data, and base their plans and actions on their data. Secondly, they approach their efforts with a systems approach, understanding that all the dimensions influence and impact the data contained within the other dimensions as well as academic achievement.

par·a·dox (păr'ə-dŏks') *n.* **Definition:** A statement contrary to received opinion.

Educators are riddled daily with paradoxes that leave many perplexed. As mentioned in the Preface and Introduction, one such paradox is that "student achievement scores are the center of teacher accountability." Another paradox that many parents and students wrestle with is, "High achievement test scores are definitive of academic success." For many, these are *statements contrary to received opinion*. Many educators wonder how they can be held accountable based solely on achievement scores that barely measure or reflect all they do in their differentiated classrooms. Many parents and students wonder how well achievement tests represent all that has been learned or accomplished. Many wonder if a continued heavy focus on achieving Adequate Yearly Progress (AYP), measured mainly by student achievement test scores that most students are *not* held accountable for, can help inspire and guide educators to inspire and guide students. As parents, educators, and researchers, we (the authors) know that what takes place in schools and classrooms has an impact that reaches far beyond test scores. We know that educators are the impetus behind the development of our students' academic success, but we also know the social and ethical abilities that they need to be successful in life.

In other words, as Dr. Spencer Kagan (2010) asks, should we focus on preparing our youth for a life of tests or the test of life? And why does it have to be one or the other? Can't we work toward both goals? By spending 8 hours a day, 9 months a year, with a child (the majority of their waking hours) are we not going to be doing both by default? One objective of this book is to apply a commonsense approach to unraveling these and many other paradoxes tied to educational leadership and assessment. Unfortunately, when it comes to using data to drive the success of education, common sense is not that "common" anymore.

We have found that the differing perceptions of these paradoxes often rests upon whether educators entered education as a *career*, driven to rid the world of incorrect verb conjugation or to build a movement of standards-based minions capable of memorizing the quadratic equation ("Houston, we have a parabola"), or if they answered a *calling* to be the educator who inspires tomorrow's citizens to move far beyond being grammatically correct and equation savvy. From what we have experienced, the best educators are individuals who answered the calling and have found a way to teach or lead with passion. They have found career satisfaction and accomplished their professional and personal goals regardless of strict standards, required curricula, and rigid standardized achievement expectations. They are able to make the required standards-based subject material interesting through creative instruction. They have built healthy relationships with students, parents, and colleagues. They are able to find a way to tap into their students' minds and motivations to learn and discover what is needed to energize higher-level cognitive processing. They understand that for educational success to occur, we must first know how our students *feel* before we can help them *perform.*

We believe that if you are to be held accountable, you deserve a more fair and effective form of assessment. We want to help you move far beyond one test score and better understand how other data and evidence exists that can help you tap into the perceptions that impact your success. We want to help you develop a more holistic data-driven support system that informs your decision making by focusing on seven dimensions that have a great impact on your success. We want to help you be less reliant on cold accountability statistics that reflect a test score and be more focused on numbers that nurture and guide your success. Statistical sanity is rare in our scholastic world, but we believe that by adding a few common-sense approaches to assessment that will necessitate change on your part, you can achieve academic excellence that prepares our youth for the test of life and a life of tests. So to get started on this journey, let's first start with a reframing exercise.

Derealization

How accurate is our perception of ourselves? Frequently our emotions and the fact that we grow comfortable with our surroundings hold us back from taking an objective look at our existence. The goal of this initial reframing exercise (and this first chapter, for that matter) is to get you to disconnect a bit from your preconceived notions or personal feelings associated with our education system in order to consider a different and possibly more objective outside perspective. As Bernard Mayer explains, "The art of reframing is to maintain the conflict in all its richness but to help people look at it in a more open-minded and hopeful way" (Mayer, 2000, p. 139).

Derealization is defined as an alteration in the perception or experience of the external world so that it seems strange or unreal (e.g., a world where people may seem unfamiliar or mechanical). Given that many educators have told us they already work within school districts that feel somewhat surrealistic, this should not be that hard for some to accomplish. So if you don't mind, we would like to try to take you into a state of derealization in hopes of helping you envision how assessing education multi-dimensionally can provide a more mutually beneficial perspective (lens) that connects all of the stakeholders and variables needed to increase achievement, improve attitudes toward education, accomplish school reform, and help our children become more intelligent contributing citizens.

Breathe Deeply and Relax

There are many wonderful movies that have been made about inspiring teachers or principals. *Dead Poets Society, To Sir With Love, Mona Lisa Smile, Blackboard Jungle, Mr. Holland's Opus, Lean on Me, The Great Debaters, Dangerous Minds, School of Rock* . . . the list goes on. Imagine you are in an empty, dark theater watching a new inspiring movie about education, but in this movie you are the star. You are getting a sneak preview! You are the star teacher or principal who is making miraculous progress in a challenged classroom or troubled school. For a moment, think about what you would want the title of your movie to be. What actor or actress would you want to play your part? Can you imagine the movie playing in front of you? Can you close your eyes and see it on the screen? Close your eyes for 30 seconds and imagine watching your movie on the big screen.

Now imagine you are in the projection room in the back row of the empty, dark theater watching yourself watch the movie about yourself. Close your eyes for another 30 seconds and try to move yourself out of your body (so to speak) so that you are several rows above, looking at yourself. Does it look like you are enjoying the movie? If the movie you are visualizing is in color, then imagine it switching to black and white. Now visualize the movie in slow motion for a more dramatic effect. Don't forget you are in the very back of the empty, dark theater, above the seats, watching yourself watch your movie in black and white and in slow motion. Can you imagine a theme song playing or hear any dialogue or conversations? If so, turn down the volume in your mind. When you have the movie in black and white and the volume is low, imagine the movie now moving in fast-forward mode. Your movie is flying by in front of you now, the climax of the movie is taking place, and your success is being celebrated. Is your character smiling? Does it feel good to be an inspiring educator on the big screen? Are you using data?

The data question was intended to make you laugh; but how did this exercise feel? Have you ever dreamed of such a movie while sitting on your couch late at night with a box of tissues and chocolates next to you while watching a rerun of one of these inspiring movies? We all deserve a chance to dream a little dream. To us, all educators deserve to pursue such dreams.

Now for Something Completely Different

Here is where the next stage of derealization begins. This second stage is where things are meant to become a little more strange, mechanical, and maybe even uncomfortable. It is an exercise we call O-PIT; the Oxymoronic-Paradox Identification Test.

Oxymoronic-Paradox Identification Test

Once again close your eyes and try imagining your movie. Revisit that part where the students are celebrating your success. Now imagine that your movie stops abruptly, like when a reel-to-reel projector malfunctions, and that as the movie begins again, a different black-and-white silent movie starts to play. This new black-and-white footage at first seems to be one of those old-fashioned black-and-white films, but, strangely enough, it is not a movie. Instead, it is a recruitment commercial, and the following scrolling text begins rolling up from the bottom of the screen like in the Star Wars movies. The scrolling text is still in fast-forward mode, so read quickly (in your best radio announcer voice) for maximum effect. But for this exercise, see if you can identify (circle, highlight, or underline) any oxymorons (contradictory phrases) or educational paradoxes in the recruitment commercial as you read.

Welcome to the Business of Education!

Are you ready to become one of the lucky and respected 3,000,000 people who work for one of the most stable, oldest, and largest organizations in America?

Opportunity is knocking because 41–50% of our new employees leave our organization within 3 to 5 years of starting! If you are highly qualified and want to pursue a fulfilling career in education at our national corporate headquarters located in Washington, D.C., one of the 51 additional corporate offices in all our nation's capital cities, one of the 5,000 local management offices located in nearly every town or county from coast to coast, or in one of our more than 100,000 satellite service centers, we probably have a position available tomorrow.

That is, of course, if we can find the money to give you a competitive low wage.

Each of our 5,000 local management offices, which we refer to as school districts, are fully capable of managing 7 to 500 of the 100,000 satellite service center locations. These satellite service center locations, which we call schools, are responsible for providing essential community services to more than 97 million children and parents in accordance with strict common education standards created uniquely different by each of the 51 corporate offices, which we call State Departments of

Education. To strengthen our efforts to achieve excellence, additional requirements come annually from our national corporate headquarters, which we call the U.S. Department of Education. To manage and constantly monitor the accountability of this massive organization and to document whether these standards and expectations are being followed and achieved, our well-organized state corporate offices require the heavily staffed local management offices to provide comprehensive reports on the performance of our satellite service locations. After our state corporate offices thoroughly review the reports, they typically issue new annual mandates and expectations to our local management offices, who effectively communicate these expectations to satellite service centers.

With such an organizational hierarchy in place, it would appear to a business analyst that our organization's national corporate headquarters follows the successful system of hierarchical management (where the corporate headquarters is actually in charge) that have made our largest global corporations dominant forces in society. But this is not the case in the Business of Education. Instead, *you* are in charge; and you are responsible for your own success or failure to meet our strict standards, requirements, and accountability expectations. Our goal of constantly increasing expectations for high achievement is what makes us successful.

[Press Pause]

So what do you think? Does this sound like a great, supportive organization that you would like to join? Did it sound unfamiliar or mechanical? Did it sound surreal, strange, or unreal? Or is it just the opposite: all too real? How many oxymorons did you identify? How many paradoxes did you identify? How many things just seemed contradictory? Did this recruitment commercial put a little damper on the movie about your inspiring career and make you forget about your dream? Well, wait one minute, because it's not over yet! Here's some more. Please keep reading quickly with your radio voice and continue identifying the oxymorons and educational paradoxes; especially those related to educational assessment.

Management Opportunities Galore!

In addition to the effective top-down organizational communication tactics used and our strategic plans that rarely require us to bother our employees for feedback or insights related to the customers (students, parents, and community members) with whom satellite service center location employees interact daily, we also are very open-minded when it comes to hiring managers (whom we call principals). In decades past, we normally only hired managers who had business management

(Continued)

(Continued)

degrees or experience, or who had served for many years as assistant managers (which we call assistant or vice principals). But today we hire a significant percentage of qualified managers with a minimal amount of management experience or preparedness. The new managers may be deficient in the skills required to handle the uniquely personal concerns and needs of the employees and customers who do not always behave rationally; but these new managers have great intentions, so we put all of our faith in them!

We stand behind our managers for at least 2 to 3 years. To ensure their success we give them on-the-job training, modernized efficient operating budgets, a streamlined support staff and organizational infrastructure, and 9.5 months to accomplish that which most corporations take 12 months to achieve. It is this type of support that gives our managers the autonomy and control they need to achieve adequate yearly progress.

With such a short time frame and so many responsibilities, our managers need only a few minutes a year to support and assess teachers (who are largely responsible for the success of the customers) by providing a thorough drive-by evaluation of their performance. As a result, teachers who in many cases are rarely observed or assessed while working with customers are also given full autonomy, control over teaching the required curriculum, one of the best vacation packages available, and allowed to work for some of the lowest salaries among college graduates. As to why 41% to 50% of the satellite service centers' teachers leave the profession within 3 to 5 years due to feeling undersupported, underpaid, and unappreciated, we are not sure.

But regardless of unavoidable staff turnover or other little challenges such as the special needs of customers skyrocketing and needed resources dwindling away due to annual budget cuts and rising costs (also out of our control), we only expect our managers to make an adequate amount of yearly progress. And to simplify the assessment of this adequate yearly progress, we only ask for one performance measure. And that is the performance of our customers (students), whom the satellite service location often has no role in recruiting or selecting. This performance measure is based upon a test score intended to measure the customer's subject knowledge gained at the satellite service locations. Additionally, instead of measuring from year to year (longitudinally) if the student is gaining knowledge (i.e., measuring if the teacher helped the student improve), we do a fairer and simpler cross-sectional measure of the students the teacher has the next year to see if they are smarter than the students from the year before. But if this goal—to annually increase the level of highly proficient customer performance—is unachievable due to an overwhelming number of variables nearly impossible to control for (for example, confounding variables such as special needs, low SES, and normal distribution of intelligence), our national corporate headquarters allows each state to change the performance measure test regularly if they find that the customers are not performing as well as expected.

As a result, nearly every state's corporate offices use a different measure of success to measure the same goal. And since the differing tests with questionable construct and convergent validity (do they actually measure what they say they measure?) have changed over the years, it is hard to say whether the schools have actually made the improvement that our national or state organizations set out to achieve. But this is not important, because the teachers and principals we hire to be responsible for the test scores that serve as the sole indicator whether they have done their jobs effectively, are the noblest workers in America!

Finding Comfort in Numbers

For some educators, this exercise produces similar results to what they have experienced in their careers. They either laugh at the irony to keep their sanity, become angry at the innuendo, or grow sad and disillusioned by this reality. By having to focus on the many paradoxes and oxymorons, the business of education has distracted them from the dream, calling, or career they set out to pursue. It has taken the wind out of too many sails and the luster out of too many dreams. The acronym O-PIT is fitting because many educators feel like they are in a pit of oxymoronic and paradoxical bureaucracy *and need help in order to be able to see through the layers of red tape and recognize how surreal the expectations have become.* In the more than 40 school districts with which we have worked over the past several years, data we collected show, and our conversations confirm, that unfortunately a large percentage of educators (young and not-so young) are growing very disenchanted with the field of education. Many of our best educators have left for the business sector or retired early. For too many, their hands and feet have been tied (slow-motion), what was once a colorful existence has turned to black and white, their voices have been muted, and in order to make it to the magic retirement age they have pressed fast-forward mode (aka autodrive) with little hope of experiencing a climactic ending in which their colleagues and students celebrate their success. O-PIT is an exercise we like to have educators complete so they can take a step back to try to get a look from the outside in and begin to open their senses to how there might be comfort in numbers that move us beyond one questionable test score. For some of you (at the least) it probably got your imagination moving or your blood pumping.

For some of you, this reframing exercise might have made you a little irritated or increased your anxiety. You might have been insulted that the ad suggested that some of our principals are underqualified or ill-prepared. You might have been appalled that we suggested that administrative offices are not doing a good job communicating. Some might be setting the book down now and writing their letters of resignation. We hope not, because there is good news to follow. But we apologize if this did increase your anxiety or insult you, because we did this on purpose. We did this on purpose, however, because educators are some of the noblest and most dedicated workers in America—even loyal to a fault.

Because we are a somewhat divided country when it comes to the goals of our education, some agree with the existing system and are loyal committed educators who will follow all the rules, while some are at the other end of the spectrum, longing for change. We have tried to make this exercise a little discomforting because, in order to get others to listen, we must often make them a little irritated. There is research that shows that when low to mild anxiety is constantly experienced, the learning process is enhanced (Ormrod, 2006a). Anxiety makes us think. So given that we are trying to share with you how to use data more effectively in education (often not an interesting topic or popular endeavor) and you or some of your colleagues might not want to admit that something is wrong with the existing model, we do this to reframe and start the debate, a rich debate that we hope maintains "the conflict in all its richness but [helps] people look at it in a more open-minded and hopeful way" (Mayer, 2000, p. 139). As Niels Bohr once said "How wonderful that we have met with a paradox. Now we have some hope of making progress."

Investing in Education

Assuming you are a stock investor or business analyst, would you buy stock in the recruitment commercial's Business of Education organization even in positive economic times? Most savvy investors would probably not. Would you be willing to work for a corporation that offers little support or financial incentives for its employees? Would you, as a skilled educator, be willing to take a management role in an organization that rarely if ever provides its managers with the data needed to fully audit and analyze the strengths and challenges of the efforts and services being delivered? Would you, as an educator, be willing to work for an organization that rarely considers other factors that indicate you are doing a good job? For most educators, the answer is, thankfully, *yes!*

The answer is yes because most people working in the education field are not doing it for money, but for much more altruistic motives. Most educators realize that high pay and high-stakes test scores are not the true measure of the rewards or success that make your job satisfying and life-defining. Most *good* educators know that there are many more meaningful ways to measure success and progress. Unfortunately, only a small percentage are taking advantage of using the other statistical performance or "value-added" management measures available that could show how well the organizations are working, how much adequate yearly progress the organizations truly are making with customers (that is, students and parents) as well as employees, and how a wide array of efforts beyond preparing for the tests (for example, using curricula, products, and programs) are contributing to the success and performance of the students. In other words, though we are being challenged to become data-driven educators, it would appear that very few are actually able or willing to do so.

Though focusing on the achievement of a customer is an admirable goal, can you think of any other thriving businesses that measure success solely on how much knowledge their customers possess? What if Weight Watchers based their success solely on how many customers learned how to diet and exercise correctly, and yearly dividends to stockholders rested solely upon how many pounds were lost (or unfortunately regained) by their customers? What if Microsoft's dividend yield was reliant exclusively upon whether their Windows users actually knew how to use their newest software proficiently? Most corporations taking this approach would not have happy investors.

Of course, education is a government-based nonprofit organization that does not necessarily *worry* about profit margins, unlike most corporations. But what if the Department of Justice was assessed using a unidimensional statistic, one number? What if the Department of Justice's Federal Bureau of Prisons performance was judged and funding determined by only considering Adequate Yearly Progress (AYP) based upon the number of convicts they turned into *proficient* model citizens? What if the Department of Agriculture's performance was assessed using only the amount of crops successfully harvested or AYP on reducing the obesity level of children eating the school lunches they oversee? Just as with the masses of educators, parents, and students who are pleading for the high-stakes testing obsession to end, most folks presented with such unrealistic and shortsighted ways to measure success would scream even louder. Think about it!

What do you think the public's reaction would be if the government stated they would not give funding to prisons that did not make 100% of their prisoners proficient model citizens within the next 10 years? What do you think the wardens and guards would need to do if recidivism is around 50%?

We all know that NCLB set out with the commendable goal of shrinking the achievement gap between blacks and whites and mandated that schools demonstrate AYP, put state standards in place, and assess such efforts through testing; but at what point did we lose sight of other government-led efforts to reform schools that were based on and recommended a broader use of meaningful variables, statistics, and practices? At what point did we decide to set aside the abundance of data we have at our disposal to more comprehensively measure academic success (e.g., increased attendance, graduation rates, college placement, Advanced Placement and International Baccalaureate assessments, or completion of vocational and technical school proficiencies) and agree to be graded on just one mark of excellence or failure? Doesn't the fact that nearly 30% of our students are not graduating from high school raise huge questions about our level of achievement and success?

The Courtship of Eddie and Eva

So who are Eddie and Eva? Believe it or not, you know both of them. But don't worry; there is no reason to run out to the mall for a present, because the wedding is not yet final. Eddie's full name is Ed Ucation and Eva's full name is Eva Luation. Yes we are talking about the courtship of education and evaluation, and we want to discuss now how this love-hate relationship began. Have you ever wondered when and why this focus on educational evaluation or assessment began? In other words, how did we get here?

Early output accountability measures began in 1895 with the introduction of spelling tests and written exams as a means to measure the quality of Ed Ucation in schools (Wynne, 1972). The Elementary and Secondary Education Act (ESEA) of 1965 required funded programs to conduct Eva Luations that used basic skills tests as the measurement of student and program success (Popham, 2001). This brought about the idea that programs and school performance could be measured or evaluated by the performance of students on standardized testing measures, and by the 1980s many states had developed statewide testing programs, which for all practical purposes were utilized in an earlier accountability system.

On April 26, 1983, the problem of low-performing schools was reintroduced to public attention by the Reagan administration's release of a report on the status of America's schools, *A Nation at Risk*. This criticism of the public education system, which basically blamed teachers and schools for the decline in student performance, was prepared by a prestigious committee, given the endorsement of Secretary of Education William Bennett, and warned that this decline would be the demise of America's industrial clout (Berliner & Biddle, 1995). With the idea accepted that America's future business prominence would only be as strong as the student test scores being produced in America's public schools, the movement toward a competitive testing environment and mandates for evaluation gained great momentum. It was this shift to a focus on testing that challenged Ed Ucation to embrace Eva Luation's higher standards and a system of accountability. Similar to many relationships, Ed and Eva have had their ups and downs, and the past ten years have been a real test of love.

During the past decade, we have all heard the words *rigorous assessment* or *adequate yearly progress* ad nauseum. Yet instead of screaming adequately enough up a corporate ladder that does not often practice the doctrine of the presidential candidate Ross Perot ("I'm all ears!"), we immediately embraced a number to parsimoniously "prove" that our efforts were worthy. Those of us in the numbers business, and a growing number of educators, have learned that one number rarely provides a sufficiently clear and valid picture to *prove* anything. Indeed, rarely does one number give enough information to *improve* anything! In fact, we strive to never use the p-word—prove. As a result, some in the education field are now taking a step back and asking, "How can we best demonstrate proven, comprehensive school reform?" And the answer, as the U.S. Department of Education stated in 1998 (and we believe to be true), will come from "rigorous, systemic, and objective procedures [needed] to obtain valid knowledge." The question we ask is how can we get educators to focus on rigorous, systemic, objective procedures when they are reminded daily that their job rests upon one not-so-rigorous, nonsystemic, subjective outcome measure: the tests?

As Justin Snider, a research fellow at Columbia University's Hechinger Institute on Education and the Media, stated in *Education Week*,

> The accountability measures of the federal No Child Left Behind Act, for instance, are based on cross-sectional rather than longitudinal data. In layman's terms, this means that we end up comparing how one set of 7th graders performs in a

given year with how a different set of 7th graders performs the following year. Experts in data analysis agree that this is a little more than problematic. A better system—one based on longitudinal data—would instead compare how the same set of students performs year after year, thereby tracking change over time. But these are not the data we currently collect, in large part because doing so is difficult and expensive. (Snider, 2010)

Although we agree with Snider's synopsis of the shortcomings of the present model, we do not agree that the data needed to improve our efforts are not already being collected, and we do not agree that such data is difficult or expensive to organize or analyze. If the development process of the next set of achievement tests could benefit greatly by developing achievement tests that can actually be studied longitudinally on the same students, then it should be done, because anything worth doing is worth doing right. If states are giving $250 million contracts to testing companies to do it wrong, it would seem possible they could use a few million dollars to do a little research and development in order to do it right. If we are spending millions to do it wrong year after year, then we are just wasting valuable education dollars. But it is not sufficient to just keep changing the tests in hopes of making an improvement. We must also utilize other data and evidence that is readily available. We must use data that tells us what we need to do to improve scores. We need a more holistic approach to accountability that provides assessments to help develop better students and educators.

Expanding the View

The February 2003 edition of *Educational Leadership* focused on the theme "Using Data to Improve Student Achievement." The articles in this edition, written by some of our nation's best educational researchers and practitioners (Marzano, Schmoker, and Slavin), comprehensively and clearly illustrated how there are many meaningful dimensions of good education that can be assessed. Yet many of our nation's best administrators have had their hands tied since that publication and have had to focus strictly on *meeting AYP*. Teachers, principals, superintendents, and school boards are far too often being forced to make decisions based on intuition, incomplete data, or skewed public opinion. There is a limited amount of information that is both empirically reliable (the same factor is measured consistently) and valid (that which is claimed to be measured is actually measured) that can assist a teacher, principal, or school district in meeting AYP and other valuable achievement norms. Currently, nonvalidated tests and curriculum-based formative assessments are often being utilized at levels from the district office to the classroom. When the job security of many of those involved rests strictly upon one number, it is not surprising to find that many of the sound suggestions made by the U.S. Department of Education in 1998, the experts published in the 2003 *Educational Leadership* journal, and the decades of research supporting a multi-dimensional approach to data-driven education have subsequently fallen on deaf ears and that we have struggled to reach this single number that represents achievement. While moving forward in time, we have gone backwards in progress by not considering other assessments that can contribute to increasing that magic achievement proficiency number as well as broadening our conceptions of education's impact on our stakeholders.

We have the data on hand to better inform our practices. We could and should collect even more data, or at least look at what we have, what we know, and what we do through a new, more meaningful, and more useful lens. We need to use data that is relevant to succeeding at our goals and make that data understandable to educational stakeholders. It would appear that part of the resistance to adopting the data-driven education model being proposed is because a large number of educators see such a process as cold and based on statistics rather than on real people. This makes great sense, because who would want the fate of their job or the quality of their child's education being dictated or determined by a simple number? Most of us want to be treated like real people with feelings and daily challenges. We want our children to be considered a priority and not just another number or test score.

Yet another problem, according to research, is that many school principals lack the necessary skills to make decisions based on data (Striefer, 2000). Beyond understanding test scores, educators also need to understand growth models and how to measure goals. There is research in the field that strongly supports placing a focus on the building of data capacity for principals and teachers. According to Glickman's work with successful schools, these schools assess and refine their own practices on the basis of an ongoing process of active research, both external and involving the school's own continual collection and analysis of student data. Glickman's research included 20 schools that showed an increase in achievement over a period of 10–30 years. In conducting the research, one of the noticeable commonalities in all of the schools was that there was an emphasis placed on using a variety of data and information to make decisions for improvement in the school programs (Glickman, 2002, p. 43).

In June 2009, the U.S. Department of Education released a request for proposals to have colleges of education apply for teacher quality partnership grants to update their teacher preparation programs to be more data-driven. These efforts to improve teacher preparation programs are due to the fact that "many if not most colleges of education are doing a mediocre job of preparing teachers," stated Secretary Duncan. And we agree that in some cases college professors should bear part of the blame for this shortcoming. Many educators have not been provided with the statistical schema one needs to be successful in data-driven thinking or education. Also, unfortunately, often due to standards and assessment requirements from states and federal departments, educators are forced to focus their limited time more heavily on data related to student behavior and standards-based curricula selected to increase achievement scores. With a limited amount of time historically given to educators for planning periods, an even lesser amount of time to focus on data, and only a few district offices providing schools with all of the data they collect in a report form that one can actually understand, educators have been forced to focus on the few measures they are given that often only tell where students are at (summative outcome data) and fall short of providing data in an understandable fashion to get all stakeholders to where they want to go (process and formative data).

Data-driven decision making is a process of inquiry, analysis, and decision-making inferences gained from the interplay of *process, formative,* and *summative* data.

> *Process data* relates to the way school reform or instruction takes place and the processes that occur as leaders lead, teachers teach, and learners learn. Included in the process data is the assessment of the routine or innovative procedural and instructional focuses that take place during the school year. An accurate analysis of the infusion and effectiveness of interventions, processes, and programs put in place to enhance leading, teaching, and learning at the school site can produce valuable data for guiding improvement.

> *Formative data* (sometimes referred to as input data) can consist of data about student, staff, and community perceptions and opinions. It can also be gathered from ongoing testing scores, similar to the approach taken by some reading curricula. Formative data can be garnered from meeting minutes and leadership or teacher effectiveness data collected from groups of teachers or students at the school. These data can guide our short-term (proximal) goals.

Summative data (outcome measures) tell what results have been obtained. Data can include statewide testing data as well as data collected for or by principals or teachers in the school or classroom; the latter may better reflect the climate, teaching, learning, and achievement at the school. These data could more accurately reflect the long-term (distal) goals that can be achieved at many levels.

The good news is that educators have some of the rigorous, systemic, and objective data and data collection procedures needed to guide and validate one's efforts currently available to them. We also know that some want to take a more data-driven approach and just need guidance and a framework to accomplish that goal. Still others need a new lens or need to adjust the one they have to get beyond the tunnel vision and anxiety (often associated with fear of failure) that currently clouds or hinders their judgment and their educational assessment and management efforts. Many just need to get beyond the fear that more data means more accountability based on numbers and adopt a way of data-driven thinking that provides a more holistic approach to focusing on the kinds of data that actually drive education. We believe that approaching education multi-dimensionally provides such a lens to better accomplish a broader spectrum of goals for educating our nation's youth. And as Johncarlos Miller, the principal in the opening story, has documented and shared, the Multi-Dimensional Education process allowed him to see what needed to be fixed, to direct his faculty's thinking to factors beyond achievement tests, and to experience double-digit increases in achievement test scores.

So What Is Multi-Dimensional Education?

Quite simply, it is a lens for you to study what you do that directs your focus to seven dimensions associated with highly effective schools. It is a lens that is focused on a multi-dimensional framework rather than on a single dimension, achievement. Multi-Dimensional Education provides a process and framework to organize data so that it can be put to work for you in a meaningful and productive way. To some extent, many already approach education multi-dimensionally. Similar to an educational researcher who collects data on numerous variables, you collect data from many points to document your accountability at the local level. The questions to be asked are whether you are considering the right data points, collecting them correctly to measure the most meaningful dimensions relevant to education improvement (at the school level), connecting these data points to achievement, and using data effectively to improve.

Figure 1.2, the Multi-Dimensional Education Process Model, illustrates the seven dimensions we will be discussing in depth and how these dimensions of formative data can organize existing process and summative data such as attendance, office referrals, suspensions, grades, and graduation rates. We have also provided an abbreviated version of our Multi-Dimensional Assessment in the Appendix. If used correctly, this lens for redirecting your vision can have a great impact on the learning and teaching climate of the school and perhaps the community. This model for data-driven education has allowed us to provide a year-to-year comparison for hundreds of schools on the most meaningful dimensions that impact school reform. But, as we will explain in Chapter 2, and as the gears in the head in the illustration at the end of the Preface suggest (see page xvi), this model is meant to be used *systemically.* Systemic is different than systematic. *Systematic* implies we do one step at a time, where *systemic* is intended to focus on many parts at one time in order to get all parts of the "engine" working together. We would like for you to first look at this dimensional model as a lens to just consider and examine the many different parts or variables reflective of what exists in your school(s). In the chapters to follow, however, our goal is help you to see how these seven dimensions work systemically to empower your data-driven thinking. We will also explain how to use new and existing qualitative artifacts and evidence, as well as multiple quantitative scales or measures, to evaluate each dimension. And in Part II of the book we will show how these dimensions relate to and empower the 4Cs.

We developed the Multi-Dimensional Education Process Model shown in Figure 1.2 based on the research to be covered in Chapter 2, and the federally funded studies that we evaluated or directed in more than 100 randomly assigned schools over a 6-year period. In the schools we studied that showed superior performance, we witnessed how they consistently excelled over their less proficient neighbors in one or more of the seven dimensions we assessed. The following is a brief description of the seven dimensions of Multi-Dimensional Education.

Dimension 1: Community Engagement

According to a host of educational visionaries (e.g., Dewey, Piaget, Vygotsky), without the help of parents and positive interpersonal

Figure 1.2 The Multi-Dimensional Education Process Model

Multi-Dimensional Education Process Model

SUCCESSFUL SCHOOLS

ACADEMIC CHALLENGES

Excessive Staff Turnover, High Drop-out and Hold-back Rates, Negative Behavior and Discipline, Poor Attendance and Retention

ACADEMIC ACHIEVEMENTS

High Student Achievement, Respectable ACT and SAT Test Scores, College or Vocational Placement, Meeting "Adequate Yearly Progress"

High Test Scores Are a Worthy Goal. Knowing How to Best Improve Student Achievement and Your Schools' Performance is Even Better.

The Goal of Multi-Dimensional Assessment is to Get Solutions not Just Statistics!

MEANINGFUL DIMENSIONS OF EDUCATION

Community Engagement	Curriculum Expectations	Developmental Perspectives	Educational Attitudes	Faculty Fidelity	Leadership Potential	School Climate
According to Dewey, Piaget, Vygotsky, and a host of other educational visionaries, without the help of parents and positive interpersonal interactions within the greater community, educators face	Schools that are surpassing the norm in America approach teaching as a science. Studies reveal they use theory to create, prepare, and deliver a rigorous challenging education.	Recent private and federally funded research into character education, socio-emotional learning, and moral development has produced empirical evidence that show increases in academic	GPA and standardized testing supposedly offer insight into one's hypothesized academic achievement. Yet most of us know a smart child who is not motivated to learn or take a test. Motivation is the key	Approximately 45% of new teachers do not make it past 5 years in the profession. Professional development is paramount to insuring that all participants fully understand the	Principals and leadership teams are critical to the success of creating an organizational culture for instructional and professional success. With poor leadership at the foundation of the organization,	Safe and caring schools are a necessity for a student/teacher relationship to grow. The emotional attachment of a student to his or her school is critical to a good education, and the school climate is a

(Continued)

Figure 1.2 (Continued)

MEANINGFUL DIMENSIONS OF EDUCATION

Community Engagement	Curriculum Expectations	Developmental Perspectives	Educational Attitudes	Faculty Fidelity	Leadership Potential	School Climate
increased challenges to achieving miracles in youth development and instructional success. What is the level of community engagement being practiced in your schools? Is it contributing to the educational success or unfortunate failures?	They use technology and enthusiasm to share such knowledge. How do the students and educators feel about your curriculum? Is your curriculum meaningful and challenging? Is the instruction meeting the many expectations?	achievement when schools focus simultaneously on academics and developing caring citizens. Are your schools focusing on the social, emotional, and moral development of students and educators? Are you practicing character right or light?	to learning, and improving educational attitudes is the answer to increasing motivation. How about considering how the student feels toward school or testing? How about seeking more information as to how one might build an intrinsic drive to learn?	basics to instructional success and continuous improvement. More thorough understanding is obtained through ongoing instructional support, and coaching. Are your teachers supported? How well are they teaching? How well are they respected?	success will rarely ever materialize. Assessing organizational management practices and communication is essential for academic achievement. How do the teachers feel about school leadership? How do the students feel about leadership?	major impact on this attachment and academic achievement. How do students, parents, and educators feel when they walk through the school doors? Do students, parents, and educators feel safe? Do your schools offer a positive learning environment?
This dimension assesses factors such as: – Interpersonal Community Engagement – Parent Involvement – Service to Community – Community Support	This dimension assesses factors such as: – Educational Rigor – Instructional Creativity – Academic Support – Differentiated Effectiveness	This dimension assesses factors such as: – Student Success Traits – School Misconduct – Compassion for Others – Behavior Issues – Discipline Policies	This dimension assesses factors such as: – Motivation to Learn – Academic Empowerment – Student Work-Ethic – Feelings Toward School	This dimension assesses factors such as: – Teacher Trust – Teacher Satisfaction – Teacher Efficacy – Organizational Support	This dimension assesses factors such as: – Leadership Satisfaction – Leadership Styles – Communication – Shared Mission and Vision	This dimension assesses factors such as: – School Climate – Student Relationships – School Liking – School Loneliness – Bonding to School

interactions within the greater community, educators face increased challenges to achieving visions of positive youth development and instructional success. As Chapter 7 will cover in much more depth, redefining and increasing parental involvement holds some of the greatest potential to unlock your achievement. How involved are your students' parents in their education and in your efforts? What is the level of community engagement being practiced in your schools? Is it contributing to educational success or to failure? When we go into schools and assess this dimension, we begin by looking at factors such as *interpersonal community engagement* (students' level of community communication), *parent involvement* (parents' involvement in school and community), and *service to community* (students' level of service to community). As we will explain in the chapters to follow, you can use the Multi-Dimensional Assessment survey we provide in the Appendix to measure all of the dimensions; you can also collect and organize other data, evidence, and artifacts to assess this dimension.

Dimension 2: Curriculum Expectations

Schools that are surpassing the norm often approach teaching more as a science than an art. They use theory-based practices to create, prepare, and deliver a rigorous and challenging education. Although in decades past teaching might have been viewed as an art, today many of our most outstanding educators use research, technology, and assessment to complement their creativity and enthusiasm in sharing knowledge. There is an abundance of research in this book that will show that it is not necessarily the curriculum used that increases achievement and performance; often the teachers in the classroom in charge of sharing the curriculum and adults in the community hold the greatest potential for bringing about improvement. How do the students and educators feel about your curriculum? Is your curriculum being shared in a meaningful and challenging way? Is instruction meeting the many expectations? When we go into schools and assess this dimension, we begin by looking at factors such as: *instructional curriculum* (perceptions of the instruction and lessons received), *instructional creativity* (perceptions of how creative your staff is in the classroom), *academic support* (perceived support given to students), and *educational rigor* (perceived demandingness of the coursework). We will explain this dimension more thoroughly in the chapters to follow, especially Chapter 5.

Dimension 3: Developmental Perspectives

Recent private and federally funded prosocial education research into such areas as social-emotional learning, service learning, and character education has produced empirical evidence of increases in academic achievement when schools focus simultaneously on academics and on developing caring citizens. Our research has identified significant relationships that begin to show how students view their character has a direct positive relationship to their achievement (Corrigan, Grove, Vincent, Chapman & Walls, 2007). As we teach our students in our learning theory classes that study such developmental models such as Piaget's, often a delay in learning can be easily diagnosed or connected to a delay in development. They are often one and the same, and in order to help our students learn we must first help them progress in development. Are your schools focusing on the social, emotional, and moral development that enhances cognitive development of both students and educators? Are you practicing character right or light? When we go into schools and assess this dimension, we begin by looking at factors such as: *student success traits* (the level of character understood and exhibited), *school misconduct* (level of student misconduct in school), *compassion for others* (how much a student thinks and cares about others), and *good deeds* (how often a student has helped others). We will explain this dimension more thoroughly in the chapters to follow, especially Chapter 8.

Dimension 4: Educational Attitudes

GPA and standardized testing supposedly offer insight into academic achievement. Yet most of us know a smart child who is not motivated to learn or take tests. Motivation is a key factor in learning (Skinner, 1969) that typically accounts for a significant percentage of achievement (10+%) (Uguroglu & Walberh, 1979). Also, one's feelings (often referred to in research as affect) about the subject matter or schoolwork play a key role and account for an equally significant percentage of academic achievement. As a result, improving educational attitudes is often the answer to improving learning and increasing test scores. In reality, if a student is not held accountable for his or her test scores and the scores do not have any impact on their GPA, moving to the next grade, or graduating, why would they try hard on the tests? One answer is that they actually feel intrinsically motivated and empowered to do well and want to show how smart they have become. Another possible reason for trying harder is that students know that the teacher and the school are held accountable for their test scores, and they like you, the educator (as well as the school), and want to do well to help you. How about considering the students' feelings toward school or testing? How about seeking more information as to how one might build an intrinsic drive to learn or achieve? When we go into schools and assess this dimension we begin by looking at factors such as *motivation to learn* (how motivated a student is to learn), *personal academic empowerment* (how empowered a student feels), *student work ethic* (how hard a student works on academics), and *feelings for school* (how a student feels about school).

Dimension 5: Faculty Fidelity

As we shared earlier in the Preface and the Business of Education derealization exercise, more than a third of new teachers leave the profession within 3 years, and half of new hires are replaced every 5 years (National Commission on Teaching and America's Future, 2008). Most likely, an equal number of "seasoned" teachers are in need of rejuvenation. Professional development is paramount to insuring that all participants fully understand the basics of instructional success and continuous improvement. But what sort of professional development should you bring into the school? Instead of taking an informal poll to determine what kind of professional development your educators want to learn more about, or hiring a motivational speaker to come in and talk about a random topic that only some of the educators are interested in or moved by, what about using data to determine what kind of professional development your educators actually need? This is what we call data-driven professional development. This dimension can get you started on the road to teacher evaluation that so many are resisting and that so many need. Our faculties need more instructional support and coaching, and evidence gathered on this dimension can help us pinpoint more accurately where our faculties need improvement. Are your teachers supported? How well are they teaching? How well are they respected or trusted? When we go into schools and assess this dimension we begin by looking at factors such as *teacher trust* (perceptions as to how much a student trusts teachers), *teacher satisfaction* (perceptions of how teachers feel about their work), and *teacher belief in students* (perceptions as to how much teachers believe in students).

Dimension 6: Leadership Potential

Principals and leadership teams are critical to the success of creating an organizational culture for instructional and professional success. That is why the Leadership Potential gear is in the center of our seven-dimension gear model. With poor leadership at the foundation of the organization, success and improvement will rarely materialize. And just as it is important for teachers to be evaluated and receive feedback, assessing organizational management practices and communication is essential for academic achievement. How do the teachers feel about the leadership teams? How do the children feel about the leadership teams? How do your parents feel about the leadership? As Fortune 500 companies learned long ago, knowing how your stakeholders or customers feel is paramount to offering the best quality service. When we go into schools and assess this dimension, we begin by looking at factors such as *leadership satisfaction* (how satisfied the stakeholders are with school leadership), *principal trust* (how much a student trusts principals), *leadership communication* (the level of communication provided by leadership), and *leadership shared mission and vision* (the connectedness of shared mission and vision between stakeholders).

Dimension 7: School Climate

Safe and caring schools are a necessity for a student-teacher relationship to grow. The emotional attachment of a student to his or her school is critical to a good education; the school climate has a major impact on this attachment and has a strong indirect relationship to academic achievement (McNeely, Nonnemaker, & Blum, 2002; Osterman, 2000). Furthermore, a good school climate has an impact on your success in retaining your best educators (Wynn, Carboni, & Patall, 2007). How do students, parents, and educators feel when they walk through the school doors? Do they feel safe? Does your school offer a positive learning environment? When we go into schools and assess this dimension we begin by looking at factors such as *school climate* (the school climate or environment perceived), *student relationships* (the quality of relationships between your students), *school liking* (how much students like their school), and *school isolation* (to what extent students feel isolated within the school). As we will explain in the chapters to follow (especially Chapter 7), you can use the survey we provide in the Appendix to measure this dimension as well; you can also collect and organize other data, evidence, and artifacts that exist to further assess this dimension.

Each of these seven dimensions has been shown indirectly or directly to improve aspects of the school experience and achievement. For example, School Climate may not often have a direct impact on achievement itself, but it does impact or drive the dimensions of Educational Attitudes, Curriculum Expectations, and Faculty Fidelity, which often do have a direct impact on achievement. Yet, just as Howard Gardner has found that there are multiple types of intelligences and there is room for more to be discovered, there might be other dimensions you might want to add to this model, or others that we (the authors) might decide to add in the future. Regardless, as Chapter 2 will illustrate, these seven dimensions are the seven dimensions most often associated with highly effective schools. These seven dimensions of data (qualitative and quantitative) are what you need to consider, focus on, and use to determine what you need to do to increase achievement and achieve positive school reform. But what is more important is addressing all of the dimensions together to create the synergy needed to achieve real lasting school reform. It is important that you assess all of these dimensions from the different perspectives of all of your stakeholders. By themselves (e.g., one dimension such as School Climate) or from one point of view (e.g., that of the student), they are limited in their ability to enhance the learning and teaching culture of a school, but together they are a powerful tool. As the model suggests, it is when we consider how these seven dimensions impact, align with, and explain or predict academic achievement and academic challenges that we can achieve greater success.

We believe that the majority of school systems can utilize a user-friendly common-sense approach to becoming more data-driven, and would greatly benefit from doing so. This multi-dimensional systemic approach can help you more comprehensively assess the *organizational efforts* taking place, as well as the attitudes and perceptions of our customers (students and parents), employees, and other stakeholders (community members). As Leonardo da Vinci once said, "All our knowledge has its origins in our perceptions." A goal of Multi-Dimensional Education is to provide such perceptual knowledge that offers meaningful and usable evidence to inform systemic practices. These data-driven systemic practices will strategically guide educators in their efforts to provide the essential professional development and systems-based management practices needed to actually achieve increased academic performance and continuous improvement.

Innovators Wanted

Much of our lives has been spent working for or with educational organizations and trying our best to help them make positive change in the services and products they provide. From our experience, we have come to live by a saying that makes good sense when it comes to organizational change: *Some will, some won't. So what.* A classic organizational change model created by Everett Rogers (Rogers & Singhal, 1996) accurately explains how we as individuals are normally distributed (i.e., on a bell curve) when it comes to embracing change. Figure 1.3 highlights how there are a few of us who are *innovators*, a few more who are willing to jump onboard at the start (*early adopters*), twice as many that will become part of the *early majority* to try it, an equal amount that might come on after a little success (*late majority*), and the unfortunate group that is labeled as *laggards* (those that rarely embrace the change proposed).

But before you think we are beating up on the laggards, let us remember that it is often the laggards who have been the dissenting voice in those unhealthy *groupthink* situations that use bullying tactics to pressure people to adopt change. These laggards are sometimes the voices of reason who screamed not to launch the shuttle *Challenger* before its unfortunate demise. It was the laggards that tried to get Ford to stop selling the Pinto in light of gas tanks that exploded upon rear end accidents. Often the laggards are the voice of reason. When it comes to educational change laggards may be actively or silently opposed. Either way they provide "drag" to the

Figure 1.3   The Diffusion of Innovation Model

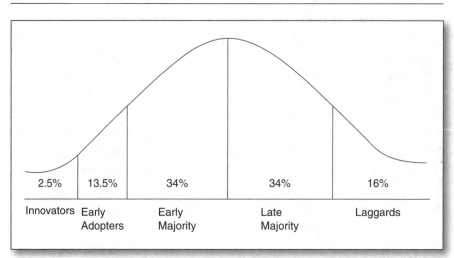

| 2.5% | 13.5% | 34% | 34% | 16% |

Innovators   Early Adopters   Early Majority   Late Majority   Laggards

gears for change. Yet even the apathetic teachers that some might encounter still might be good teachers. And instead of alienating some of our best teachers, we should listen respectfully and consider their concerns.

Rogers's model reminds us that change takes time and not all will adopt change immediately (or sometimes ever). Many of the early majority and the late majority need to see evidence (qualitative or quantitative) that change is taking place and that it is change for the better. But in order for change to start, we need innovators. And in order for change to have a chance to succeed these innovators need early adopters by their side to build momentum. Change in any organization is difficult to achieve. Throw in the role of unions and policies such as tenure, and cloud those waters with a democratic process that is willing to consider or at least listen to all views from the likes of parents who do not always behave rationally, and suddenly your challenges are doubled if not tripled. But many people in the teachers' unions are just looking out for the welfare of those they represent. Many of our tenured teachers who have grown comfortable in old habits and are now fighting change were once incredibly energetic teachers, ready to embrace change in hopes of inspiring more students. And many parents simply want change focused on providing the best for their children. If we are able to show evidence, we can bring more onboard. We can rejuvenate our peers. If we can provide them with evidence that short-term goals have been accomplished, we can get them onboard for long-term goals. But if our long-term goals are unrealistic, the laggards and late majority will rarely ever join us in our efforts to create systemic change.

They call it *normal distribution* for a reason. We are human, and it is normal that we are distributed on a bell curve when it comes to IQ, willingness to change, and many other things. Yet for positive change in education to occur, dedicated innovators are needed. We hope that you are one of those who can lead the way, and that we can help you with the process.

We must emphasize that we are not afraid of academic excellence. We all have children at various ages from pre-K to university, and we expect excellence in their academic efforts. We know that test scores are important. We expect good test scores from our children as well as from the students we teach. But there is much more to educating students and improving a school than relying on a *single* test score or *single* mode of assessment. You deserve a much fairer and more informative growth model that better documents your accountability. Educators need true assessment that uses rigorous, comprehensive, and, when possible, valid means to determine what we can celebrate and what we must do to improve the outcomes of all stakeholders.

We are on your side. And we have written this book to share how you and other educators can be more successful and satisfied when it comes to the demand for data-driven education or accountability. But the first step is to improve our data-driven thinking.

Debunking the Myths of Education Assessment

There are many myths that complicate the paradoxes of education and education assessment. When such myths are embraced as truths, this magnifies the challenges that must be overcome. So before we end this chapter, let's take a few more minutes to consider a few of the myths this book seeks to debunk.

Myth #1: Educators Need to Become Data-Driven

You probably don't need to become data-driven because you are already data-driven. But as we have attempted to illustrate, many need to change the way they are driven by data. As we have stated, and as a majority of our friends in education agree, the biggest challenge educators face is getting this high-speed chase to increasing achievement scores under control. As the Rand Corporation's report *Making Sense of Data Driven Decision Making (DDDM) in Education* points out:

> New state and local test results are adding to the data on student performance that teachers regularly collect via classroom assessments, observations, and assignments. As a result, data are becoming more abundant at the state, district, and school levels—some even suggest that educators are "drowning" in too much data (Celio & Harvey, 2005; Ingram, Louis, & Schroeder, 2004). Along with the increased educator interest in DDDM has come increased attention from the research community to understand the processes and effects of DDDM. Yet there remain many unanswered questions about the interpretation and use of data to inform decisions, and about the ultimate effects of the decisions and resulting actions on student achievement and other educational outcomes. (Marsh, Pane, & Hamilton, 2006, p. 1)

In other words, to improve the approach to data-driven decision making in education, we need to reassess what data are important to our goals and organize them with a process or framework that makes more sense.

Myth #2: Teachers Don't Need to Be Evaluated

As college professors, we are evaluated every semester. Our raises, promotions, and tenure are partially determined by these evaluations. And though we might sometimes dread reading and reviewing our teaching evaluations, they do provide us with a reliable measure as to how our students perceive the instruction we are providing. Also, though there are always a few students who are not happy with a class or a teacher and provide somewhat frank, blunt, honest feedback that might make one a little sad, for those of us who teach well there are always a great many more positive comments. There is normally a silver lining to celebrate and good feedback to build upon.

These evaluations allow us to see how our instruction is perceived and how we as teachers are received. Faculty evaluations allow us to see how well we are communicating with our students. And though assignment grades and tests may provide summative data that show

Figure 1.4   Truth Through Assessment

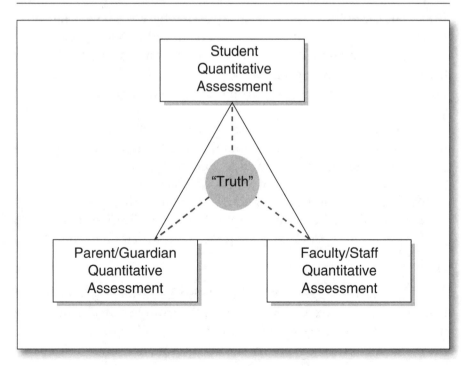

how much knowledge and understanding is being gained by the student, faculty evaluations provide the formative data we need to determine how best to increase the scores on the summative data. They also provide us with a longitudinal assessment of teachers, so that one can see if improvement is being made or if intervention is needed to help our struggling colleagues.

We have worked with a great number of school districts. The data we provide school districts have at times been questioned by teacher unions and by school-level administrators. But always, after we have had a chance to explain how our multi-dimensional data can and should be used to provide a fairer assessment of teacher effectiveness and the information we need to improve our instruction, the tune changes. In one district we worked in, the teacher's union had complained repeatedly to the administration and school board that they would not stand for this type of assessment of their schools or teachers. After coming to the training on the data eventually collected on their participating schools, the union's representatives left the meeting early stating that they were on their way to the superintendent's office to tell him that they recommend that this data approach be taken in all of their schools. They realized that having many data points to illustrate how well we teach is much fairer and more objective than having a principal drop into the classroom a few times a year to write up a report based on one or two short observations. Principals cannot accurately or fairly assess how well a teacher does based on a 10-to-50-minute scheduled observation once a year.

This is not a new debate. One reason the issue is still discussed is because it holds great promise to improve teaching. But it must be done fairly and correctly. According to Marsh and Roche,

> Researchers and practitioners (e.g., Abrami & d'Apollonia, 1991; Cashin & Downey, 1992; Feldman, 1997; Marsh & Roche, 1993) agree that teaching is a complex activity consisting of multiple dimensions (e.g., clarity, teachers' interactions with students, organization, enthusiasm) and that formative-diagnostic evaluations of teachers should reflect this multidimensionality (e.g., a teacher is organized but lacks enthusiasm). (Marsh & Roche, 1997, p. 1187)

As Figure 1.4 suggests, you should also ask students, parents, and peers what they perceive. This is where the truth lies. And whether or not you or the teachers in your building are willing to agree to have these evaluations serve as an accountability measure within your schools, it cannot hurt for teachers to initiate this effort on their own and complete regular self-assessments. Teachers need to be evaluated. We all need feedback to improve.

Myth #3: We Can Achieve 100% Proficiency

Any good teacher knows that a test on which every student gets a 100% is probably not a very accurate assessment. It was probably too easy. Any class where all students leave at the end highly proficient according to assessments given throughout the course, is quite possibly a class that gives numerous proficiency tests that are too easy. Normally, in our classes we have a wide distribution of students with differing abilities and motivation to succeed. But in America, with a heavy reliance upon standardized testing and accountability issues in place due mainly to NCLB, as well as signs of an increased focus on proficiency continuing under the new administration, one might consider the historically controversial debate relating to the normal distribution of the intelligence quotient (IQ) to shine a little common sense on this myth.

To begin this discussion, we must first go back to France and look at why Alfred Binet created the IQ test. In 1905, Binet developed the test to better determine which children were not suited for public schools (Ormrod, 2006a). In other words, the test was *not* created to see how smart a child was. This is just the opposite of the ubiquitous Internet tests for IQ that exist today to see how smart we are compared to our friends. To some, Binet's approach might seem to be backwards, but when you consider the goal of his test, it was quite useful. It was useful because it provided a tool to see who actually needed help. He did not set out to show that everyone was a genius. He did not continue changing the test to allow the test takers to have a greater chance of scoring higher. He continued working to make the test more accurate in truly assessing intelligence and determining which small percentage of students were not suitable for public schools. As Figure 1.5 illustrates, IQ is normally distributed, and theoretically only a very small percentage of students would fall several standard deviations below the average IQ of 100.

The theory that individual differences in intelligence are distributed in accordance with a normal distribution (bell) curve was proposed by Thorndike, a leader during the earlier 1900s in the field of educational measurement (Thorndike, 1927). However, Burt (no relation to Ernie) suggested that a strict focus on the normal distribution of IQ could lead to an underestimation of the number of gifted children

Figure 1.5   Normal Distribution of Intelligence

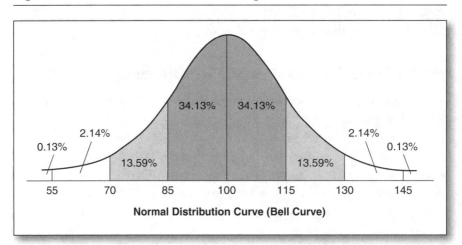

within a school (Burt, 1963). Regardless of the school of thought to which one subscribes, the mass of research does suggest that there is a wide variability of intelligence across children of like ages. As Figure 1.5 shows us, however, we know that the majority (68%) of us fall within one standard deviation of the average IQ (100). We also know from research that rarely (no matter how much we study) can one increase their IQ by more than 15 points, or one standard deviation (Flynn, 1999). This bell curve shows us, in laymen's terms, that some of us are very smart, some of us are not so smart, and most of us are in the middle or average. If the objective of our standardized achievement test is to measure how intelligent our students are in relation to core subject areas such as mathematical abilities or reading comprehension (which, by the way, are related to doing well on an IQ test), then what makes us think we can change the normal distribution of our students' intelligence? Why are we thinking that we can miraculously pull so many of our students from the low achievement side (on the left) or the middle to the high-achieving side (on the right)? Shouldn't we expect our achievement scores to also follow the bell curve? Therefore, one might question whether a challenging curriculum and intensive instruction in a public setting can actually improve intelligence significantly enough to ultimately lead to test scores reaching 100% proficiency.

One might argue the criterion-referenced test requirement of NCLB is a fairer approach, less dependent on a forced normal distribution, and more reflective of student content mastery. The hope of 100% proficiency even on a test that, theoretically, everyone could pass remains an unobtainable goal in many circumstances; studies show that student scores on criterion-referenced tests can be normally distributed or can be negatively skewed due to the test being a minimum proficiency test (Fusarelli, 2004). Therefore, because intelligence is one of the strongest predictors of high achievement, even for criterion-referenced tests, IQ and mastery remain difficult to separate.

As Bruce Feirstein once said, "The distance between insanity and genius is measured only by success" (Feirstein & Spottiswoode, 1997). However, if success (100% proficiency) is most likely an unobtainable goal (as science and 10 years of NCLB has shown us) and for that matter possibly insane, we educators will most likely continue to be frustrated with our failure to document successful or adequate yearly progress in achievement. Having proficiency as a goal is admirable, even essential, because as the old saying goes, "If you aim at nothing, you'll hit it every time." The goal of this text, however, is to help you set realistic goals for the data you use to guide and document your success. And if we know that all of our students fall somewhere on the bell curve in Figure 1.5, wouldn't it be a much more realistic goal to take a more personal approach to helping every child improve rather than expecting every child to be 100% proficient?

Still, the questions remain: When test scores increase, to what might that increase be attributed, and what does it represent? Could a significant increase in test scores be due to increasing intelligence, more demanding curricula, creating better test takers, or possibly increasing the motivation to learn within children? Or is it possibly due to "improving" or "updating" the test? The verdict is still out on this conundrum. Yet with teachers, parents, and students expressing concerns about too much high-stakes testing, one might wonder if the not-so-proficient national scores are a reflection of a lack of motivation or an effect of testing burnout. One thing is certain: For many who teach, it is very clear that not all of our students are going to become brain surgeons or rocket scientists. Many are predisposed and nurtured to perform several standard deviations below the genius level, and sometimes below average. Thus, the challenge is to prepare our students, no matter what their level of intelligence, to do the best that they can in the modern-day world of standards-based and norm-referenced education while preparing to become a contributing citizen.

Theoretically, children are more motivated to perform to their highest ability when they are inspired and feel a need to make their mentors proud. Theoretically, children are more likely to accomplish such goals in learning environments that offer a supportive, caring, and constructive avenue to academic success. With current efforts to increase proficiency rates across all children falling short of nearly all stakeholders' expectations, we believe it is time to get beyond this paradox and myth of education assessment and focus on the dimensions we know will actually improve achievement and contribute to total school improvement.

Myth #4: There Are Three Kinds of Lies— Lies, Damned Lies, and *Statistics*

Have you ever stood at a crosswalk where the *Do Not Walk* signal seemed to take forever to change? If you are alone, you are not likely to cross the street against the signal, because you do not want to be singled out for breaking the law. Yet if a group of people is standing there waiting and then begins to cross the street together, we usually join in, somehow feeling that the numbers justify the infraction. There is comfort in numbers. And yet many people still fear numbers—statistics.

What we have found is that folks tend to fear numbers because often those numbers (statistics) are presented in a fashion they do not understand. They fear numbers because in the past they have been held accountable to standards that make use of numbers that were not fair or accurate. But the honest truth is that numbers do not lie, liars do. Unfortunately, as Andrew Lang once said, we "use statistics as a drunken man uses lampposts—for support rather than for illumination." This is often the case when it comes to educational statistics. Our goal in this book is to help you get beyond this statistical limitation and begin to use statistics to drive what we do and not just provide a lamppost to lean against.

Recently we were in a school on the East Coast giving a workshop to faculty and support staff. We were showing them statistics that related to the level of trust in teachers. The first slide we presented showed that students in that school had a very low level of trust in their teachers. You could see disbelief on the faces of some of the teachers in the room. The next slide showed a similarly low level of trust in the teachers by parents. At this point one of the teachers stood up and said, "You are a liar! You are making up these numbers!" Another teacher screamed an "Amen!" We explained that these statistics were gathered from surveys given to all of the faculty and to more than 300 students and their parents. We asked (with a smile), "Given that we live more than 1,000 to 3,000 miles away from here, how do you think we were able to get these 600 people to give consistently negative answers to these questions? Do you think we called all of them up in our free time?" Silence filled the room as we went to the next slide, which showed how the educators in the room thought that students do not see them as trustworthy. The slide showed that the majority of teachers in the building also felt that many of their colleagues were not seen as trustworthy. We asked them, "Can any of you explain these numbers?" And slowly, one by one, they began to express how as a group they needed to work on building trust because they didn't even trust each other.

This is one example as to how holistic numbers (meaningful statistics) can help teachers have courageous conversations. This is just one example of how a simple statistic on a variable (trust) that has great impact on our ability to provide quality instruction can guide a data-driven conversation to improve all that we do as educators. This is the difference between this book and other books on data, research methods, and analysis. We will not be teaching you how to run statistical analysis. We will not be teaching you how to design a perfect random trial experiment. We will be helping you to collect the data and evidence you have and how to collect additional data and evidence you need. We will be helping you to better organize this data under a seven-dimensional model so that you can understand and use this data to become more successful in what you do. This is not just another book on data analysis. This is a book about a process and framework to make qualitative and quantitative data, statistics, artifacts and other evidence more meaningful and useful to educators.

First Steps

1. Consider how you typically approach and embrace new ideas (proposals for change presented either by you or by others) and how the educators you work with will behave in relation to Rogers's notion of the diffusion of innovation.

2. Begin thinking about how the seven dimensions of Multi-Dimensional Education are perceived in your school by all stakeholders.

3. Begin thinking about how the Multi-Dimensional Education seven dimensions and the existing quantitative and qualitative data, artifacts, and evidence you have on your schools are connected and how such data could be a part of your model for growth.

4. Consider how you might begin to have courageous conversations with a few of your colleagues regarding the best approach for getting others to buy into a positive, multi-dimensional change process.

2

The Seven Dimensions to Guiding Systemic Data-Driven Thinking

In a school district we will call Vinigan Grove Unified Schools, two Building Leadership Teams (BLTs) have gathered to review their respective data. Each school has received their Multi-Dimensional Education data reports for the second year.

The BLT meeting at School One begins with a few introductory remarks from the principal concerning the lack of substantial progress in achievement proficiency for this year. Sighs and moans fill the room, and one teacher remarks, "I just can't teach any harder." The principal tells everyone to relax and passes out the summary report of the testing data. The staff notices that there are some aspects of the comprehensive academic assessment that show progress over the last two years. Yet there are other areas that seem to have remained the same, and an overall literacy score actually dropped from the previous year. They quietly continue to study the test scores; strangely enough, not one person mentions that the test this year was different from the test taken last year.

The assistant principal then leads a discussion on what the BLT feels it can do next year to improve in the area of literacy. "There is money available to put toward our challenges. We just need to decide which ones and what to do." Some people suggest getting everyone retrained on the reading program. Others suggest attending a reading conference or having a consultant come in to work with the faculty at the beginning of the next school year.

(Continued)

(Continued)

"What about the parents?" one teacher asked. "Surely they could do more." Everyone agrees with this, but the discussion moves on. "Our attendance was much lower this year as well," states another administrator. All agree, but no one mentions the swine flu that was rampant during the school year. It is then decided that the BLT will recommend that the parent-teacher committee schedule a professional development program to focus on better communication with the parents concerning the importance of reading and getting the students to school on time, since the attendance officer stated this was a problem. The BLT also decides to investigate getting further training on the reading program.

Next, the assistant principal explains that one third of the staff has asked for transfers and several others are retiring by the end of the year. "Well, this isn't the easiest school to teach in," states the guidance counselor. "I've been here 10 years, and 20% to 30% turnover a year seems about right. You just have to be committed to being here." Several others agree, while others quietly chuckle. "We should try to do something special for the incoming teachers," states Jerome, a fifth grade teacher. "Jean is on the hospitality committee. I will speak to her about this issue." The principal then announces that only 30% responded to the e-mail sent to the teachers containing the 5-item climate surveys. "Most of the data appeared pretty positive, about the same as last year. It would appear from the faculty responses that the students are, in general, happy to be at the school," he added as he passed out the results from the teacher survey. "Based on the teachers' remarks concerning the students, however, it appears we should work on respect next year." It is decided that the climate committee will be charged with coming up with some ideas to improve respect in the school during the next year and that at least a half-day will be spent on strategies to improve student respect towards adults. After one hour, the meeting is adjourned. Designated individuals from the BLT will talk with the various committees about the decisions made and seek their help.

School Two's BLT has already presented their data to the entire faculty. Each faculty member received a copy of the Multi-Dimensional Education data report the staff has used for the past two years to improve their school reform goals—including their academic outcomes. Now the BLT is meeting to have a more in-depth discussion of the data and to make recommendations. Each of the seven assessed areas (Community Engagement, Curriculum Expectations, Developmental Perspectives, Educational Attitudes, Faculty Fidelity, Leadership Potential, and School Climate) is being examined during this meeting. The data are based on responses from staff, parents, and students in the school. The survey used to collect the data utilized reliable and valid scales. The BLT is also looking at data collected by the school relating to behavior incidents, attendance, retention, and other variables.

The guidance counselor speaks first. "I was especially pleased to see that the faculty, parents, and students trusted the teachers and the administration. I don't know if that led to the increase in test scores, but perhaps it played a part."

"I don't know if that is the key," replied Kara, an eighth grade science teacher. "I do know that when I studied the report, the students and parents felt that our curriculum expectations were stronger, with a lot of support for instructional creativity from both the students and the parents. They seem to like what we are doing."

"Did you notice the teacher satisfaction with their working conditions was also quite strong this year?" observed the assistant principal. "I have always felt that a happy teacher teaches happy kids!"

"I think there is some positive data on so many fronts," replied the principal, "However, I am also concerned with an increasing number of students stating that they felt lonely in the school. They trusted the teachers but still felt isolated from their peers. I don't think we have a serious bullying problem but I wonder if our reduction of advisor/advisee from 20 minutes to 8 minutes a day resulted in a sense of isolation. We cut back time for getting to know each other on a more informal basis."

"Perhaps it is because they are just having trouble moving from the elementary school to the middle school. Is this a sixth grade problem or a seventh and eighth grade one also? If it is sixth grade, then we should meet with the sixth grade team as well as our feeder elementary schools to develop some strategies to help this transition and work on building team connectedness," stated a sixth grade teacher.

"Well, why don't we go through the data scale by scale, and see if we can infer any patterns that are positive and others that may require more focus in the next year? Why don't we start with the data concerning the Developmental Perspectives of all the groups and go from there? What are the students saying about this area?" asked the principal.

The meeting goes on for the next few hours, with the staff making notes on the large Post-It paper pasted on the wall. They work to compare last year's data to the present data. The BLT works to determine what will be celebrated the next week at the end-of-the-year party, as well as briefly presenting additional concerns drawn from the data that will need additional committee focus in the coming school year.

Doing or Being?

For quite some time now, research has suggested that if we truly want to improve the quality and productivity of our learning environments, we should focus on variables in education that measure *doing* and not focus as much on *being* (Bloom, 1976, 1980; Mood, 1970; Wolf, 1966). In other words, as Bloom and others proposed, we should focus on that which we can change and not on variables over which we have little control. The introductory story about the two schools (located in the same district with similar demographics and nonacademic barriers) shows how schools take different approaches to using evidence to make data-driven education decisions. While School One focused mainly on achievement scores and briefly touched on parent involvement, teacher retention, and a few behavioral issues, School Two put more effort into looking at the same concerns as well as at additional data on multiple dimensions of education. School Two used all of the data they received (including the Multi-Dimensional Assessment report that both were given) while School One left a number of reports to gather dust in the principal's office. School Two understands that if we cannot change unproductive patterns in the classroom or school (or possibly our achievement proficiency), then we need more information on variables that are possibly related to or causing such patterns and how they can be changed (Anderson, 1972). School Two looked at what they are *doing* related to many dimensions of education and the support they are giving to all stake-holders (educators, parents, and students).

For instance, though socioeconomic status (SES) might be one of the variables most predictive of student success, and without mythical money-growing trees or unprecedented resources we probably are not able to change the SES of the families in our community, we might be able to change the level of parent involvement (Figure 2.1). Though low-SES parents often are perceived not to be as active or engaged in their children's schooling as are more affluent parents (a perception

Figure 2.1   Doing Versus Being

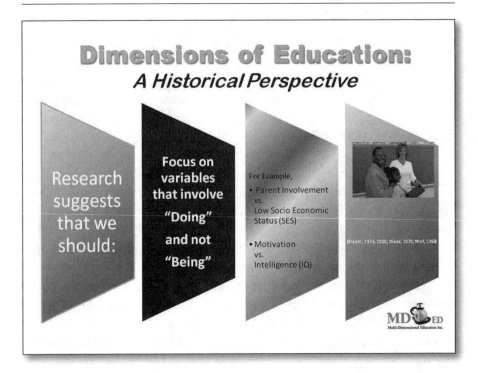

that research cannot confirm or deny), we have found that a large percentage of lower-income parents still have as strong if not a stronger desire for their child to get a great education and become successful. The challenge is determining how schools can turn this desire into action. By looking at data that identifies your challenges with parent involvement and introducing efforts such as College Club (a club that brings all stakeholders together to truly help educators help parents to help students become college and career ready, a strategy we will elaborate on in Chapter 6), we often can get a large number of parents involved who would normally not be involved at all. By looking at data that helps to determine what parents think about what we are doing, and using data to figure out what they need or want in order to get involved, we have a greater chance of impacting both of these nonacademic barriers (SES and parent involvement).

We believe that focusing on data that relates to *doing* can help a school focus its lens on that which it is actually capable of improving. If we know that research shows us intelligence is somewhat innate— inherited from nature and not nurture-dependent or changeable (Simonton, 2001)—and we also know from research that children who enjoy learning and like or trust their teacher are more likely to be motivated to try harder on tests and complete assignments (Corrigan & Chapman, 2008), then common sense would suggest that we should focus on collecting student data that helps us increase motivation.

Yet in an educational world where common sense is not that common anymore, we still continue to focus on variables and data points of *being* that we can rarely change. For instance, we often hear from school personnel that they work with what their community brings to the school. They often state, for example, that more than 60% of their students qualify for free and reduced-price lunches. They say that the neighborhoods they serve are crime-ridden and that their school climate is a direct reflection of what you see on the streets. However, research (Ellis, 1988) shows that in one study after another a good school climate as appraised by teachers (no matter what neighborhoods they serve) is correlated with variables such as

- teachers' trust in principals,
- teachers' belief that they can get help when needed,
- teachers' belief that they are respected, and
- teachers' belief that they are involved in decisions.

All of these bullet points are variables we can impact and improve. For many this just means making educator outcomes or perceptions a priority.

In many schools, students come from low-SES backgrounds, high-crime neighborhoods, and communities that will most likely never be revitalized in the near future. However, in many of these schools you do not find teachers or administrators blaming the majority of their problems on the community. In many of these schools the problems are not even visible, because the educators within the schools understand the importance of both trust and respect, as well as the best means to help their students. They do not lean on the data lampposts and use low SES as an excuse. They understand that these kids deserve and want a safe place to spend their day. They understand the troublemakers are normally a very small percentage of the student body, and with a bit of relationship building combined with focused instruction that supports various students' abilities, educators can make school the best eight hours of their students' day. By establishing consistent rules and procedures and helping the disadvantaged students wash away their developmental delays, they can see gains that many more affluent schools might not be able to achieve. Often it is not the communities that we can rejuvenate, but rather the educators, students, and parents. And no matter whether you are a seasoned, tenured educator or a new teacher who needs additional support and training, by focusing on the doing (or not doing) you can often bypass the challenges of being held accountable for the being.

Effective Schools and Corn-fusing Research

Most of you have visited, attended, or worked in enough schools to know that highly effective schools (e.g., schools you would want your own child to attend), feel very different from less effective schools. Sometimes, when you walk in the door, you can just feel it or see it. The more time you spend in a highly effective school, the more you start to identify characteristics (programs, processes, practices) that make you think, "Hey, we should try this in my school." As you begin to make a mental list of what these highly effective schools are doing differently, you begin to see what we mean by *multi-dimensional.* They don't just do one thing. They do many things simultaneously. Each part of what they do complements the system they have in place. And the really good ones do it right, not light. The best schools closely monitor what they are doing. They assess effectiveness, and they have open lines of communication to discuss how to continually improve what they do.

Yet the more effective schools you visit, the more you realize that rarely do any two of them use the same model to achieve success. They might have common characteristics, but most often we have found that they have taken different paths and shine in different areas or dimensions. What works on one side of town or on one coast might not work as well on the other side, and each school has its unique contextual challenges to overcome. Some have really good leadership and excellent parental involvement but some challenges with faculty. Others have great teachers but a mediocre leader, and yet somehow they create a school climate that motivates students to attend, learn, and succeed. Regardless of their challenges, they all seem to have identified what works for them and have capitalized on their strengths in order to minimize their challenges. They have been able to find the catalyst needed to achieve success, and they remain patient and vigilant during the sometimes laboriously slow learning curve required for positive change to take hold (Fullan, 1991; Sarason, 1990).

Despite all of the research, books, success stories, and literature available on how to become the school about which all those inspirational movies are made, we still have only a limited understanding of how a school becomes effective. There is not an abundance of research that connects the dots for us to determine all of the components we need to put in place in order to become highly effective. Because most research on highly effective schools is largely correlational and based on narrow definitions of academic success centered around standardized tests, we often do not know if these schools are becoming effective because of the listed characteristics or if the characteristics are the natural result or outcome of becoming effective (Kelley, Thornton, & Daugherty, 2005). The good news is that we do know which dimensions are associated with or most often relate positively (correlate) to the success experienced by these effective schools. But before we get into some more specific research on the multiple dimensions of education associated with successful schools, let's spend a little more time discussing the limitations and shortcomings of correlational research and what happens when we only consider or focus on evidence related to a few variables.

To be honest, as researchers who have published numerous correlational studies, we do this because frequently the sample of schools or students we study is not large enough to justify and meet the assumptions demanded of a more comprehensive statistical analysis using a large number of variables. We do this because often we are only given a short amount of time to administer a survey, so the questionnaire must be short, thus limiting the number of variables we can examine. Some researchers might only publish a correlation study because, although they studied a great number of variables, the only significant results identified were related to just a few of the variables studied. And, of course, most journals only want to publish significant results. This is unfortunate, because often it is when we do not find the results or significant relationships we expect to see that we realize that something else is afoot—that something else needs to be considered. Also unfortunately, there are very few journals that want to publish a research report longer than 25 to 30 pages. And it is quite difficult to write up the literature and results on multiple variables or dimensions within those page limits. In addition, as many know all too well, correlation analysis offers a convenient way to complete a dissertation or thesis: Write a short literature review on a few variables and show that they are or are not related. As a result, our journals and databases are filled with endless studies doing simple correlation analysis. This is problematic because often a correlation study that catches the attention of the media or district can be shortsighted and even provide a misleading analysis. In the worst-case scenario, correlation gets confused with causation, and some are led to believe that a specific variable has actually caused something to happen.

A couple of years ago, one of the 24-hour cable news networks ran a story on how research had discovered a significant correlation between corn and the increase in autistic children. The way the story was presented suggested that corn might be responsible for the increase in autism. Think about this for a minute before you stop eating corn or feeding it to your children. How many children do you know who don't eat corn? Not just corn, but also the large number of processed corn products that are part of most children's diets. Whole corn, corn flour, cornstarch, corn gluten, corn syrup, corn meal, corn oil, and popcorn are just a few common forms of corn consumed or used as ingredients. Then you have baking powder, caramel, confectionary sugar, glucose, dextrose, fructose, vanilla extract, monosodium glutamate (MSG) . . . the list goes on of other common ingredients that usually contain or are made from corn or corn syrup. Would you think that a large percentage of kids with autism might consume some form of corn? A correlation study identifying a significant relationship between the evils of corn and autism basically tells us that kids with autism eat corn. But so do a large percentage of kids without autism. We are not big gamblers, but we bet if you replace the variable of autism with low achievement you will probably once again find a significant relationship ("Corn causes low achievement"). And if you replace low achievement with high achievement you will probably find a significant relationship to corn again ("Corn causes high achievement"). So corn might be significantly related to high and to low achievement. It is true that high levels of mercury have been found in corn syrup, and it is also possible that a diet with less corn (and definitely fewer processed foods) *may* help in the battle against autism. But to say corn causes autism is an overstatement. This is one example demonstrating how we must be careful in how we react to data that is not complete or comprehensive enough to serve as a foundation for change.

Another important part of understanding a correlation is how strong the relationship is and whether it is a positive or negative relationship. This might challenge your math abilities a bit, so get out your calculators if you want, or just read along. To avoid singling out another study or author, we will use a hypothetical correlation study. Let's say we read a study that shows there is a correlation between illegal drug use and GPA. The study states that a significant negative relationship exists between illegal drug use and GPA with $p < .0001$ (we have less than one in a thousand chance of being wrong) and r (the statistic representing the correlation) is $-.2$. What does this correlation study tell us?

It shows that when one variable goes up the other goes down. So the more illegal drugs a student uses, the lower the GPA plummets. Makes good common sense, correct? That's why they call it dope. But first you must understand that r represents the strength of the relationship and that when r is squared (r^2) it represents what statisticians call "variance accounted for." In other words, if we square .2, we get .04. And if we turn .04 into a percentage, we get 4%. Therefore, what this study is saying in laymen's terms is that illegal drugs account for 4% of the variance, impact, or reason for this study's sample of students' GPA. So the logical question normally asked is what accounts for the other 96%? This is a good question! Well let's make a list: amount of time spent studying, amount of sleep, course load, nutritional intake, number of classes missed, IQ, SES, extracurricular activities, tutoring, gender, motivation to learn, academic self-esteem, interest in the subject material . . . the list goes on. The point of this exercise and miniature statistics lesson is to show that if we look at the data or statistical results connecting only a few variables, we are only looking at a very small percentage of the variables impacting the total system and ignoring other variables that might have a greater impact. We must consider all the data and move beyond an overreliance upon correlation analysis that only looks at a few parts of a multivariable system.

Meaningful Dimensions of Education

While there is much correlation research published in education journals, there is also an abundance of contemporary and historical research documenting that a great number of dimensions have been thought to be relevant to educational leadership and overall academic success. The term *dimension* is often used when categorizing the different factors or clusters of variables related to a specific area of concern (e.g., School Climate). The term is also often used to organize the components and steps that practitioners and researchers want the reader of their studies to focus on. For instance, the National Association of Secondary School Principals (NASSP, www.principal .org) suggests that there are 10 dimensions on which principals should focus: *setting instructional direction, teamwork, sensitivity, judgment, results orientation, organizational ability, oral communication, written communication, development of others,* and *understanding own strengths and weaknesses.* To some extent, all of the ten dimensions could be assessed to see how well a leader is following the ten steps. Whenever we can figure out and simplify what it is we need to focus on and *do* in order to be successful, it is a good thing. But in order to be an effective educational leader, whether in the school, classroom, or community, we also need to focus on what others are doing and the many variables that impact our being.

For decades, researchers and practitioners have studied or approached education multi-dimensionally. According to Robert C. Kelley, Bill Thornton, and Richard Daugherty,

> Researchers have attempted to quantify the leadership process and establish relationships between dimensions of leadership, school climate, teacher effectiveness, and student learning (Deal & Peterson, 1990; Maehr, 1990; Waters et al., 2004). Early research by Brookover (1979), Edmonds (1979), and Rutter, Maughn, Mortimore, and Ouston (1979) found that correlates of [variables linked to] effective schools include strong leadership, a climate of expectation, an orderly but not rigid atmosphere, and effective communication. These researchers and others suggest that the presence or absence of a strong educational leader, the

climate of the school, and attitudes of the teaching staff can directly influence student achievement. (Kelley, Thornton, Daugherty, 2005, p. 18)

Such research provides support for a multi-dimensional approach to continuous improvement in education. Such research begins to show how *good* education and leadership is systemic and not systematic. A good approach to education challenges us to look at all of the parts of the system and not systematically address one issue at a time. To do this, educators need to move beyond the challenges of the last ten years of NCLB's accountability model by taking a step backward to consider what research discovered in the past as to what works in education.

We are often asked by our college students if using "old" studies is a smart thing to do. For some reason, many people think that the challenges of today's education world are very different from what educators had to deal with in the past. But from our perspective, this is not always the case. If you watch the inspirational movies we mentioned in Chapter 1, which span six decades, you will see many of the same challenges in the plots (e.g., unmotivated students, bad behavior, lack of support for educators, and poor leadership). If you do a thorough review of the historical education research, you will find that many of the same variables we discuss today have been studied for decades. Many times, what we identified just a few decades ago is now buried in the basement of a library or gathering dust on a bookshelf in an office, forgotten in our pursuit of excellence and the demands of new policies. In educational research, we often see new publications that claim to have uncovered new evidence, but in reality, if the authors had just completed a more thorough historical review of the literature related to their topic, they might have found that such evidence was discovered in the past.

This happened to us while working with the U.S. Department of Education on a project to develop new models and measures for efforts to focus on school climate. We were among the 35 experts they had convened to develop the model and measures; after participating in meetings and numerous conference calls with the Department of Education staff, we decided to do a little digging into what was discovered on school climate in the 1970s and 1980s, when *school climate* was the buzzword. We felt that too much of the conversation was being spent on trying to formulate new definitions and measures of school climate, and not enough time was being spent exploring possible existing well-researched models and measures that had gone through extensive validation studies. Why try to reinvent the wheel?

Upon spending a few hours searching for articles on research databases, and then a bit more time in the musty basement of a university library, we came across a great number of *old* articles that provided the insights we were looking for to add to the conversation. One of the articles (saved on one of those crazy old microfiche tapes) held many answers to the questions we had been debating in Washington, D.C. It was a meta-analysis of studies on school climate (Anderson, 1982). *Meta-analysis* basically means an analysis of the analyses; this meta-analysis was an analysis of 200 references or publications related to school climate. So instead of having to read 200 different pieces of research published prior to 1982, we were able to read Carolyn Anderson's opus on school climate. Beyond the article's insights into the many different components of school climate studied by hundreds of researchers and practitioners, it also provided support for our multi-dimensional model. Suddenly, the lesson we had taught so many times to our students once again provided the answers we wanted to add to the conversation on school climate at the federal level. It also identified evidence that further complemented our efforts to continually improve the Multi-Dimensional Education seven-dimensional model.

Anderson addressed how there are two types of models: *additive* and *mediated* models. As she explained, "The simplest models are purely additive. That is, they assume that variables directly influence student outcomes in a separate but additive way" (p. 384). While operationally easy to use, these models do not adequately reflect reality, where many highly related variables are constantly interacting (Burstein, 1980; Levin, 1970). Anderson explained that, in the mediated model, some variables appear to mediate others so that the effect of the distal (long term) variables on student outcome operates through the effect of the more proximal (short term) variables. In other words, in order to accomplish your long term goal there are a great number of short term variables that will impact and predict if you are able to accomplish this goal. And as a result, under a mediated model, you should be including these many variables as part of your focus.

In 1972, Dyer used this mediated model in a simple form to suggest that environment (of family, school, and community) affects pupil achievement by first affecting attitudes (of parents, teacher, and peers). Basically, Dyer found that the students' home, school, and social environments influence the pupil's attitudes (self-perception), which finally and directly affect achievement. In other words, they discovered nearly four decades ago what we have been helping schools put in place for the past six years: If you want to increase achievement, you must focus on multiple dimensions of data to improve and connect areas such as the curriculum, community, climate, and character. Needless to say, this finding spurred us on to do more research to see if there were other research projects or educational initiatives we had not yet discovered that had used this systemic approach.

Although our previous research had revealed how others had used the term *dimensions* to describe characteristics of highly effective principals and highly effective schools, we found that very few had looked at gathering data comprehensively around the dimensions we identified as being the most promising attributes of successful schools. Although for our federal research efforts we had investigated each dimension within our model separately as we developed each dimension of the model and the scales needed for an educational index to measure each dimension, we decided after finding Anderson's article that we had not completed a thorough enough literature review on how others before us approached educational research multi-dimensionally. To shorten our own learning curve, we decided it would be worth our time to look for more lessons learned so that we would not just repeat history, but rather learn from it. So, throwing aside any prejudice we might have against research completed decades ago, we decided to put on our Indiana Jones hat and start digging.

Another meta-analysis we found was based on an examination of 48 studies and reviews published prior to 1982 (Borger, Lo, Oh, & Walberg, 1985). In this publication, the authors identified nine constructs related to highly effective schools: *leadership, school climate, physical environment, teacher-student relationships, curriculum, instruction, finance, evaluation,* and *parents and community.* We were astonished at the similarities of their dimensions to ours. In their research, they found that the above nine dimensions were the most often identified predictors or contributors associated with highly effective schools. (As a side note, would you categorize these nine constructs or dimensions as falling under the *doing* or *being* category? In other words, which of these dimensions could we realistically make an impact on or change for the better as educators?)

When we continued to dig deeper into identifying historical research related to the Multi-Dimensional Education approach, we began to see a pattern in the dimensions that past research has identified and the research we were completing. For instance, research funded by the U.S. Department of Education in the late 1980's identified eight *dimensions of excellence: school climate, leadership, teacher behavior, curriculum, monitoring and assessment, student discipline and behavior, staff development,* and *parent involvement* (Dusewicz & Beyer, 1988).

Dusewicz and Beyer developed scales around these dimensions to "collect data on key variables represented by the school effectiveness research as being related to excellence in education" (p. 2). (These scales can be found fairly easily online.) Upon the discovery of dimensions identified by Borger, Dusewicz, and Beyer, we were once again amazed at the similarities of their dimensional models to ours. At first this was somewhat alarming and slightly disappointing. We slowly started to realize that what we had discovered and developed was nothing new, just forgotten. But as researchers who seek to find validation of what we claim and practice, it was quite rewarding and insightful to read the discoveries made before our efforts. And this research didn't stop in the 1980s, like parachute pants.

Robert Marzano, a highly respected expert in the field of education who has completed decades of excellent research, has identified 11 factors that influence achievement (Marzano, 2003a; Marzano, 2003c). Though the factors Marzano proposes might be worded differently, they are quite similar to the constructs or dimensions that we use. As Figure 2.2 illustrates, he encourages educators to look at

Figure 2.2   Marzano's Factors of Influence

Dimensions of Education:
A Historical Perspective

According to Marzano, the Factors
Influencing Achievement Are:

1. Guaranteed and Viable Curriculum
2. Challenging Goals and Effective Feedback
3. Parent and Community Involvement
4. Safe and Orderly Environment
5. Collegiality and Professionalism
6. Instructional Strategies
7. Classroom Management
8. Classroom Curriculum Design
9. Home Environment
10. Learning Intelligence/Background Knowledge
11. Motivation

"Doing"
or
"Being"?

www.marzanoresearch.com

dimensions such as curriculum, community involvement, school climate (for example, environment and relationships), educational attitudes (motivation), instruction, and communication. When you look at these dimensions or factors, how would you categorize them—doing or being?

These studies and practices show us that education, or more specifically academic achievement, is rarely improved by focusing on a single test. "Drilling and thrilling" will seldom develop students who possess intellectual curiosity or motivation that improves educational outcomes. A thorough review of the research completed during the past 40 years tells us to focus on the many parts of the system we need to develop highly effective schools. Research also shows us that rarely does a new curriculum or product have the ability to change our achievement or success on its own. It is the synergy of many efforts (dimensions) on which we need to focus in order to truly turn our schools around. And it is data on these dimensions that will help us determine what needs to be done.

As Schmoker (2001) points out regarding how effective schools approach the use of data,

> They [effective schools] aren't satisfied with data until data have life and meaning for every teacher, every pertinent party. They use data to create and to ensure an objective, commonly held reality. . . . The use of data allows for organized, simplified discussions that merge to create focused priorities and productive action. (p. 51)

Easy as Cake

Some might think that creating a system of many variables to feed your data-driven thinking is difficult, but it doesn't have to be. Consider the following scenario. It's late in the evening, and you just finished watching one of those baking contests on a food channel. As a result you are now hungry and surveying your kitchen. You ask yourself the question, "What are the ingredients needed to bake a delicious chocolate cake?" You decide you need butter, oil, eggs, flour, sugar, baking soda and powder, a pinch of salt, some artificial vanilla (with corn additive), and of course chocolate; lots of chocolate! We know that if we follow the directions of the recipe, mix the ingredients together correctly, and bake to perfection, we will reap the benefits of one of the most wonderful inventions known to humankind—cake. Now imagine after you have pulled out all of these ingredients, you discover that your oven is broken. But since you are so hungry, you must eat each of these ingredients separately. How does two cups of flour sound for a nice snack? Or maybe you love Elvis and feel the need to eat three whole sticks of butter. Or maybe you hear the theme from *Rocky* playing in the back of your mind and you want to chug a few raw eggs. No? Chugging raw eggs, downing several sticks of butter and somehow swallowing several cups of dry flour don't sound good to you? Of course not!

With the exception of chocolate icing, very few of these ingredients would be very tasty on their own. But combine these ingredients and put them in an oven for a set period of time and you have a delicious cake. Yet if you remove an essential ingredient such as flour or allow another ingredient such as salt to have too much impact, suddenly the cake is no longer wonderful. In a nutshell, this is the basic concept behind systems theory. The sum of the parts working together (*synergy*) is normally more powerful than the individual parts operating separately or alone. And if we remove or augment one or more of the parts, we no longer have the same system creating the same output.

We can apply this cake analogy to simplistic approaches often used by schools. How often have you heard that if you will just put a new program in a school, it will solve the dropout problem or the literacy problem? The promising program may make an impact, but rarely will it make a significant impact that "solves" the problem or has a long-term effect. The reason is quite simple: A simple solution rarely solves a complex problem.

In education, we often fail not due to the inherent weaknesses of the innovations themselves but due to the nature of the change process (Marzano, Zaffron, Zraik, Robbins, & Yoon, 1995). Specifically, we often fail because we rarely can take the change process in schools from a level of *first-order change* (more psychological in nature and reflective of our doing) to a level of *second-order change* (more ontological in nature and reflective of our being). First-order change often fails because we try to introduce new components to an existing system rather than adopting new components that allow us to create a new system. This is one of the reasons schools and districts frequently err in their efforts to be data-driven. They add the demand to be data-driven to their efforts, but they have no system or plan for helping educators interpret and use the data (Marzano, 2003b).

Schools are complex organizations, and a systems approach is required to actually accomplish what is referred to as *systemic change*. If we only focus on improving the instructional performance and effectiveness of our teachers while ignoring problems with our school climate, we will rarely achieve long-lasting positive results. No matter how well a teacher can teach, he or she cannot overcome the anxiety experienced by students if they do not feel safe or valued within the learning environment. We cannot improve the morale and character of a school if the leader in place is the antithesis of good character and negatively impacts morale. We must approach change systemically. We must focus on all parts of the possibly disconnected existing system in order to make the repairs or replacements required by the new system. We must figure out which parts will allow us to create a new system if we are going to be able to make improvements.

For decades, systems theory has been used successfully within the field of organizational management to help leaders improve their organizations. It is a theory that helps many to visualize and, to some extent, take a more objective look at the organizational system within which they work. Below are a few other terms from systems theory we would like to briefly share with you to help you better visualize applying a bit of theory and utilizing the Multi-Dimensional Education framework. Now we know some might think, "More theory? Come on, guys!" But how many theories can bake a cake? Systems theory holds great promise for guiding educators when it comes to data-driven thinking. These terms begin to give data life and meaning for every pertinent party, as Schmoker suggested. By considering how these terms relate to the many parts of the system surrounding educators, you can see more clearly how you are working within a system that most likely needs to adapt and adopt new components, and how many of these terms begin to highlight much of what you might be experiencing and need to embrace. Let us consider the following terms that we think can help you create a system around the Multi-Dimensional Education Process.

- *Entropy.* This is a measure of energy that is expended in a system but does no useful work and tends to decrease the organizational order of the system. In other words, think about wasted or negative energy being expended in your school and how you can redirect it.

- *Feedback.* A well-functioning system continually exchanges feedback among its various parts and participants to ensure that they remain closely aligned and focused on achieving the goal of the system. Communication is key to success. Where does feedback need to be improved?

- *First-Order Change.* First-order change is probably best described as *surface change.* This type of change is usually superficial and is often characterized by the cliché "the more things change, the more they stay the same." Thus, behaviors within a system are altered, while the system's structure (i.e., the rules governing that behavior) remains unchanged. This type of change is just scratching the surface but not necessarily making a difference. In other words, this systematic change is not yet impacting systemic change.

- *Homeostasis.* This is the tendency of a system to maintain internal stability, owing to the coordinated response of its parts to any situation or stimulus tending to disturb its normal condition or function. Everett Rogers's Diffusion of Innovation Model, discussed in Chapter 1, offers an explanation as to why this is often the case when trying to change a system. How do we get all onboard to counteract the homeostatic nature of our schools?

- *Open System.* This is a system that regularly exchanges feedback with its external environment. This is the goal. Just like we expect our students to be, we must also be open to listening and sharing in order to learn and improve. We must be open to changing the whole system of how we use data in order to find a system that can benefit from data.

- *Second-Order Change.* If we are actually able to adopt new ways of thinking (first-order change) and then also able to act based on new rules and premises, second-order change can then occur. This is the goal. This is real change.

- *Equifinality.* The same end result may be achieved via many different paths. As we stated earlier, when we study highly effective schools we find that often they take different paths to achieving success.

Considering the terms above, have you ever felt like the stakeholders in your school were putting plenty of energy toward what was thought to be a worthy endeavor but little or nothing resulted from the energy expended (entropy)? Have you ever worked in a school that did not communicate well with its stakeholders or listen to them (feedback)? To fix the apparent challenges in your school, have you agreed to changes that never seem to work within the structure you operate by (homeostasis and first-order change)? Or did you adopt a system more open to change that regularly exchanges feedback with the many parts internal and external to all you do (second-order change)? This is our goal. We want to help you see how and what is needed to change. We want to help you better connect the many parts (dimensions) of your system in order to create a new system for achieving success.

The point is this: If we continue to apply Band-Aids to our most obvious academic challenges while not paying as much attention to related aspects that also need attention, we will only continue to experience frustration and, at best, short-term relief. Our goal is to help you see the education process within your school as a system. We want to help you better assess or diagnose these essential dimensions for highly effective schools. Figure 2.3 illustrates how good data combined with strategic systemic planning and data-driven professional development will improve the educational outcomes of children, the support you receive from parents, as well as the performance and job satisfaction of your colleagues.

The Multi-Dimensional Education Systemic Model

As stated earlier, we developed the model for Multi-Dimensional Education one dimension at a time. By initially studying more than one hundred randomly assigned schools and more than 35,000 educators, parents, and students in the five states we were hired to evaluate, we set out to discover why the good schools were successful. As we studied each successful school, we methodically began adding dimensions to our model that captured what these schools did best. In our first year we had four dimensions. By the third year we were up to six dimensions, and by the fourth year we had developed the seven-dimensional model that you see in this book.

But, as we explained in Chapter 1, the initial seven-dimensional model was designed and meant to serve as a logic model. The logic was that as the seven dimensions improve, academic challenges would decrease, academic achievement would increase, and over time schools would become successful. However, as our measurement tools improved and caught up with our theory and research efforts, we began to see data-based evidence that these dimensions were interconnected, complementary, and identifiable to some extent in all of the schools. We discovered that schools were all using the same ingredients but not the same amounts. For some reason some were not producing the same delicious cake. And just as Alfred Binet devised a test to determine to what extent students were intelligent in different areas (IQ), we discovered a measurement tool that showed us how schools varied across these seven dimensions. We began to see how these dimensions provided a way to diagnose what other schools needed to improve. We discovered that by assessing all

Figure 2.3 The Multi-Dimensional Education Assessment Process

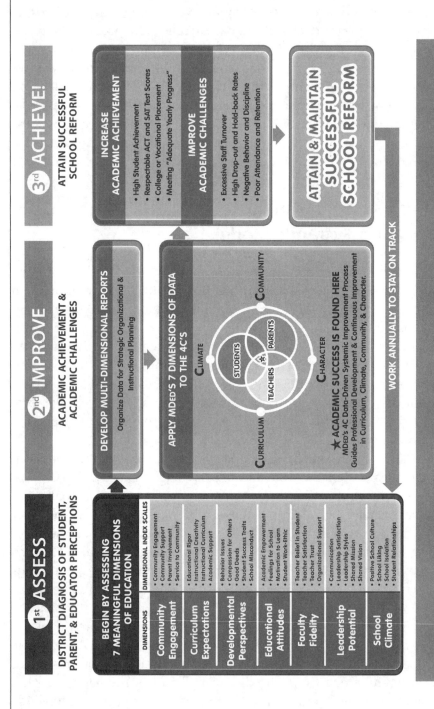

stakeholders in these schools on these seven dimensions, we could capture the pulse of how people were feeling. And that is when we started calling what we do MDed (pronounced like a medical doctor would—M.D. Ed), because to some extent we were providing the vital signs that educators needed to diagnose their ailments and vitality. As we have discussed, we believe that this seven-dimensional model for assessment can better inform what you are doing in your first-order change efforts as well as help you reach second-order change that holds greater promise for improving your being. No matter whether you use the Multi-Dimensional Assessment provided in the Appendix (similar to what we use when evaluating schools) or other qualitative or quantitative assessment tools that relate to the MDed seven dimensions, or you organize your own evidence and existing data under the seven dimensions, by focusing your new lens on these seven dimensions of data you can begin to make strategic positive systemic change.

As Schmoker (2001) has found, successful schools "do not just collect data, they revere it" (p. 51). By assessing seven dimensions essential to your success and incorporating them into a new data system that educators understand, embrace, and can use to inform their practices, Multi-Dimensional Education can become a compass that is guided by meaningful data collected on your school. Therefore, in order to begin looking at these seven dimensions as a system, let us now consider how they interact with and impact each other. Let's take a look at how they all provide part of the impetus needed to change academic achievement and challenges. Please note and remember that some of these dimensions are directly correlated to achievement while others are indirectly correlated.

Dimension 1: Community Engagement

An abundance of research (which will be discussed in Chapter 6) has shown how Community Engagement is quite beneficial to academic success. A sense of community can provide benefits in terms of increased student achievement and motivation to learn, which falls under our Dimension 4 on Educational Attitudes (Bryk & Driscoll, 1988; Comer & Haynes, 1991; Welhage, Rutter, Smith, Lesko, & Fernandez, 1989). Community engagement also can reduce student feelings

of alienation, which interacts with Dimension 7 on School Climate (Bryk, Lee, & Holland, 1993; Wellhage et al., 1989). It can create a more engaged community that goes beyond benefiting students and also benefits teacher morale and collegiality (Dimension 5, Faculty Fidelity), teacher-administrator relationships (Dimension 6, Leadership Potential), and even school-parent-community relationships (Dimension 2, Curriculum Expectations) (Bryk & Driscoll, 1988; Comer & Haynes, 1991). We believe that once you read Chapter 7, you will become a firm believer (if you are not already) in how this dimension can be one of your most powerful tools.

Dimension 2: Curriculum Expectations

Often, when a school system we are assessing looks at our second dimension, they think we are going to assess the curricula that they use in their schools. This is rarely the case, however, because this is not what we are interested in studying. As the U.S. Department of Education's What Works Clearinghouse and other organizations such as the National Science Foundation have discovered, there are not many curricula that can be identified as significantly effective when used across a large sample of schools. The failure of Reading First to produce such evidence provides just one example supporting this claim. We believe that the difficulty of identifying generalizable evidence on the effectiveness of curricula is not due to curricula being ineffective; quite the contrary, we believe that many of these curricula hold promise for helping educators help students learn. We believe the lack of consistent research findings is usually due to the fact that the quality and consistency of curricula delivery varies greatly. We also know from firsthand experience the challenges of trying to produce sound and significant quantitative evidence when conducting a study within multiple schools that differ greatly. Thus, the lack of statistical evidence showing that various curricula produce significant impacts on learning that can be generalized to all schools is probably explained by the fact that no matter how good the curriculum, learning any subject matter depends mainly upon the person in charge of the room teaching it. And as many educators know, though they might be surrounded by excellent teachers, they also can name a few that are not so excellent.

Therefore, we focus more on what constitutes good teaching. Similarly to the way in which Harvard University's Tony Wagner has helped many educators refocus on three new Rs (*rigor, relevance,* and *relationships*), in this dimension we focus on how the instruction, curricula and subject matter shared by educators are viewed by all stakeholders. If you by chance saved a textbook from your university courses on educational psychology or curriculum and instruction, you can find an endless array of what researchers and practitioners have discovered produces quality learning. Yes, rigor, relevance, and relationships are important, yet so are results. The results from teachers that do a good job of being creative in their instructional styles and providing the support students need (no matter which curricula they are told or allowed to use), can have a great impact on (Dimension 3) Developmental Perspectives (Ormrod, 2006a). The results which come from a teacher who understands Vygotsky's Zone of Proximal Development and provides each individual with the level of rigor that pushes them just enough can be the catalyst for shaping that individual's attitude toward education and learning (Dimension 4). The way one teaches and the experience that comes from one's teaching is what defines how one feels about one's job (satisfaction) and belief in students (Dimension 5). Classroom climate is directly related to perceptions of School Climate (Dimension 7). Being surrounded by good, qualified, and motivated teachers is an important component of success. Knowing which teachers need help or which teachers deserve recognition can help you to improve whatever curriculum you adopt. Chapter 5 will provide you with more insights into how to make your curricula most conducive to success.

Dimension 3: Developmental Perspectives

To some extent, one's view of this dimension once again depends on whether one entered education as career or as a calling. The philosophical foundations of the educator's role in the development of a student (or whole child, if you will) date back at least to the teachings of the Greek sages. Although Aristotle's efforts to teach Alexander the Great how to be a great person rather than the conqueror of the ancient world did not go necessarily as planned, if one does not see the

need to focus on the overall development of students as a means to increasing their learning, it is probably because one has not yet had a student come back to say how one changed the student's life and inspired them to greatness. Many teachers who have been blessed with such praise tell us that this type of evidence is better than any data that can be collected. Even if the debate continues in some circles, from our experience, the better a teacher is at helping a child develop into a better person and helping them to see the role of education in achieving their true potential, the greater the chance for success, both in a life of tests and in the test of life.

Beyond the research to be addressed in Chapter 8 on effective prosocial education efforts such as social-emotional learning, civic engagement, service learning, and character education, there is an abundance of foundational theory that you were provided, most likely as a preservice teacher, that supports this dimension. You probably remember learning about Locke, a British philosopher who viewed the child as a *tabula rasa*, or "blank slate." According to Locke, in the beginning of life we start with nothing; it is the experiences that we gather that shape us. Erickson's (1950) psychosocial theory of development illustrates that, in some stages of development, children need to autonomously expand their intrinsic initiative and ask themselves questions related to who they believe they are and what their place in society is. However, at each stage of Erickson's model, the child acquires attitudes and skills that contribute to the development of an active, contributing member of society. Therefore, in a number of Erickson's stages, a child is somewhat reliant upon those in the roles of parents, teachers, adults, and peers, and interaction with them, to help in the process. Vygotsky, in his sociocultural theory, proposed that these social processes account for the higher mental processes, which are not genetic endowments (as cited in Wertsch, 1985). Psychologists such as Bruner believed "that individual development could not be understood without reference to the social and cultural context within which such development is embedded" (Driscoll, 2000, p. 240).

Regardless of whether or not we think that, as educators, we should help in the development of students' personality, behavior, or character, most of us have either heard about or, unfortunately, experienced a class in which the students were *not* motivated to become something special, to behave well, or to care about others. And when we have a class that has such not-so-nice or not-so-well-developed children, we often experience challenges in teaching (Dimensions 2 and 5) and in the climate of our learning environment (Dimension 7), as well as with attitudes toward education (Dimension 4). Often the difference between good students and bad students depends upon what the students believe about themselves. And the Internet is filled with stories about how one educator made the difference in a child's life. Chapter 8 will provide you with more insights into the power of developing character for all stakeholders in your building.

Dimension 4: Educational Attitudes

Dimensions 3 and 4 are tightly related. While Dimension 3 addresses students' social and behavioral development, Dimension 4 is focused more specifically on the development of students' attitudes toward education. The field of educational psychology is an "academic discipline that studies and applies concepts and theories of psychology to instructional practice" (Ormrod, 2006b, p. 4). Basically, educational psychologists study how learners learn and what variables help them to be successful. A number of variables  (e.g., affect—feelings and emotion for a task, motivation, goal setting, self-efficacy) hold great potential for helping students reach higher levels of achievement. For decades, motivation has been studied by a great number of psychologists, such as B. F. Skinner. What we have found is that motivation is one of the keys to learning. If a child is not motivated to learn about a subject, the level of intelligence of the student or educator does not matter. If a student does not believe that they are capable of mastering a subject, they will lack the confidence they need to be successful. If they lack motivation, a sense of self-efficacy, academic empowerment, and positive feelings for school or subject matter, this will provide many challenges to the educator.

Therefore, Educational Attitudes have an impact on the learning climate (Dimension 7), the ability of faculty to be successful (Dimension 5), and Curriculum Expectations (Dimension 2). Since these attitudes can be strengthened or weakened by the environment and academic support they have at home, you will also find a strong connection to Community Engagement (Dimension 1).

Dimension 5: Faculty Fidelity

Dimension 5 complements Dimension 2 (Curriculum Expectations) by expanding our view from *how* we teach to our relationships with those we teach. If you reflect back on the best teachers or professors you have had, what characteristics of the relationships with them

come to mind? Were they caring? Did you trust them? Did they seem happy or satisfied with their roles as educators? Did they believe in you? We have asked these questions many times to preservice and experienced educators, and we typically receive the same answer: *Yes!* And quite often these same teachers were the hardest and most demanding.

The fidelity (devotion, loyalty, and faithfulness) of teachers is the true indicator of teaching success. Educators can be "highly qualified" (i.e., have a certification or degree saying they know what they are teaching) but still not have the fidelity to be a successful teacher. Therefore, if they are not passionate and diligent about the subject matter they teach and do not develop relationships with students that allow them to share that fervor, they often will create additional challenges related to Developmental Perspectives (Dimension 3), Educational Attitudes (Dimension 4), and the learning climate (Dimension 7). And of course, when a student is not happy with a class or course, the leadership team (Dimension 6) encounters additional challenges of one sort or another.

Dimension 6: Leadership Potential

Quite simply, this dimension has an impact on every dimension we measure. On nearly every analysis we have run, we have found Dimension 6 to be strongly correlated with, and to some degree predictive of, the other dimensions. In our studies, one definitive conclusion is supported by both qualitative observations and quantitative data: if leadership is lacking, all else will most likely fail. In the schools where we have witnessed bad leadership, the outcomes resulted in a failure to make positive change or the leadership was changed. Leadership is crucial to all of these dimensions, which in turn guide how we successfully respond to academic challenges. In Part II of this book, and more specifically in Chapter 4, we will address how leadership can be improved by using the seven dimensions of data.

Dimension 7: School Climate

A student's positive connectedness and the quality of relationships with others in school have been shown to promote psychological health, (Kasen, Johnson, & Cohen, 1990; McNeely, Nonnemaker, & Blum, 2002; Whitlock, 2006), to help develop a positive self-concept (Reynolds, Ramirez, Magrina, & Allen, 1980), to reduce bullying (Peterson & Skiba, 2001), and to reduce antisocial behavior (Kuperminc, Leadbeater, Emmons, & Blatt, 1997). In Chapter 7, we will provide you with an abundance of research that shows how

school climate or culture holds a strong indirect relationship to the high achievement you seek. The research will also expand on how climate is connected to all of the other dimensions. If the school does not provide a safe, supportive, and caring atmosphere, you will encounter issues with community and parent engagement (Dimension 1), classroom challenges (Dimensions 2 and 5), and student attitudes (Dimensions 3 and 4). If the school does not provide a positive atmosphere for learning, the challenges in regard to Leadership Potential and Faculty Fidelity (Dimensions 5 and 6) are endless.

When we *systematically* approach each of these dimensions, what we will produce are seven gears that typically do not have enough power to turn on their own. When we *systemically* address all of them, pull them together around Leadership Potential at the center, and allow the gears to connect, we then can create a mechanism able to generate the synergy needed to empower data-driven thinking.

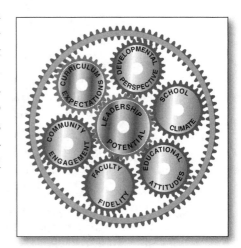

Eeny, Meeny, Miny, Moe

As we hope you are beginning to see, there are many factors that affect whether a school is able to meet its goals. The issue is whether you have enough meaningful and accurate information, and when possible *valid* and *reliable* data and evidence, that the decisions made are not simply based on what one feels, but effectively address all of the issues or concerns at stake. The challenge is how to select what data to use. How do we empower our data-driven thinking? The challenge is to get beyond the old systematic approach (additive model), in which we add one effort to fix the system, and to begin to embrace the systemic approach (mediated model), in which we must address many dimensions simultaneously. Feelings and intuitions are fine and have their place in life and leadership. Indeed, they add much to both. But by using qualitative and quantitative evidence (insights, artifacts, and data on the essential dimensions related to educational excellence), educators can often confirm their intuition, inform their decisions, and document details about the challenges and how to address them.

Now, imagine that you are the superintendent of the two schools in the story we started with in this chapter. Both schools' students and families reflect the same SES—the schools are carbon copies of each other. Each school has the same opportunity to hire qualified faculty and staff. Each school has monies to either invest in professional development or to purchase programs that they *think* are needed, and can utilize the evaluation services provided by the district to pinpoint what is *actually* needed. In fact, each school had the same data, but only one looked at the dimensional data report provided. Which school do you think would have a greater chance of meeting their academic, social, and ethical goals? If School One is only looking at achievement data and a few *homegrown* survey questions, while School Two is focusing on seven of the dimensions most often associated with highly effective schools while also considering achievement data and behavioral data, then research and common sense would clearly indicate that the second school is better able to make informed decisions. We have experienced the same basic story in numerous districts. Every time, it is the school taking the data-driven thinking approach that School Two does that is able to more often accomplish second-order change.

If we consider the abundance of sound longitudinal research, we find that there is a convergence of a limited number of dimensions that will truly impact the learning of students and lead to school improvement. Based on this research, we believe that knowing the views of *all* stakeholders within a school community is of paramount importance for the school that desires to improve in all aspects, including achievement. We further believe that sound research can be used to focus the attention of schools and their stakeholders onto seven dimensions that provide a complete 360-degree assessment of their situation. The next chapter will build on this idea.

The Paralysis of Analysis

Before we end this chapter, we want to share with you one more lesson about using data in educational settings. When we started providing the Multi-Dimensional Assessment to schools, we discovered that not only did they find our data interesting, but they wanted much more detail than we were providing in our reports. Educators often asked us if they could have a report that provided the mean response for each of the questions on our survey. At first we thought that this was a good sign and said that we would be glad to offer such a report. Then one day we witnessed a group of educators in a training session going through the survey item response report one question at a time. Since our survey replaces several (four to eight) surveys currently used in schools, it is longer than most, with over 100 items. The idea is to survey students once a year with a comprehensive survey that takes about a class period to administer rather than expend multiple class periods throughout the year administering many different surveys and contributing to survey burnout.

As we watched the educators go through the report that day, we noticed that they were taking a lot of time discussing each survey question. They stopped to discuss and debate why their students and parents were answering specific questions the way they did. At one point they brought us over and said, as they pointed at one question on the survey, "This is what we are going to focus on this spring. We want to know why students feel they have very few people to turn to for help in our school." Had we allowed this process to go on for much longer, the training day would have slipped away, and the educators would have only made it through half of the survey; they would have focused on 1 question out of 100. And though this approach might be beneficial to getting educators talking about data, it is not the best way to spend our limited time.

When you start to organize your data into the seven dimensions we are proposing, you will be astonished at how much data you have. You will have specific statistics such as attendance rates, dropout rates, and behavioral incidents. You will have numerous scales, possibly within a single survey, that measure the dimensions through an assortment of variables (for example, motivation to learn and trust in teachers). You will have achievement data. And if you try to go through each statistic or survey item one at a time, you will truly discover what we mean by the paralysis of analysis. Just imagine how you would feel going through each question on your achievement test. You would probably find yourself somewhat paralyzed. You will feel overwhelmed and possibly unable to move. Your brain will turn from numb to dumb.

We want to help you better understand and gather data you need to make a difference in increasing achievement and so much more. And we do this by helping you to focus on seven dimensions. The Multi-Dimensional Assessment we provide you in the Appendix measures seven dimensions by using constructs or scales that measure at least two variables per dimension. And each of these scales has 4 to 12 items or questions. The goal is to get you to look at your data through a lens that studies seven dimensions. In considering the totality of the dimensions, you will not have time to look at each item; instead you should look at outcomes of each scale (variables such as school isolation) under the dimension. In addition, one item in a scale or survey is not a reliable measure of anything.

For example, reflect back to a time when you thought you were falling in love. Maybe you told the person you loved them, or they told you they loved you. When this happens for the first time, often the person telling such news wants to know if the receiver feels the same. So, when the answer does not come back quickly, the one professing love may ask again "Do you love me?" And sometimes the answer is even more delayed, "Uh, uh . . . Yes, I love you too." But due to the delay in the answer, the teller might not be convinced that the receiver actually does love them, so they ask questions such as "Are you sure?"; "Why do you love me?"; "What about me do you love?"; and "When was the first time you knew you loved me?" Frequently, in order to get a more reliable measure of something we must ask more questions. This is why scales and surveys have multiple questions. We need to consider how the questions combined make for a more accurate and robust measure of that which we wish to assess. This is what is called, in a nutshell, *reliability.* And if we focus on one question, we ignore the power of all of the questions combined to give us a much better measure.

The reality is that you have too much data to consider; what you must do is combine the most meaningful statistics and survey or scale results to make generalizations about the perceptions, behaviors, and actions taking place in your school. Often, when we combine different measures or scales together to measure a certain topic (for example, Leadership Potential) we refer to these as *educational indexes.* Indexes are used in many fields to combine multiple measures together. For example, economic indexes are comprised of indicators such as unemployment rate, jobs created, and consumer confidence. When we add measures together, we can get a better sense of how we are performing. This is easy to see when you compare focusing on one question used to measure consumer confidence to using a complete measure of consumer confidence complemented by measures of the unemployment rate and the number of jobs created. One of the goals of the Multi-Dimensional Education Process is to help you get a broader, more accurate picture of what is taking place and what needs to change.

Next Steps

1. Do some research into how *good* Building Leadership Teams utilize data to make decisions to improve all aspects of the school experience for all stakeholders.

2. Develop an understanding of the seven dimensions of education and how each has an impact on the development of a good school.

3. Do a little research on how organizations use systems theory to manage their many challenges.

4. Consider how you might begin to use the Multi-Dimensional Education model to guide your management or instruction efforts, similarly to the way in which Fortune 500 corporations manage their employees and customers by focusing on many aspects that relate to their "bottom line."

3

Connecting the Data
Dots to Achievement

A benefit of working in many different school systems across the nation is the opportunity to see in action the continuum of how data are used at the district, school, and classroom levels. The observations we have made in these settings have validated many of the propositions we make in this text to help educators take a more data-driven thinking approach to education. What we have found is that open lines of communication are the key to connecting the data dots between the multiple levels of data collection and data dissemination that takes place from the district office to the classroom. If we are not careful we can easily find these lines disconnected.

This disconnection was most evident this past year when we collected data in a school district using our Multi-Dimensional Assessment (MDA). Three different people come to mind when we think about the disconnection of data collection and data use in this district. We first have the district data person, who is responsible for proposing a system of data collection and use. The next person is a school principal, who is having trouble understanding what the district data person is proposing and even more trouble fitting such requests into a timeline. Last is a teacher, who in this case is collecting the data requested and wishes that at least some of the data collected could be shared to help her in the classroom.

This district has a strong commitment to collecting and using data to drive the organization and they have a great data director who has vast experience in research and evaluation. This data-director is truly committed to doing the kinds

(Continued)

(Continued)

of deep analysis that, if data were collected through a strict research-based methodology, ideally would allow for better prediction of student achievement and an understanding of the many factors that might be affecting student achievement. What we came to realize in this district, however, is that data were not being collected in a fashion that would permit deeper analysis to be performed due to many limitations of the data collection process, nor were they being shared with those in the classroom who wanted to know the results. We also realized that the passion of the district data director and the collection of data that ensued from this passion were often perceived by leadership and teachers as unrealistic, overwhelming, and disconnected from what was happening at the school sites.

It was nearing the end of the school year and it was time in this district to do some end of the year surveying of students, teachers, and parents, as well as time for the end of the year tests. Our three participants were very busy, which is the common ebb and flow in most school systems, with the biggest flow coming at the end of the year. It was crunch time, and the data director was getting several assessments together and getting them out to the schools with the correct instructions and coded surveys for each student, parent, and educator. The schools had already administered 5 surveys this year for the data director and they were a little shocked that she had three more in store for their last few months. In addition and even more importantly, the student achievement tests were quickly approaching and the window for their administration had been set. This was a very important time of year for the data director and much of the analysis and value of data collected in the school district hinged on getting these last surveys and assessments returned before the end of the school year.

Meanwhile, this was also a very busy time for the principal. Yet despite everything on his plate, the principal was working to coordinate all of this data collection at the school site. The principal was busy explaining to staff the window for student data collection in regard to the student achievement tests and also explaining the additional survey pieces needed from students, parents, and educators that would take place shortly before the student achievement tests. The principal knew that part of his duties also entailed getting buy-in of the teachers to take seriously the collection of these survey data and he was going to great efforts to get good responses from all stakeholders.

But these last surveys to be administered would make for 8 surveys he had agreed to collect this year and several teachers were growing weary. Instead of calling the data-director, he called us and asked, "Since I have two other surveys to administer this month before the testing week, would you mind if I put the two other parent surveys in your parent survey's envelope so that they can complete all three at one time? By the way, I have a teacher in my office that is not real happy about having to complete more surveys." We could hear the teacher's not-so-happy tone when she asked us through the speakerphone, "How will this survey help me?" The teacher in his office was concerned she wouldn't have time for all of these latest data collection requests and explained to the principal that she was worried they would take away from valuable time and hurt her students' achievement scores.

What we were seeing in this district were three different folks working from three different reference points and since there was not a great amount of communication and clear understanding for the planning and purpose of the data, we had the makings for a difficult situation. The district, school leadership, and teachers were not on the same page. To make matters even more challenging, this district chose to collect the MDA during this window and it was the new survey on the block. The district's hope was to replace the many surveys they took during the year with our one survey that measured nearly all they collected. Our main office happened to get several calls asking which survey was ours and whether or not ours was the teacher satisfaction survey or the parent satisfaction survey. We came to realize very quickly the district had too many surveys going out and what the principal explained was there were actually three parent surveys going out at the same time.

Needless to say, there is a lot going on in schools, especially at the end of the year. Yet it is important to collect data. The internal motivation for the data director, school leader, and school teacher in regard to data collection though is very different. The data director envisions this process as necessary for understanding how the school is functioning and in reality the data collection process is primary to the data director's job. The school level leaders may have varying views of the importance of the data collection and some may see the importance more than others. In some instances and depending on the circumstances it may be viewed as compliance to the district leadership and something that needs to be checked off the list of things to do. For the teacher the range of needing this data collected and using this data may be very unclear. The student testing data is an obvious one that teachers whether they like to collect or not can understand, but all of the survey data in the case of this school district would at least for most teachers be hard to stomach. Teachers are the first to discuss the problems with data collection and how it detracts from the instructional time, so for many teachers oversurveying them and exerting energy to comply with a district wanting to collect a lot of data is a real conundrum. As a result, most schools need help in figuring out a process of data collection that fulfills the goals of the administration while providing the data results back to educators in a meaningful and understanding format that connects the dots.

This chapter, "Connecting the Data Dots to Achievement," is where we lay out a road map to help leaders and teachers take a more tactical approach to collecting, analyzing, and taking action with data. Connecting the data dots to achievement is a primary goal; connecting the dots can take great intentionality and sophistication, but can result in great rewards. It is important that all stakeholders, from the district office to the classroom, have the same understanding of the data collected and why it is collected. In education, there is a wide spectrum between those who choose not to engage in data-driven education and those who have a comprehensive approach to the issue. As you consider the ideas set forth in the chapter, reflect on where you or your organization is on this spectrum. Many of the points discussed here need to be considered within your operating context. To assist you in this reflection, provided in the Appendix is a Data Needs Assessment (DNA). The DNA is a start to helping you understand what data you might have and what data you might need to collect. One form is for the school-level administrator, and the other form is for the individual teacher. Each DNA helps to quantify and provide a picture of where you or the organization is on the data-driven educator continuum. This DNA can create a focus on some first steps toward making data-driven education more of a reality. The DNA forms are focused around the pitfalls of capacity, fear, and organization to help you better consider how to proactively avoid the pitfalls that often thwart data-driven thinking efforts.

Planning for a Better Cruise

As a teacher shared with us one day regarding the demands of data-driven education, "This is not the cruise I signed up for." For many, the journey into data-driven education has turned out to be a long, frustrating trip. But there are also success stories that illustrate the role of data in guiding efforts toward school improvement as well as student achievement. These stories tend to follow a similar plot, in which data was used to create goals to meet specific needs, and in the end the needs were met and the goals accomplished. What is often missing in the synopsis of these stories is the process of data-driven thinking that makes data-driven decision making possible and the conditions conducive to reviewing data and providing an environment where goals can be set and attended to. When properly done, though, accountability and improvement can be effectively interwoven, but it requires great *intentionality* and *sophistication*.

This intentionality and sophistication is realizable; case studies with principals in Florida demonstrated that data can be used to actually inspire discouraged teachers and give teachers new motivation and confidence in knowing that their students can do better (George, 2001). Teachers in Florida who had a negative attitude toward students' ability to learn were corrected when the principals provided SAT scores from the previous year's seniors (George, 2001). The teachers were amazed at how well students scored and were encouraged that the students had been learning. This shows that it is possible to use results for positive change by just considering additional outcome variables. Until educators can be provided with data suggestive of results as well as progress, however, it is somewhat unlikely that change will occur.

Much of the literature explains that better, more sustainable decisions and goals can be made when leaders use data. Educators need to collect good data on what is happening in the school and the school instructional programs. These data can provide information for steering school improvement. Guskey (2000) notes that "clearly, if an educational reform is to succeed, any decision about introducing it should be founded on accurate information" (p. 114). The reality is that data can provide the means by which to measure the effectiveness of implemented reforms.

Anytime we start planning for a trip, we have to take a look at the options we know and even consider some of the great trip advisory services that are free on the Internet. These trip advisory services tell us what others have experienced on trips and what we might expect in the way of food, accommodations, and activities provided. If we are planning to travel to a new location, then we are likely to do considerable research on the places we want to visit. As you consider the many trips you will take during a journey to data-driven thinking, it might help to first consider the structures you already have in place to help make data-driven education a reality.

Response to Intervention (RTI)

Response to Intervention (RTI) was originally developed to target those students on the bubble of possibly needing special education services (Fletcher, Coulter, Reschly, & Vaughn, 2004). The RTI push was made as a proactive response to the explosion in the number of students being labeled with some kind of learning disability in the last ten years. The RTI process has many key components; the process of using data to identify students for intervention and support is one of the highlights of this structure. The process focuses primarily on student achievement and student challenges (behavior). RTI seeks to use data to identify those students who will need intervention early in the school year, to intervene, and then to systematically monitor the impact of the intervention on students.

The process of RTI is very much an action research process; it is a good structure for analyzing data, implementing interventions, and then monitoring impacts on students. What is incomplete about the RTI process is that it often overlooks quality data about the overall picture of the school and even how the educators treat the greater student body and think about the climate of their classroom and school—all equally important factors beyond student achievement and behavior data. One thing to consider, given the differences in how RTI is implemented across the nation, is how exactly the RTI process is defined. Is RTI just for those bubble students? If so, then we need to think more about how we are serving all of the students. Given the differences in RTI implementation that we have seen, it seems important to understand the RTI process as a mechanism within a larger systems process concerned with data-driven improvement.

Professional Learning Communities (PLCs)

Professional Learning Communities (PLCs) have been one of the most widely adopted approaches to improving schools and classrooms (Hipp & Huffman, 2002). PLCs are widespread throughout districts and schools; the work of Rick DuFour and his colleagues in writing and promoting PLCs is truly monumental. PLCs encompass many of the components needed to promote good school environments and help teams of leaders and educators work toward common educational goals.

As teachers and administrators in the 1980s and 1990s, we were fortunate to be a part of PLC processes or similar learning team structures that were started in our schools and that are still in place today. We observed that one of the most productive elements was the opportunity to meet regularly with grade-level and discipline-specific teachers to review data and discuss how we could make improvements to instruction or curricula. We remember great conversations at these meetings about the expectations placed on students and how we were creating environments where these students could meet those expectations. We used only student achievement data in our PLCs, however, and usually it was summary data. In hindsight, if we had some benchmark or common formative assessments to discuss, it probably would have made for stronger discussion and planning. Our leadership teams also had a PLC; they used this opportunity to look at schoolwide issues, and on occasion would present some of their work in faculty meetings.

What we liked most about the PLCs was the way they helped to create an environment for discussion about students and a chance to review data related to the students. Participating in a PLC was a great professional experience. As with RTI, though, it would appear that

PLCs are not always the same across all schools. In fact, we have visited schools where PLCs are taking place but attendance is not mandatory and the PLC process seems more like something to be complied with and less something that will lead to improvement. We have observed fractured staffs in schools that are not willing to engage in the PLC process, causing that process to be something talked about rather than implemented. Like any initiative, PLCs vary in effectiveness and utility from school to school, from grade level to grade level, and from leadership team to leadership team. The other thing not specified in the PLC process is the depth or breadth of data needed; this is because use of data is an encouraged but not always a required part of the PLC process. PLCs do not claim to be a systemic model for school improvement, but rather another promising piece of the puzzle. However, PLCs are powerful, and when implemented with fidelity and buy-in can really cause great things to happen in schools. The PLC must fit into a larger school improvement process and framework as a means toward an end and not an end in itself.

Positive Behavioral Interventions and Supports (PBIS)

Positive Behavioral Interventions and Supports (PBIS) is another widely adopted behavior management system already being implemented in many school districts. PBIS was initially a system aimed at assisting students with severe developmental needs develop more appropriate routines and practices through nonaversive strategies (Sailor, Stowe, Turnbull, & Kleinhammer-Tramill, 2008). Since the early inception of PBIS, many schools have adopted it schoolwide, and by the late 1990s School-Wide Positive Behavior Supports (SWPBS) was created. SWPBS has demonstrated some level of effectiveness (Horner, Crone, & Stiller, 2001); it provides a way to identify student behavior problems and formulate a plan for dealing with these problems that will minimize the cost in administrative time. It is a focused approach that uses behavior data (and in some cases student attitude data) to implement policies and procedures that can help to reduce behavior problems. Even more importantly, SWPBS brings consistency to how behavior is dealt with at the classroom and the school level. SWPBS provides for better communication to the students on how incidents will be handled and what kinds of behavior are not acceptable. SWPBS can do a lot to improve the consistency and management of discipline within a school. Again, similarly to what we have seen with RTI and PLCs, these initiatives are only as effective as the fidelity and buy-in that accompany their implementation. SWPBS would also benefit from more data on the overall school climate, especially information on how the educators and parents are viewing the school from a number of dimensions. SWPBS focuses on discipline, which we know is very important to making sure the academic side of the house is in order; but it is not a complete model for school improvement, nor do those promoting it consider it to be such. It is one leg in a much longer journey.

There are a number of great resources available for getting educators and leaders attuned to good practices in education that use data. In your district, you might have others in addition to the three discussed here. At times, the availability of so many options can even complicate the process of school improvement. We have all seen educational organizations that adopt one program after another without giving any single approach the time necessary to bring about the cooperation and support that may lead to the desired results. Sometimes, waiting for summative results takes too long. Sometimes, schools expect that interventions will somehow immediately increase academic achievement. But, as many have learned during the past decade, changing scores is not easy or quick. It takes more than an intervention; it takes a functional system of many efforts. This is why it is helpful to develop or to better implement a data-driven approach that includes process and formative assessments of ongoing and new programs, processes, and interventions. There is much to be learned in this approach; in order to succeed, it will be necessary to take a look at the possible problems we may encounter on the journey.

The Potential Pitfalls of the Journey

A journey really implies a number of shorter trips that we plan. We plan trips every year, whether they are family vacations or trips to visit friends or relatives in other parts of country or world. In planning trips we often reflect on possible pitfalls: for example, those that we might learn about in travel warnings for international travel, or those involved in visiting relatives you actually would rather not visit. Consideration of pitfalls is a key factor on the journey to be a data-driven educator, since this journey will be made up of many trips. The pitfalls in starting on the journey fall into three thematic categories: (1) capacity for data use; (2) fear of data, and (3) organization of data.

The problem of capacity is that most educators are not trained adequately in testing or measurement; assessment literacy is therefore a major concern (Popham, 1999). While teachers and administrators do not need to be experts in psychometrics (statistical measurement), they must have some level of assessment literacy (Webb, 2002). On the other hand, as Wayman (2005) notes in his research on data use, "The mere presence of data does not automatically imply that useable information is available; educators need support to use data to its fullest extent" (p. 3). An additional capacity issue is that of time. Considering the time problem in light of the training problem, Edie L. Holcomb (2004) explains, "When we're overwhelmed with the list of things we know we should do, we resort to completing the things we know we can do" (p. 30). Many who are untrained and who lack confidence in their ability to be a data-driven educator are likely to devote their time and efforts elsewhere by default. This is not to discount the fact that in education there is too much on your plate and not enough time to do it all. This being said, the importance of data-driven education and the requirement to demonstrate that you are data-driven must cause you to pause and create the time and infrastructure for that work. You cannot, however, do this alone. You should approach the problem with shared leadership in mind. You deserve and should request help from your colleagues and superiors. We can tell you that when educators ask their district data experts for help, the answer is normally an enthusiastic "Yes." And when leaders explain that they want to create a fairer growth model to document their school's success, the answer is the same from their colleagues.

Data and results often cause fear, not only among leaders but also among teachers. Teachers may often be leery of setting achievement goals within their own classroom. While educators take pleasure in seeing student achievement results go up, there remains a fear of setting goals and then anticipating the results (Stiggins, 1994). This fear can cause conflicts and can reveal problems with how students are being taught, who is teaching well, and who is teaching poorly. Fullan and Stiegelbaures (1991) point out that efforts to use results can be difficult when people fear the reality that results indicate. Schmoker (1996) points clearly to the reason we in the schooling business avoid data and results.

> The reason is fear—of data's capacity to reveal strengths and weakness, failure and success. Education seems to maintain a tacit bargain among constituents at every level not to gather or use information that will reveal where we need to do better, where we need to make changes. (p. 123)

Data can point to areas of need and weakness.

Another difficulty is organizing data to make it more user-friendly for purposes of planning, dialogue, and monitoring. A number of studies have noted the problems involved with the organization of data, use of technology, and data-driven supports that assist in getting data into formats that can be used for planning (Bernhardt, 2003; Mandinach, Honey, & Light, 2006; Wayman, 2005; Wayman, Stringfield, & Yakimowski, 2004). Having not enough or too much data to organize and not having data presented in a fashion you can use are major barriers. The seven MDed dimensions are the framework needed to determine what data you need to focus on at the school level; the 4Cs are a way of using dimensionally organized data to improve our journey toward maximizing achievement.

The Power of Data to Perpetuate Change in the Journey

Data provides the user with new information and a way to test or affirm our intuitive beliefs about what is taking place in our schools. It is easy to accept what we believe intuitively and act upon it. Without the presence of data, however, our intuition often becomes the only information we have to act upon. Research on successful organizations shows us that there are five important stages for data-driven organizations to consider (Savin, 2000). These five stages were noted as the leadership steps in successfully implementing a data-driven system within the organization. The steps are: (1) assessing current status and planning for buy-in, (2) initiating data collection, (3) ensuring data integrity, (4) utilizing data in assessment and improvement, and (5) benchmarking goals and systems evolution (p. 54). It is important to consider these key steps as you begin this journey. You need to begin by assessing your current state, which will involve using a number of measures, not just test scores. The use of multiple measures will also help you to create buy-in, as most will feel more comfortable with many measures rather than being held accountable for just one or a few measures. Data collection has to be intentional and organized. You have to consider the data collection in light of the dimensions or areas of improvement that need your attention. The data has to be of quality. There is no better way to decrease buy-in and increase skepticism than to gather and report bad data. When you collect data, you then need to demonstrate how data will be used to guide improvement at the school level as well as the classroom level. Lastly, you have to develop and record goals toward which progress can be measured. These are the broader steps of an approach that involves intentionality and sophistication.

The importance of setting goals cannot be overstated. An organization with clear goals and purpose can provide the environment in which employees feel secure in their jobs and how those jobs relate to the purpose of the organization. In these organizations, people are ideally striving toward the same goal; this can create a unified environment (Peters & Waterman, 1982). The fact remains, though, that in schools, tradition has been to refrain from setting data-driven goals. However, according to Glickman's (2002) work, successful schools engage in action research that is an ongoing process of assessing and refining the school's practices. Engaging in practices using data at the school and classroom level can lead to positive changes and a better focus on what is actually happening at the school site. It is ultimately people who make decisions resulting in the changes that improve conditions in the school site or classroom. But what is the map that gets us to the place where these kinds of decisions can be made? The map has to be a consideration of the data collected and an understanding of the data within the context of the work taking place in schools. Without the collection and review of data on a regular basis, many of us are left with blind intuition, which at times can be serendipitously effective, but in the greater scheme of the school improvement landscape is an inadequate tool.

The Process, the Pain, and the Pleasure

This idea of process, pain, and pleasure is captured well by Csikszentmihalyi (1990),

> It does not seem to be true that work necessarily needs to be unpleasant. It may always have to be hard, or at least harder than doing nothing at all. But there is ample evidence that work can be enjoyable, and that indeed, it is often the most enjoyable part of life. (p. 145)

There is a wide range of value and satisfaction that those within schools find in the work they do. From kindergarten to twelfth grade, teachers try to instill in students the importance of hard work and the virtue of doing a good job no matter what the task; yet some are more successful than others. The process of becoming data-driven in education may cause many to pause for a moment and think about looking at things differently; both personally, with regard to what you can control, and externally, with regard to what you cannot control. This is another educational paradox to ponder as you begin to consider the evidence that shows how the leadership and instruction in your organization is perceived: Are you perceived as working hard? As doing a good job? In essence, school improvement and school reform is as much about changing the organization as it is about changing people and changing ourselves.

Being an educator is a career or calling that is, to most, a very personal matter. And rightly so, because there are very few jobs where individuals are personally responsible for so much throughout every work day. This is understandable, since teachers are expected to be solely responsible for everything and everyone in the classroom from the time the bell rings and the door closes. This responsibility is equally demanding for school leaders, given that the classroom doors are closed the majority of the day and the leaders are to some degree responsible for everything else in the school. The process of being an educator can often be painful, but through hard work and continuous improvement we can also find pleasure in it.

A process for being a data-driven thinking organization really involves a focus on data collection, communication, culture, time commitment, and usable data with structured tools to allow for planning. The data collection is a given, as obviously it is hard to be data-driven without data. Later in the chapter we will discuss the kinds of data that are readily available and the kinds of data that need to be collected. Also provided in the Appendix are several survey and evaluation tools you can choose to use, as well as references within the chapters of tools that already exist.

The importance of communication in the process cannot be overemphasized. It is the communication from leaders at the school site, as well as how stakeholders perceive the process, that really makes an amazing difference in whether or not an effort to be more data-driven ever gets off the ground. Studies (Mason, 2002; Mieles & Foley, 2005) show that communication and culture are key to data-driven decision making. These studies also show that when leadership is experienced in using data, a school organization is more likely to adopt data-driven inquiry approaches and more likely to be able to create a culture where data is valued and used. This time commitment is very important to making data-driven education a reality. Many schools and districts have found it difficult to allocate the necessary time for data analysis and reflection (Feldman & Tung, 2001), but those schools and districts showing most promise typically have existing structures such as PLCs or grade level teams that provide a setting for data-based review and planning.

To be successful, any data-driven education initiative must take into account the need for these structures. In the beginning stages, an organization must get these structures into place. Once that is done, the next thing to consider is how to provide educators at the school level with actionable data. This is data they can actually sit down with, understand, discuss, and begin to use in the decision-making process. In addition, there are some inquiry questions and data dialogue steps that can help focus a discussion on the data and the information it provides. Many such discussions get held up when the data is not in a format that is easy to use or for some reason there are concerns about the quality of the data. It is important that there be enough data available to allow those involved to distinguish between more important and less important data. Our framework will assist you toward this end. Therefore, in this chapter we propose an approach to collecting and discussing the data not as accountability data, but rather as data that is applicable to better understanding what is happening in our schools or classrooms. We also propose using triangulation wherever possible with the data you are able to collect. Triangulation will be explained more in the pages to follow. As the opening vignette highlights, you might also need to sit down with the district data team to explain what you want to do and ask them for help.

Triangulation Versus Strangulation

From our work with schools, we have come to realize that, from the point of view of educators, end-of-year test scores are more about accountability and less about applicability. In other words, we are forced to be accountable for data that can rarely be applied to improving our performance. It should go without saying that end-of-year test scores give us little guidance in helping those students currently in our care. We are much better served by benchmarks, monitoring assessments, or common assessments that can be given and graded quickly and then considered for what they indicate about the current state of instruction for these students. The applicable data needs to be data trustworthy and free from the broad-reaching arms of federal and state accountability. In selecting data closer to home, many of the communication issues about using data can be lessened, especially if there is grade level buy-in on the most important data pieces to examine. Triangulation can also go a long way in helping to create buy-in and give people a sense that the data is there for action and not for accountability.

In research and evaluation work, we are constantly faced with the need to justify the conclusions we make based on the data we have collected. In our work with hundreds of graduate students on master's theses, we have come to teach the method of triangulation, and we encourage them to adopt that method. Triangulation is basically when one collects or compares data from three sources that measure the same idea. Triangulation is not only a good research and evaluation strategy, but also a good action research and data-driven discussion strategy. Triangulation is simply "a way to corroborate data and eliminate the bias that may be inherent to some forms of data" (Gay & Airasian, 2003, p. 215). Triangulation provides a way for us to cross validate data we have collected by comparing it to other sources. Triangulation can relieve the feeling of strangulation many sense from the existing use of accountability data.

Most educators involved will understand from the onset that it is a myth that we are going to get a completely unbiased or perfect understanding of student performance based on any single piece of data. Another reality is that we may not be able to get our hands on three pieces of data, so in that case we need to find at least two good data points for consideration. Table 3.1 provides an illustration of how we might go about triangulating data on several important areas of school and classroom planning.

Table 3.1   Triangulation of Data

Data Review Areas	Data Source 1	Data Source 2	Data Source 3
Student Achievement in English Language Arts (ELA)	District Benchmark Assessment in ELA	State Standards Test in ELA	Student Portfolios (qualitative)
Student Behavior Challenges	Student Referral Records	Student Survey on Self-Reported Behaviors	Student Journals (qualitative)
Community and Parent Satisfaction	Community and Parent Surveys	Records of Parent Involvement in School (# of parent aides)	Interviews With Parents and Community (qualitative)

You can triangulate data points to get a better measurement of something such as achievement, but you can also triangulate between participants. For example, as our Multi-Dimensional Education charts have shown, we often strongly recommend triangulating perceptual data between students, parents, and educators. Another important point to make here is that not all data you collect need to be in numeric format. Data can also be qualitative in nature and could involve more description through words or thoughts collected through interviews, journals, quick writes, or other narrative forms that can help you understand many of the factors involved in student achievement. Often, by analyzing qualitative data or evidence, you can begin to identify recurring themes or ethnographic insights specific to your school culture that allow you to give a little more meaning to the numbers you collect. For discussion of tests or student performance, you may be stuck with looking at numeric or quantitative data, but when you begin to dig into the social factors in schools and look at school climate or student motivation, many times some more qualitative evidence will better guide your understanding of what is occurring with students.

If you don't believe us, after the achievement tests are administered, provide your students with a chance to complete an anonymous feedback form. (Possibly even better, do it before the tests.) On this one-page form we suggest you ask three questions:

1. Do you think the end-of-the-year achievement tests are important? *Yes* or *No? Why?*

2. What are your reasons for wanting to do well on the test?

3. What can we do to get you to try harder on the test?

We suspect this simple qualitative exercise will identify much to discuss.

Even at the teacher or building leadership levels, a satisfaction survey with some room for comments can provide a greater understanding of what people think. Allowing educators to respond to some open-ended questions can often yield some qualitative data for consideration and discussion. The quantitative data often helps us understand the "what" of the challenge we are trying to better understand, and the qualitative data guides us in understanding the "why." Consider Table 3.2 as it relates to the different forms of quantitative and qualitative data we might go about collecting or already have on hand in a school.

Table 3.2   Quantitative and Qualitative Data

Data Area	Types of Quantitative Data	Types of Qualitative Data
School-wide Student Achievement	• Report Cards • Test Scores • Benchmark Scores • Language Acquisition Scores	• Student Portfolios • Student Exhibits • Student Interviews • Student Focus Groups
Instructional Program Data	• Teacher-student ratios • Number of students enrolled in Advanced Placement • Teacher Education Levels • Student Retention	• Teacher and Administrator Portfolios • Professional Development Agendas • Staff Interviews
Behavior Data	• Referral Reports • Number of Detentions • Student Absent Records • Student Surveys on Behavior • Parent Surveys on Student Behavior	• Student Interviews • Student Journals • Observations of Student Behavior • Parent Interviews on Student Behavior
Teacher Evaluation Data	• Administrator Evaluations • Student Evaluations of Teachers • Teacher Peer Evaluations • Teacher Self-Evaluations	• Teacher Interviews • Administrator Narrative Response to Teacher Evaluations • Peer Narrative Responses to Teacher Evaluations • Teacher Narrative Responses to Self-Evaluations

There are a great number of quantitative and qualitative pieces available to use as you begin to select data to review. Table 3.2 provides an overview of some data pieces in certain areas that might be considered. Specifically, the teacher evaluation section may not contain many data pieces that you currently collect, but we are becoming ever more aware of the needs and policy demands for teacher evaluations. In thinking toward the future about teacher evaluations, looking into evaluation pieces beyond just the administrator evaluation will be important for getting teachers in agreement with a comprehensive teacher evaluation component. To assist with getting started in this endeavor, we have provided several versions of a teacher evaluation in the Appendix for your use.

Building Your "Bucket List"

This subheading is not intended to suggest we think data-driven education will kill you and you should make your bucket list today. Instead we encourage you to start filling your buckets with the valuable data you have and need to empower your data-driven thinking. Beginning the process of identifying, collecting, and gathering data is the first step toward beginning to connect the data dots and creating a culture for data-driven thinking in your school. For many reasons, this can be a pivotal part of the process; most importantly, it must be begun with the end in mind. For this reason, we encourage you not to be overzealous as you think about all the data you have, need, or want to collect. This process has to start with some intentional, sophisticated intuition as you think about your school and what data you really need to look at. To get you thinking about the data needed, we propose you consider putting the data into the seven-dimensional buckets. Begin by considering the seven dimensions of the Multi-Dimensional Education model. All seven are important, but the reality is that you will most likely have to focus more on the dimensions that are presenting the most challenges. As we begin to conceptualize the data, we will need to have discussions around the seven dimensions. It is important to understand that organizing of data in this way can be beneficial for both schoolwide and classroom use. Please remember that we are on your side, and our intention is to help you organize and collect meaningful data that can actually be understood and used in your school to make change. By simply administering the MDA provided in the Appendix to your students (and possibly parents and staff), you can begin to fill all seven of your data buckets. But to follow are other data you might have or want to add to complement the process.

The primary focus of Community Engagement (Dimension 1) data usually is parents, but even at the classroom level we have to at least consider the larger community. The thing most schools and teachers want to know in this area is how parents are being involved in the educational process. To what extent are the parents really helping the student be successful? Are there barriers to the students' success that are coming from family issues and other problems in the home? Whether you are trying to get families more involved in the schooling of their child or trying to get families more involved in what is happening in the school, the data is important, and there are many forms of data available. You might also consider assessing how active your students are in the community. Finding or collecting these data points can begin to help you understand where you are on this dimension. Chapter 6 will provide you with a good amount of evidence as to why these types of data hold great promise for increasing your success. Here is a list of some things you might want to consider collecting in the bucket of Community Engagement:

- Parent and community satisfaction data
- Student data about parental involvement
- Student journals on how parents are involved in student learning
- Teacher input on the perceived involvement of parents at the school and with students
- The level of service to the community being performed by your students

Curriculum Expectations (Dimension 2) encompasses not only what you expect from the students, but also the data pieces, such as test scores, that enlighten you as to how students are actually performing. In some cases, it might be the bucket you tend to focus on most. If you consider the current state of data-driven education at your school, you might find that most if not all of the data you look at is about the instructional program; discipline data might be a close second. For this reason, the Curriculum Expectations bucket may already be full, and it might just be a matter of selecting the most accurate and applicable data for this dimension rather than collecting more.

What is possibly missing from this bucket are data and qualitative insights to help you understand what students, parents, and educators think about the curricular expectations at the school, and the extent to which the school and educators have been able to communicate those expectations and provide the needed means to help students meet them. Beyond performance data, do we understand how students and parents perceive the rigor and quality of instruction? Is the educator's understanding of rigor in line with that of the students and parents? This is not an easy task, as parents and students bring a myriad of perceptions as to what rigor really means. Collecting data in this dimension can help align those perceptions, understand them, and if needed provide the initiative to work on communicating what the perception should be. This dimension also reveals whether students feel supported by tutoring and other structures intended to help them be more successful. This is a big bucket, and may be one you have to watch carefully or it might get too full. But don't forget that the Multi-Dimensional Assessment (MDA) and teacher evaluations in the Appendix can contribute meaningful data to this bucket. What is important in this bucket are not just the student outcomes, but also understanding if we are setting the right expectations and how the other stakeholders are viewing these expectations. The kinds of data you want to put into this bucket are

- parent, teacher, and student perceptions of the curricula's rigor and creativity,
- formative data related to the support for low-performing students,
- artifacts related to the quality of instruction from parents, students, and teachers,
- evidence related to teacher performance, and
- data related to student achievement.

Developmental Perspectives (Dimension 3) is a bucket in which you can place much of the behavioral challenge data and in which you can begin to consider what data will be needed to work on the discipline and developmental challenges within the school and classroom. Under Developmental Perspectives, you want to begin to consider data you already collect, such as that related to disciplinary referrals and school discipline policies. It is important to note that discipline data comes in a variety of forms; we have found there is often little standardization of discipline data across districts (or even across schools within districts, for that matter). The coding and reporting policies for referral data are often independently formulated at each school site. And as principals change at the school, so do the policies. This should be considered as you begin to gather this data and think about its quality. An important aspect of understanding Developmental Perspectives (and discipline data, for that matter) is understanding how, and how consistently, the teachers are implementing the discipline policies. This reminds us of a school in which the faculty felt there was a huge cheating problem, but the discipline referral data on cheating did not reveal much of a problem. The problem was that each teacher was dealing with cheating in the classroom and not reporting it back to the office.

Note the student success traits data in the list of data that follows. These are what many refer to as *character traits:* elements such as honesty, integrity, compassion, and concern for others. While these are not behavioral issues, they do represent the traits we would want to develop and foster in order to proactively deal with behavior issues. For example, if we have a school where a lot of teasing and bullying occurs, then we need to work on concern for others and build in structures that will help students care about other human beings in the building. Chapter 8 will provide you with a deeper understanding of the research and rationale behind this bucket's focus on behavioral-based developmental issues. To gain a good understanding of Developmental Perspectives you really need to collect several forms of data, including at least the following:

- Referral reports broken out by types of referred behavior
- Teacher data showing what discipline issues the teachers are having the most challenges with
- Focus group responses on the social-emotional concerns of the school
- Student self-reported misconduct and success trait data (see Appendix for the MDA)
- Parent input showing what parents believe to be the discipline issues at the school

Educational Attitudes (Dimension 4) data helps you to understand the complex area of student motivation and feelings for school (affect) and how such attitudes are impacting the student achievement at the classroom and school level. According to Timothy Seifert (2004), student motivation can be analyzed based on several contemporary theories, including self-efficacy theory, attribution theory, and self-worth theory. These theories can help us in understanding the ways students are motivated. By collecting indicators that will help us in understanding motivation levels in the school and classroom we can use data on a practical level. Student motivation data can come in many forms, and it should come from many different perspectives. In schools we work with across the nation, we find that this area of Educational Attitudes reveals the most disconnection between parents, students, and educators.

In our estimation, motivational data is really an untapped resource that many times can explain the rationale for why students are not doing well. How often have we heard low test scores attributed to low levels of student motivation? It is an easy way to discount a number of other things that might have caused poor test performance; in reality, using student motivation as an argument places the blame on the students. It is true that student motivation is a cause, but then we have to ask ourselves what we have been *doing* to address student motivation. For many, trying to tap into the motivation and educational attitudes of students seems like the Holy Grail or black box of education.

Wouldn't our jobs as educators be much more fulfilling if more students came to school highly motivated? For that matter, what if every teacher came to work highly motivated? We understand that in schools we frequently do not specifically focus on trying to improve motivation or affect of students. Many educators do not make plans on how to target educational attitudes, and yet we realize that these attitudes often hold the key to unlocking the potential that students don't yet believe they have. Often, insufficient attention is given to building those success traits in Developmental Perspectives and addressing motivational issues within our schools with intentionality and an understanding of the data surrounding attitudes. To adequately begin the conversation on student motivation and educational attitudes, you at least need to think about the following:

- Student data on self-reported motivation, academic empowerment (self-efficacy to achieve), and feelings toward school (which can be measured using the MDA in the Appendix)
- Teacher feedback on their perceptions of the student levels of motivation and work ethic
- Parent focus groups on how motivated they believe their child to be
- Student interview data on what motivates them to want to do well in school

If Dimension 2 assesses rigor and Dimensions 3 and 4 assess relevance, Faculty Fidelity (Dimension 5) basically measures the relationships among rigor, relevance, and relationships. It is important for district-level administrators to consider, but it is also something that must be shared with teachers so that they understand how they are being perceived by students and parents. Efforts such as Improving Teacher Quality and Teach America are clear road signs pointing to the importance of improved teaching as the impetus for school improvement. Gaining better insight into what is happening with the teachers is crucial to improvement. Teachers are really the first and last line of defense. Unfortunately, we spend a lot of time attributing failure, and less time attributing success, to teachers. Many spend even less time understanding the other factors that may or may not be causing a teacher to succeed or fail. Faculty fidelity data is a bucket providing us a view as to how teachers are perceived, whether or not teachers feel personally able to make a difference with students, and whether or not the organization is supportive of the teachers. The evidence and information under Faculty Fidelity might consist of some of the following:

- Data on trust in teachers, teacher efficacy, and satisfaction (as captured by the MDA)
- Teacher evaluations
- Peer reviews
- Feedback on whether or not the teachers feel supported by the organization to do their jobs

Leadership
Potential

The bucket of Leadership Potential (Dimension 6) is a bucket usually carried by just a few people at the school site, and at small schools only one person, the principal. It takes a courageous leader or leadership team willing to really look at these kinds of data. This bucket is very personal and yet very important, because we know that as leadership goes, so goes the school. Any school improvement effort that does not consider how the leadership plays a role in the process is likely to fail. We have been in schools using our surveys in which leaders are a little reluctant to have students, parents, and educators report on the leadership potential currently in place. We have even had schools choose not to administer our survey because the leadership did not want to see the results. In other schools, leaders have embraced the self-reflection that can be provided from understanding how the stakeholders in the school perceive the leadership. Oddly enough many leaders really appreciate these kinds of data, because they usually only take blame or get accolades for improved student achievement scores. Administrators and leadership teams find Leadership Potential data something they can use to take action. These data often provide a clearer direction for how they might go about communicating better, proposing a clear vision, and sharing the leadership mission to others in the school. Some of the data pieces that leaders and leadership teams need to collect are

- Data on satisfaction in the leadership from teachers, students, and parents
- Focus group feedback on the vision or school mission from teachers, students, and parents
- Data on the communication of the leadership from students, parents, and teachers

School Climate (Dimension 7), as well as classroom climate, consists of a number of important data points from students, parents, and educators that need to be considered. These data inform you about how the climate of the school or classroom is perceived and what steps might need to be taken to change perceptions. These are often the environmental factors associated with what is happening in the organization and how the environment might be detracting from the success of the organization in improving student achievement. School and classroom climate data help us understand the perceived environment of the school, school safety, student relationships, school liking, and a number of other factors that contribute to a positive or negative school climate. Our recent work with the Office of Safe and Drug-Free Schools, and the new funding for education agencies to take steps toward improving school climate, are evidence of how this work has quickly moved forward and become important in public education policy. In the fall of 2010, a number of states were awarded Safe, Supportive Schools (S3) grants to specifically address school climate and other school environmental factors. These new state awards require state and local educational agencies to participate in the collection of data around school climate. In the proposal for these funds, there are also plans to develop a growth model of accountability that takes school climate measures into account for purposes of tracking growth in positive school climate indicators and decrease in negative indicators. In simple terms, as Chapter 7 expands on, a good school climate seeks to promote a learning environment where students first feel safe, secure, and valued, and secondly feel they can be successful.

School Climate

There are a great number of organizations that measure school climate, school culture, school environment, and safe schools. This work has been done for years and has been overshadowed by the demands of accountability for improved student achievement. Once again, there are a number of data pieces available to get started on looking more closely at this dimension, and even more instruments that can be used to collect these types of data. Realistically, most schools receiving Safe and Drug-Free Schools or title money are already required to collect some of these data and may already have the data available. The list for school climate data and information could be long, but here are a few necessities you should have on hand to begin your School Climate discussion:

- Feedback related to the safety of the school from parents, students, and educators

- Data related to student relationships and how students treat each other from student, parent, and educator perceptions
- Data related to student attachment to school
- Insights related to how teachers foster a positive climate within the classroom

Crossing Items Off the Bucket List

With a better understanding of what data we need to put into our seven buckets, we would now like to discuss a seven-step process (see Table 3.3) to put this data to work for you. This is the same seven-step process we will use in Chapters 5 through 8 to help you apply the seven dimensions of data to improving the 4Cs.

STEP 1: Ask the Right Questions

In the last section, we walked you through thinking about the data related to the seven dimensions of school improvement. Keep those seven-dimensional buckets in mind as we move into the phase where we lay out the actual work of being data-driven. We have to begin by asking the right questions; otherwise, we will be stuck gathering all kinds of data that may not really help us plan for or organize toward improvement. In the last section, we went through the data available in each dimension, but before you collect data, you will first want to ask questions that might help you determine what data you need. A good way to start thinking about the questions needing to be asked is to begin with the dimensions. If you are a school or district just beginning to think about School Climate and how your stakeholders view it, you might begin by asking the question: How do students perceive the climate of our school? To this question you may need to add a question that digs a little deeper into School Climate wherein you ask: What areas of School Climate do

Table 3.3 Seven Steps to Informing Data-Driven Thinking

Steps	1	2	3	4	5	6	7
Tasks	Ask the Right Questions	Collect and Organize the Data	Discussion and Reflection on Data	Set Goals and Target Planning	Implement Systemic Change	Monitor and Fine Tune	Evaluate and Communicate the Outcomes

students note as low or problematic areas? As is true with any inquiry process, often the initial question at first only leads to more questions, but ultimately a better understanding of what is happening comes out of the discussion.

STEP 2: Collect and Organize the Data

So far, we have talked a lot about data and data collection. The next step is to organize the data in a fashion that will eventually allow for discussion and planning. This is often easier said than done; fortunately, school systems continue to make technological improvements in this regard. The ability to quickly process data and get it ready for analysis is becoming better every day. We have found it is best to present in easy formats—ideally charts, graphs, or simple tables that do not confuse those using the data. It is best to stick with percentages and mean scores when preparing data, as these are the descriptive statistics that may be most usable. Good usable data should also be provided at some disaggregated level. For example, you may need to look at the scores of boys and girls separately. It may be important for you to disaggregate the data by grade level to better understand if certain student-reported problems are more apparent at some grade levels than others. In California, we have such diversity when it comes to student language acquisition that in many schools it is necessary to break student achievement data out by language levels in order to understand student achievement. The real key is that data be easily understood in the visual format used and that the format does not confuse or create more questions. The work of analyzing data can then move forward. To follow are some simple formats for data that with a little explanation can get people into conversations about how the data reflects on the school or even the classroom.

As you consider Figure 3.1 as a sample piece of data that could be used for beginning a discussion about possible issues or even things to celebrate at the school site, look closely at how the data is laid out so that the scores of all respondents (parents, staff, and students) are right next to each other, which allows for some comparison of each stakeholder's perspectives on each dimension. An addition to this chart is a grand mean that is the combination of the student, staff, and parent scores into one total score. These scores are on a 1–5 scale, which is clearly noted by the scaling at the bottom of the chart. Each of the participant's scores are represented by a different shade, which

Figure 3.1   Overall District Dimensional Mean Score

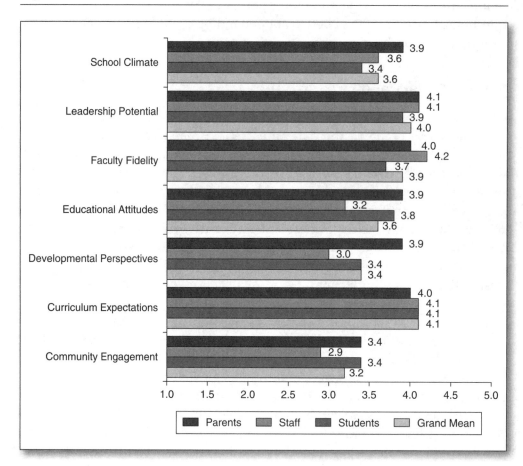

help distinguish between the participants. Additionally, the actual score is added to the end of the bar, so we know exactly what the score was for each participant group. The advantage to data in this kind of chart, if you do not have a person or company providing evaluation services, is that you can create it relatively easy with a spreadsheet software program.

Tables are another option for organizing data; they often allow for the display of more data than charts, but can also become very "busy" with data and may be overwhelming. Student achievement data often lends itself better to tables, especially if we are considering the use of a number of different measures over the course of a school year. One district we work with uses the same benchmark assessment three times over the course of the school year to look at how students are performing. They start by looking at the score by grade level; the example in Table 3.4 is specific to a seventh and eighth grade middle school. In the case of this school the data was specifically targeting a reading comprehension (RC) assessment that had three reading passages (see Table 3.4).

The next sample of student achievement data is from the same school, but shows a disaggregation of the English Language Learners. This data sample is targeted at the eighth-grade students (see Table 3.5).

Depending on your school system's use of data warehousing programs and the types of data available, many of these kinds of data may be readily available by a couple of clicks. In some cases, software or web-based data systems have canned reports that allow you to drop the data into the tables or charts you want to create. If your district does not have these kinds of data management options, many of these kinds of charts and tables can be easily made using a spreadsheet software program. If you are using spreadsheets, be sure to allow enough time for these to be made. It can often be done by office staff, but be sure to give clear direction and guidance on exactly what you want created, and make sure the results get proofread by a few sets of fresh eyes before discussing.

Table 3.4   Student Benchmark Data: Fall to Winter Mean Scores

Grade 7 Benchmark	Number of Students Completing the Passage	Fall Score (All Students)	Winter Score (All Students)	Mean Difference
Passage 1	108	6.50	6.96	0.459
Passage 2	110	4.83	5.06	0.230
Passage 3	102	4.14	4.21	0.068
RC Total	102	15.47	16.22	0.757

Table 3.5   Student Benchmark Data: Fall to Winter Mean Scores for English Language Learners

Grade 8 Benchmark	Number of Students Completing the Passage	Fall Score (ELL Students)	Winter Score (ELL Students)	Mean Difference
Passage 1	78	7.73	6.24	−1.488
Passage 2	83	6.99	4.85	−2.138
Passage 3	81	5.83	2.72	−3.113
RC Total	78	20.55	13.81	−6.739

STEP 3: Discussion and Reflection on Data

Once we have determined some questions for inquiry and organized the collected data, the next step is to begin analyzing data. As noted throughout this chapter, the analysis or organization of data is much easier if we have structures like grade level teams or PLCs in place that provide meeting times and an established group for discussions around data. If we happen to be in a larger setting like a teachers' meeting, it will be beneficial to all involved to break up into groups of 4 to 6. When we get groups beyond this size, it can be difficult to keep the conversation focused and allow for enough time for everyone to be able to share opinions and concerns. There are a number of great resources available as you begin to plan to have these data discussions and analyze the data. Bruce Wellman and Laura Lipton wrote *Data-Driven Dialogue: A Facilitator's Guide to Collaborative Inquiry* (2003), which is a rich guide to setting up collaborative groups and using strategies and techniques to facilitate data dialogues. This guide provides information on establishing teams and tools for facilitating the use of data in the pursuit of common goals. Edie Holcomb, in her book *Getting Excited About Data: How to Combine People, Passion, and Proof* (2004), provides additional resources on how to create collaborative structures where discussion can take place and people can get passionate about what the data is telling them about their school. We suggest you start with a few simple ground rules as you embark on analyzing the data you have put together.

Ground Rules to Data-Driven Thinking and Inquiry:

1. Start with an intuitive question such as "What do we think these data are going to tell us about our school or students?" before looking at the data.

2. Make sure everyone at the table has a chance to share some thoughts or points about the data—this can be easily done with a "whip around" where everyone has to say something about what is being reviewed.

3. Start with some broad statements about what seem to be trends or ideas emerging from the data—have someone chart these and call them *big ideas*.

4. Make a list of strengths and weaknesses that seem to emerge from the data—chart or have someone record this information as well.

5. Go back to why the data was collected in the first place and the questions we want to answer using the data. Begin to answer those questions, or at least make educated guesses as to what these data tell you about the questions you posed.

6. Determine if more data will be needed for future meetings, and how possibly to pursue collecting and monitoring follow-up assessments on these same data in the future.

From this point, we can move into really looking at our challenges and determining what we might consider setting as goals or target areas of improvement for turning these concerns around.

STEP 4: Set Goals and Target Planning

Setting goals and beginning the target planning process are really what the results of data-driven thinking are all about. The weaknesses revealed by the data and the knowledge we have of our school and students should provide us with some insight into what we are doing at the present to deal with some of these weaknesses and what we might consider doing in the future. Resources on goal setting are abundant (Hollenback & Klein, 1987); we like to use a simple acronym SMART: *specific, measurable, attainable, realistic,* and *timely.* It would be nice to say this is something we created, but it is often credited to Peter Drucker, who in 1954 wrote a book called *The Practice of Management.* We are sure many reading this text have come across this acronym before. There are other ways to attend to goals, but SMART goal setting is a time-tested and proven process for actualizing measurable and attainable goals.

Specific. A specific goal is more likely to be met than a general one. You need to consider the six *W*s when setting a specific goal:

- Who: Who are the people involved?
- What: What is it we want to accomplish?
- Where: At what location is this taking place (school, classroom, or district)?
- When: When do we want this goal accomplished?
- Which: Which of these requirements meet this goal? Which present challenges to meeting the goal?
- Why: Why is this goal worth accomplishing?

For example, a general goal might be "to spend more time inter-acting socially with students." A specific goal would be "with my students, to take part in a playground game at recess once a week to build stronger social bonds and trust."

Measurable. A goal has to be something that can be measured and monitored. It is better to set goals with measures in mind from the outset than to set goals and then create measures for them. To deter-mine if a goal is measurable, you have to ask how you know it will be accomplished and what measure will you take as evidence that the goal was accomplished.

Attainable. We set goals in order to succeed, not to fail, so the goal needs to be something you believe is achievable. Setting a goal that is reasonable and attainable is more likely to motivate you to do the work it will take to meet the goal. If you have a goal such as 100% proficiency, you might be more likely to give up because you do not believe it is attainable.

Realistic. In considering whether the goal is realistic, you might want to look at your track record first. Do you or your organization have a track record of meeting these kinds of goals? Is the goal something that, with careful and thoughtful planning, could be accomplished? Attainability and realism really go hand in hand in the SMART goal planning process. Another thing to be cautious of here is setting too many goals, which can be another way to demotivate yourself or your team. A smaller set of clearly defined and targeted goals is much better than a larger set of goals that there is not enough time, energy, or resources to accomplish. At the same time, don't set goals that are too easy and require little effort, as this really negates the intent of trying to make improvements.

Timely. You need to identify a future time when the goals should be accomplished. The time needs to be spelled out; set a date when you will revisit or monitor the goal. The goal should also address major weaknesses at the school or classroom level that need immediate attention. The timing for tackling and accomplishing such goals must also be attainable and realistic. Just as with the development of a child, change is a gradual, slow process. Patience is a virtue. The SMART approach provides a good framework for setting goals and creating a plan for reaching them.

STEP 5: Implement Systemic Change

What is it going to take to accomplish these goals? Actions have to be taken, and something needs to be implemented. More importantly, you have to assign people something to do in your effort to meet the goals. Implementation is often the Achilles' heel of goal setting; we often find it to be the weakness of many professional development programs for teachers. In our work in schools, we often find teachers willing to attend professional development, but not always so willing to implement what they learn into their own classroom practice. Research by Finkelstein and Grubb (2000) shows that often professional development fails to translate into change in classroom practice. We would make the same argument about goal setting; without a plan for who is implementing and what is being implemented, there is not likely to be much movement toward accomplishing the goals we set. When you set goals, you should also be creating task charts that delineate who will be doing what toward accomplishing the goals. Task charts also help you hold each other accountable for the work to be done.

STEP 6: Monitor and Fine Tune

Many get a yearly physical examination (or at least should) for a variety of reasons. In goal setting and planning for improvement, checkups are very important. Your team will need to come back together after a certain amount of time and see how your efforts are progressing. It is time to look at the task charts again and determine whether the work is getting done and whether there may be a need to redistribute certain tasks or abandon things that don't seem to be working. At this point, access to data that could give you an indication of the progress being made will be useful. Monitoring should be intentional and take place on a regular basis, ideally every time the group has a chance to convene to discuss the goals and progress or lack thereof being made toward accomplishing them.

With monitoring comes a certain amount of fine tuning. As mentioned above, you may choose to abandon certain things that do not seem to be working, or you may choose to focus greater attention on aspects of your plan that do seem to be working. This is where you have to be flexible and take into account the many different things that might be going on in the school that can impact your progress. Schools and classrooms, as you have come to know, are fluid places where you cannot always be set in your ways, and sometimes you will have to make quick decisions about things you had set out to do in order to accomplish your goals. This reminds us of a school we assisted; one of the strategies they put into place for helping students was Saturday Technology Fun Days, a very creative idea set forth by the leadership team and championed by a couple of teachers at the school.

The goal for these labs was to actually help students with their academic language through a number of innovative technology workshops. There were six Saturday sessions, scheduled by two teachers who were going to get some extra-duty stipends to do the Saturday labs. Great idea; kids were actually interested, teachers were excited, it was part of the plan, *but* there were no extra-duty stipends for Saturday work available. There were, however, extra-duty stipends for after-school tutoring and it was time to adjust the policy. The duty stipends were adjusted to pay teachers for the Saturday work and they moved on toward accomplishing the goal. Not all of the fine tuning will turn out like this little story, and you might lose team members who had great ideas but are assigned to new positions or laid off; unfortunately, we have seen this occur recently. These are the conditions under which you must still maintain a focus on accomplishing the goals you set while fine-tuning them to respond to whatever roadblocks you encounter.

STEP 7: Evaluate and Communicate the Outcomes

At some point, given the measurable goals you have set and the timeline you have given yourself, you have to face the music. Ironically, if you have followed the steps previously outlined and have put your best effort forward, you might be pretty excited to see what outcome you have achieved. It is also true in goal setting and efforts toward improvement that if you have worked hard and targeted your energy toward accomplishing a goal, you are likely to feel good about how far you have gotten. This being said, you know that you may not always meet your goals, so you have to consider the alternative. What if you didn't set any goals to begin with? If you set no goals at the start and didn't target any improvements, it is likely nothing really changed. And even if change did take place, it is hard for you to attribute that change to anything you intentionally did. You can take credit for improvements, but deep down inside you may wrestle with how those improvements actually came to fruition. The improvement process and meeting or aiming at goals helps you to be more intentional and possibly motivated by the actions you choose to take to address weaknesses in your schools or classrooms. On the other hand, you may have actually accomplished the goal; you have something to celebrate and to explain to people. We also know you will have learned a lot in the process, which will serve you well in future goal setting.

Teachers (or school leaders, for that matter) are not always experts in public relations. When we attend conferences, we (the authors) are often baffled at how sessions on public relations are some of the most frequented. There is certainly a need for better communication of results and the good things that are happening in schools. The news media is typically poised waiting for something bad to happen, like another shooting or teacher indiscretion, so you have to take advantage of the times when things go right in the school and let people know. At the least, these accomplishments need to be presented at faculty meetings or at the parent-teacher association meeting. If you have a school newsletter, then these need to be reported there as well. Most schools have moved to a web-based communication system (for example, School Loop, RenWeb, and School House) that offers another way to get this information out to the community. Simply put, you need to spend some time celebrating, and you need to let others know why you are celebrating.

Discovering the Hidden Picture

Often, when we consider only a few points of data to guide our way, they are about as useful as a random blinking dot moving across a radar screen. The dot blinks and tell us something is there that needs our attention. By connecting the many data dots provided by using the seven dimensions to your academic achievement and challenge data, however, we begin to discover the hidden picture these dots outline. We can begin to see on our radar screen just how broad the picture is that we need to focus on, and how many other dots need our attention. And, as an air traffic controller knows, we must pay close attention to all of the dots on our screen in order to avoid a crisis.

In addition to the data we suggested putting into your buckets, we also urge you to explore the tools we have provided in the Appendix to help you in your efforts. Our goal is to simplify the data collection process; the surveys and measurement tools in the Appendix can get you started quickly. The Appendix is organized to provide you with the surveys, rubrics, and planning forms you need to collect data that you might not have. However, before ending this chapter, we want to address the possible anxiety you might be feeling about actually going out and collecting the data we have suggested. To some, this might feel a little overwhelming. If it does, rest assured that there is an easier qualitative route you can take to get started; it is explained in the next chapter. But we would also like to make a few suggestions as to how you might get some help with this effort to truly embrace data-driven thinking and become a more data-driven educator.

The first line of help you could approach is the experts who handle the data needs at the district level. In most situations, you will find the data person or persons in your district will be excited to hear that you want to use more data to drive your thinking and decision processes. Often, a brief meeting with these individuals can provide the quantitative assistance you need to get your school approaching education multi-dimensionally. The many colleges and universities in your community or state offer another resource. Institutions of higher education, and more specifically schools of education, are being challenged to become more data-driven and to help educators leave their campuses more qualified to understand and use data to do the same. As professors, we are expected to provide service to the community for our tenure and promotion. As professors, we are also normally expected to do scholarship (research) for our tenure and promotion. Quite often you will find professors, or qualified graduate students, looking for such service or research opportunities. Once again, a few quick phone calls to schools of education can identify an expert (or expert in training) to help you with this endeavor. With this approach in mind, you might not even need to leave your district to find the help you need. There might be a colleague among your faculty who is searching for a dissertation or thesis topic to research. You might find a parent with such expertise. You now understand how data based on the seven dimensions can help inform and guide your efforts. Collecting, organizing, and analyzing such data might prove a stretch to your abilities. But if you can't afford to hire a professional evaluator or pay for services to evaluate your school multi-dimensionally, you might find the help you need to accomplish the goals of Multi-Dimensional Education just by asking your stakeholders. But before you start asking around, let's move on to Part II where we provide you with a bit more guidance how to get started more easily using the 4Cs.

Next Steps

Start developing your Multi-Dimensional Bucket List (see Appendix for forms).

1. Reflect on data you currently use and whether it is easily understood and useable.

2. Consider how you might use triangulation to help you improve the use of your data.

3. Develop a timeline to implement the seven steps of data-driven thinking, and begin to address each step.

4. Consider what mechanisms you already have in place (RTI, PLC) and consider what data is being used along with these mechanisms.

5. Evaluate your school's capacity for data use.

6. Address fears around the use of data in your school.

7. Consider the current organization of the data you collect or provide, and how you might improve the organization of data.

PART II

Improvement

Now that you have a deeper understanding of the Multi-Dimensional Education process and a better grasp of why and how we can use the seven dimensions of education to better assess what we do in schools, we want to move forward in applying this data-driven thinking to improvement. The way that we have helped schools use data to improve is by applying the data to four areas that hold great promise for increasing achievement and overall school success. The 4Cs of *Curriculum, Community, Climate,* and *Character* will be covered in depth in Chapters 4 through 8 in order to explain the research supportive of these four areas, how the seven dimensions feed and empower the 4Cs, additional strategies to focus your data-driven thinking, and seven steps to insuring long-lasting systemic change. Also, to help you accomplish these tasks, we will provide you with more rubrics, planning charts, and goal-setting tools to help you get a better grasp on what works well in your school and what needs improvement.

Chapter 4 begins by providing an overall description of the 4Cs and how they are related to the seven dimensions. Chapter 4 introduces and describes a new way to do "walk-throughs" in your school based on the 4Cs and seven dimensions, and how to secure the collaboration of all stakeholders, including shared leadership, in this effort. Chapters 5 through 8 then address each of the 4Cs individually in order to provide you with a comprehensive understanding, rationale, and plan for improvement.

While Part I focused on introducing the parts or dimensions of the systemic approach we are proposing in this book, Part II moves you closer to putting the systemic approach to work in your school. This is the section where all of the pieces come together. Part II expands on how qualitative observations can greatly complement the quantitative evidence you collect or gather. Part II is intended to help you see even more deeply how the seven dimensions can inform your efforts, and provides greater focus for the new lens that will allow you to see the school improvement horizon clearly.

4

The 4Cs Framework for Shared Leadership and Planning

Revisiting the fictional Vinigan Grove School District (see Chapter 2), we find two principals who are taking two different approaches to educational leadership.

Principal One, Dr. Miwae, runs a tight ship. His expectations are high for his staff. He demands excellence and truly wants the best for his school and students. His office bookshelves are lined with a spectrum of texts on how to be a good manager and leader. Next to the framed diplomas and military service plaques hanging behind his desk, there is a small sign that reads "The Buck Stops Here!" He knows that the success of his school rests upon his shoulders. He takes this responsibility seriously and works very hard to ensure success. He is the first to arrive in the morning and the last to leave at night. From the minute he awakes in the morning until the minute he closes his eyes at night, his job consumes his every thought. He is a great individual and truly a dedicated educator.

To achieve his goals, he concentrates heavily on controlling every aspect of the school's efforts. If he is not in a meeting, then he is constantly either walking the hallways keeping the students in line, popping into classrooms unannounced to monitor his teachers, assigning new duties to his administrative staff, or sitting alone in his office, planning. Though others report to him regularly to provide updates and make suggestions, in strategically managing his school he relies

(Continued)

(Continued)

primarily on his insights to intuitively address each and every incident and individual. When a problem arises, he reacts quickly to put the fire out. He sees his intuition and confidence as key elements to his success. He is not afraid to make unpopular decisions. And with an authoritarian style of leadership that demands compliance, it comes as no surprise that his nickname is Sergeant My-Way-or-the-Highway. As a result, though the school is a safe place and is run efficiently, with strict rules and procedures, many teachers do not last long before transferring, students and parents complain regularly to the district, and achievement is not increasing as expected.

Principal Two, Mrs. White, is a very caring person. When she accepted the position, she promised her staff, faculty, students, and parents that her door would always be open. She explained to them that all she can do is try her best to lead the school in the right direction, but it would take a team effort to accomplish real change. From her experience as a teacher and administrator, she was very aware of the many different personalities she was responsible for leading. She knows that every day she will deal with both happy people and grumpy people. She knows that she will have to work with very smart people and not-so-smart people. She often jokes with others close to her that they might call her Snow White, because her whole day is typically spent dealing with individuals that some might call Dopey, Grumpy, Happy, Bashful, Sneezy, Sleepy, and Doc. She is the first to arrive at the school and the last to leave. She loves her job, but still finds time to enjoy her life outside of the school. She is also a wonderful individual and truly dedicated educator, but her approach is very different from Dr. Miwae's.

Mrs. White sees schools as complex and demanding social systems challenged by many differing individuals' concerns; as a result, she seeks to get consensus and buy-in from all stakeholders on many issues. She tries to get others in the school to share in the leadership. Instead of reacting quickly to problems and taking little time to reflect, she is more retrospective and proactive in her approach. She identifies what needs to be fixed, and takes the time needed to consider data and evidence that can provide greater insight. She discusses the issues with others, organizes the possible approaches, considers the outcomes, and then works with a team to try to develop mutually beneficial plans to strategically address what the system needs for successful results. Instead of seeking compliance, she tries to find an acceptable approach that works for all to achieve continuous improvement in what she refers to as her 4Cs: *curriculum, community, climate,* and *character.* And for the record, she does not whistle while she works.

As we learned in Chapter 2, *Equifinality* means that there are many paths that can be taken to achieving similar results. As we all know from experience working with principals and other school-level leaders, there are many different types or styles of leadership. Therefore, how we achieve success through data-driven thinking can rest upon a great number of leadership approaches taken and decisions made. As we can surmise from the story of the two principals, these approaches might be as different as Snow White and Sergeant My-Way-or-the-Highway. Ideally, many would probably benefit from leadership that finds a happy medium between the two different leadership styles. Yet, depending on what leadership paradigm you subscribe to or are guided by, accomplishing first- and second-order change and creating the synergy needed to get all of your dimensional gears moving is impacted by the characteristics of the leadership style or system you practice or work under. Remember that first-order change involves changing efforts to add to the existing system, while second-order change requires adding new components to develop and adopt a completely new system. As Figure 4.1 illustrates, there is a wide spectrum of leadership characteristics. And though each end of the spectrum holds benefits and challenges, you must first consider how leadership can adapt or find a happy medium in order to allow positive data-driven systemic change to occur naturally and to some degree strategically.

As a colleague of ours, Dr. Paul Chapman, often shares with educational leaders, Snow White in many ways is an ideal leader for schools. She has many redeeming qualities that help her to manage the many challenges educators face. Although this is not a book on leadership styles, we want you to think about leadership styles from Snow White to Sergeant My-Way-or-the-Highway. We want you to consider how leaders can benefit from considering data, regardless of one's style. We must recognize that leadership often needs to change in order to allow for a more data-driven approach to inform successful educational decision making. Dr. Miwae's authoritarian approach and heavy reliance upon intuition might provide some immediate sense of sanity to the controlled chaos, but it also may preclude any

Figure 4.1   Spectrum of Leadership Characteristics

Authoritarian	↔	Shared Leadership
Compliance	↔	Continuous Improvement
Reactive	↔	Proactive
Spontaneous	↔	Strategic
Identifies	↔	Organizes
Systematic	↔	Systemic

teamwork, or preclude the data gathered from making systemic change. Under Principal White, on the other hand, her open-door, kumbayah, patient approach to building consensus might truly create a healthy culture, but it might also create challenges to getting a majority to agree upon the change that is needed within a suitable time frame.

4Cs for Applying Your Data-Driven Thinking

No matter whether you have the expertise, shared leadership, or outside assistance to pursue Multi-Dimensional Education through a more heavily quantitative process, or you will be beginning this journey reliant more on qualitative evidence, the process is basically the same. The seven dimensions are what you will use to organize your data (buckets), and they will also serve as indicators of your strengths and challenges. The seven dimensions of evidence are what you will apply to improving the 4Cs. Figure 4.2 represents the 360-degree three-step process we use when working with schools. The MDed360 is the structure we used to organize the three parts of this book. The theme of Step 1 is *Assessment.* If you do not assess, how do you know what you think you know? How do you know how your stakeholders feel about the seven dimensions? If you don't have data or comprehensive evidence, how can you be sure your intuition is correct? As you assess the seven dimensions you start to move into Step 2: *Improvement.* In Step 2, we have found that there are four areas that schools can really look at for improvement. These four areas, the 4Cs of systemic improvement, directly relate to addressing student challenges and facilitating student achievement. This is what you want, correct? Most educators want to improve academic achievement, help kids get better at school, and help teachers experience fewer disruptions. So these are the things most educators want to devote time and effort toward.

One of the authors remembers all too well serving as vice principal in charge of discipline in a large school of more than 2,400 students in California. He was in charge of discipline for male students with last names M-Z. There was not a day that went by, unless it was a half-day or the day before vacation, that he did not have at least four or five boys sitting outside of his office. He realized that the kids would not get in trouble on half-days because they did not want to get stuck after school. They didn't get in trouble the day before vacation because the kids did not want to get grounded the day before vacation. Unfortunately, very few school days are followed by a half-day

Figure 4.2   Multi-Dimensional Education's Systemic Improvement Process

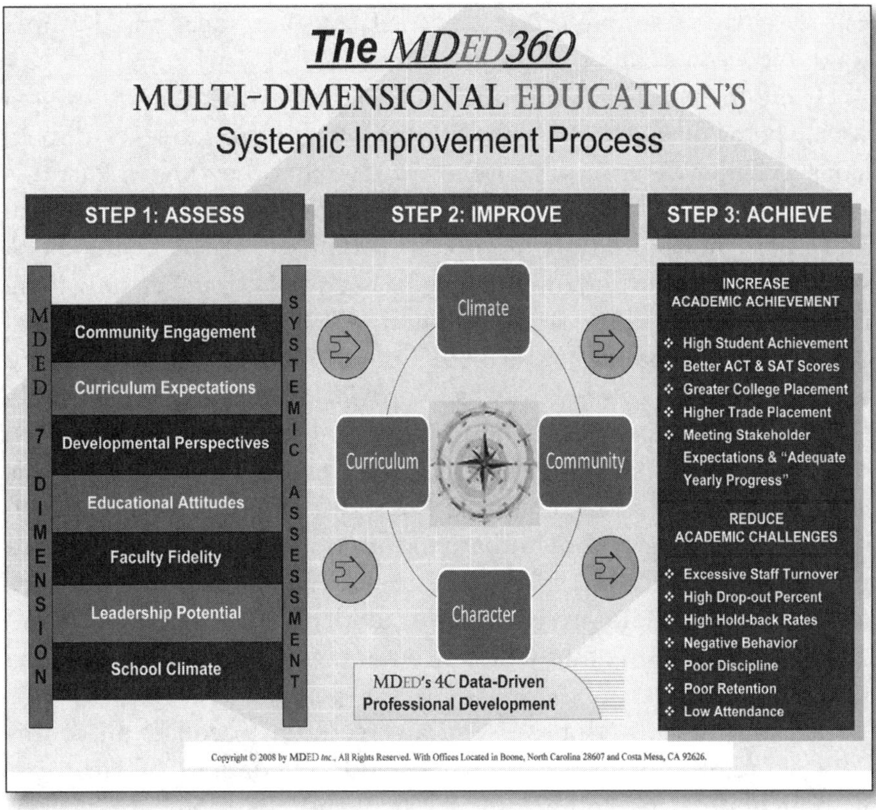

or a week of vacation. He realized that the problems he encountered on a daily basis were often related to challenges in the classroom or curriculum, community, school climate, and character. To improve achievement and to address these challenges, which rarely just go away on their own, the Multi-Dimensional Education Process focuses on applying the seven dimensions of data to the 4Cs. But just as the dimensions required Leadership Potential to get the gears moving, the 4Cs require shared leadership.

In this chapter and in Chapters 5 through 8 we will break down and unpack the 4Cs. We will consider some of the ideas and notions that fall under the 4Cs of systemic improvement and how you can begin to think differently about improvement as well. We will also share how all of the seven dimensions connect in order to empower the 4Cs. Last, under *Improvement,* we will look at how a school can improve in these areas. This is where the power of this system rests. Once you have the information (data or evidence on the seven dimensions) and you realize and document where improvement needs to be made, there is always something in all of us that says "I need to do something." So how do you go about this planning or strategic process? We have a simple process that will give you ideas and a framework for accomplishing improvement.

If the theme of Part I of this book was assessment, and our goal was to help you see how highly effective schools use the seven dimensions to better determine how they know what they know, Part II is focused more on how to organize and apply data to your educational and instructional leadership efforts to improve. Part I of this book sought to provide you with the schema needed to visualize how there are at least seven dimensions of data predictive of success, and that connecting data points across these dimensions is critical to achieving success. Part II of this book seeks to provide you with a user-friendly framework that can assist you in utilizing data in a data-driven decision making (DDDM) process. Part II, and more specifically this chapter, is aimed at facilitating a process for putting data and evidence (qualitative and quantitative) into operation in your school's practices and procedures. We want to give you a simple framework to inform your data-driven thinking and organize your evidence-gathering efforts. In other words, we now want to help you put data to work in your school.

It's only fair . . . right? If you are required to collect all of this data, shouldn't you also be provided with this data in a format that you can understand and use at the school and classroom level? Part II is intended to help you focus on data as a tool to be applied rather than something to be held accountable for.

However, much of the data that must be collected are, quite honestly, of little use or interest to those working at the school level. You know those data reports that make you ask, "Why am I compiling this stuff again?" Therefore, as Chapter 3 explained, you may need to set aside some of the not-so-helpful accountability data and focus on collecting and organizing data needed to assess the seven dimensions associated with highly effective schools. To help you accomplish this task, we have provided you with surveys and evaluations in the Appendix, as well as recommendations of other surveys and measurement tools to use. But we know that, for some, initially conceptualizing how to collect seven dimensions of data becomes a bit too cumbersome, possibly even overwhelming. Some might want to start with qualitative insights (stakeholder observations, focus group discussions, and the like) and the data you have on hand before beginning a more extensive quantitative data collection and analysis process similar to what we provide to school systems.

This is one reason why we created the 4Cs model. With this model, you can either jump in the water and collect all of the qualitative and quantitative seven dimensions of data needed to deeply inform the 4Cs, or you can slowly wade in and begin by focusing on assessing just the 4Cs of the system that we will fully explain in Chapters 5 through 8. As you might know, qualitative research often provides a thematic analysis of the evidence or insights associated with a subject of study. Thematic analysis often aims to discover a better *understanding* of why something is happening, rather than just *knowing* what is happening. The 4Cs of systemic improvement provide you with four themes for conducting such investigations. However, when you use qualitative insights only and do not support those insights with evidence and numbers to justify the perceptions, you are often left with analysis based upon words. And when you just do a quantitative analysis, you are often forced to make decisions just based on numbers. Both approaches can benefit from each other; this is what is referred to as *mixed methods*. Mixed methods allow you to combine your qualitative insights with your quantitative measures to provide the *why* to accompany the *what* that you have found. Although you can use the 4Cs to do a qualitative analysis at the start, we want to stress that taking a mixed methods approach using your seven-dimensional buckets of data can ensure greater success in assessing your strengths and concerns and applying such knowledge to improving outcomes.

Connecting the Seven Dimensions to the 4Cs

No matter which route you choose to get started on taking a Multi-Dimensional Education approach to DDDM (full submersion or wading in slowly), it is important that you understand how the seven dimensions connect to the 4Cs. As the dimensional gear model introduced in Chapter 2 highlights, in order for the seven dimensions to work, you cannot afford to ignore any of the gears. The seven-dimensional gears work together as a system. And if one of the dimensional gears has a problem with the clogs not connecting to another gear, or a gear needs a bit of oiling to lower the resistance it is exhibiting, or, even worse, a dimensional gear is moving in the wrong direction, you will find your system for synergy malfunctioning. This is what our data often shows us when we work with a school that is experiencing extreme difficulty: One or more of the dimensional index scores are significantly low. The dimension is not working, and it must be fixed while still considering the other dimensions and 4Cs.

Not only do the seven dimensions complement and drive each other, they also help the 4Cs gears to get moving, as Figure 4.3 illustrates. The seven dimensions drive the 4Cs. We developed the 4Cs based upon feedback from educators and policy experts we worked with that wanted a simpler way to put this model and the data we collected for them into action. Instead of focusing on all seven dimensions, they asked if there was a way they could focus on just a few to begin. We, however, feel strongly that none of the dimensions can be ignored or receive delayed attention. We understand the desire to focus on fewer factors; educators are overwhelmed with a massive to-do list, and it might seem insane to some to try to find time to focus on so much at once. Unfortunately, in our experience when a school only focuses on a few dimensions, the experience ends in frustration. This is due to the shortcomings we explained earlier related to a systematic rather than a systemic approach. When we began to look more closely and critically at our seven dimensions

Figure 4.3   Dimensional Connection to the 4Cs

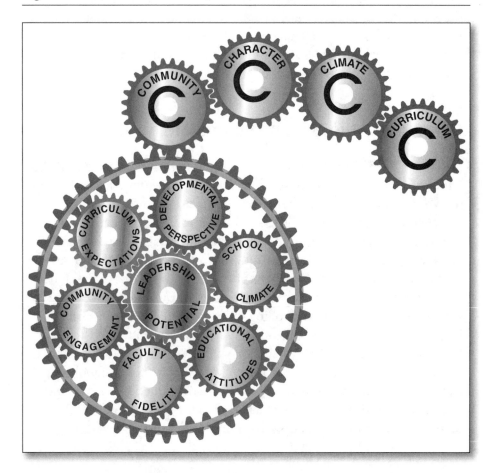

with this suggestion in mind, however, we began to see a pattern. We began to see a pattern in which the schools that were using our seven dimensions of data were also applying the information to the 4Cs of systemic improvement. Our research has actually shown how the dimensions complemented each other and were connected through and within the 4Cs.

All of the dimensions complement or are interconnected to each other. And as we would like to discuss now, they also empower each of the 4Cs. Let's start with the dimension of Leadership Potential. In reality, the dimension of Leadership Potential is one of the biggest drivers for all of the 4Cs. If the leaders are not leading the way or bringing the stakeholders together to focus on the agreed-upon tasks, none of the dimensions or 4Cs can be improved. But our research also identified that each of the 4Cs had primary dimensions that were more closely aligned to the specific 4Cs.

For example, under the 4Cs area of Curriculum, the primary dimensions beyond Leadership Potential are Curriculum Expectations and Faculty Fidelity. For Community, the primary dimension of data to be applied is Community Engagement. For Character, the primary dimensions are Developmental Perspectives and Educational Attitudes. And for Climate, the primary dimension of data to focus on is obviously School Climate. Yet from our past experience, we have seen firsthand how the Developmental Perspectives and Educational Attitudes of students can either positively or negatively impact the School Climate. If you have a group of students who do not care about others or school, improving student, faculty, and parent perspectives on School Climate will be more of a challenge. The effect on School Climate is the same if we find negative perceptions and attitudes associated with Curriculum Expectations, Faculty Fidelity, and Community Engagement. Data collected on the primary dimensions should be considered first when assessing the 4Cs, but we should not discount or ignore the contributions the other dimensions of data hold for improving each of the 4Cs. In Chapters 5 through 8, we will address in more detail how the dimensions inform and empower each of the 4Cs. In those chapters, you will also notice how the gear illustrations highlight the primary dimensions for each of the 4Cs.

In reality, no matter whether you use the MDed Seven Dimensions or the 4Cs to organize the data collection process, you will by default be assessing much of the same thing. As we will explain shortly, when you walk through your school with the 4Cs Framework rubrics, much of what you observe, note, and assess will fall under one of the dimensions as well as one or more of the 4Cs.

Mental Notes

As we explained in Chapter 3, we want you to fill your buckets with valuable data. As you go through the process, you will see that the golden nuggets of information will bring attention to themselves by shining brightly. Or in the case of Snow White, maybe they are diamonds you have mined. When you have identified the shining data you need, it becomes easier to connect the dots between the data points (consisting of the seven dimensions, academic achievement, and academic challenges) that more comprehensively explain your strengths and concerns. For those of you who do have a slight fear of numbers (numerophobia), the level to which you quantify this information or data points is up to you. In fact, for the exercise we are about to introduce, we just want you to think of the data as observations or mental notes that you might make as you walk through your school. As our gear-head illustration in the Preface suggests, we want you to use the gears to drive your thought process and focus on achievement. We want you to use the dimensional and 4Cs gears to generate a different kind of thinking; data-driven thinking. And by getting you to think about your school using these gears, we can start to provide you with a new lens or vision on what really needs to be focused on in order to improve and make systemic, lasting change.

We want you to use the MDed 4Cs Walk-Through Rubric to begin collecting insights and observations around the 4Cs of Curriculum, Community, Climate, and Character. Basically, the MDed 4Cs Walk-Through Rubric is meant to serve as a visual organizer and log. Each quadrant of the rubric represents one of the 4Cs. Within each quadrant, you have a space to fill in what you see as strengths or concerns within your school. In addition, within each quadrant you have a space to fill in what evidence you observe that supports either the perception of a strength or a concern. Some schools have printed up enough walk-through rubrics for the administration, staff, and faculty to use during a school week. After providing a little guidance and explanation on the seven dimensions and 4Cs, they asked the educators and staff to spend the week completing these forms. In other words, they spend a week observing what is taking place in the school and classrooms. They make notes as to what these strengths and concerns are and also what possible evidence exists to substantiate their perceptions of the strengths and concerns.

As discussed in Chapter 3, this evidence can take many forms. Such information could be anecdotal and qualitative in nature. The information might just represent an insight from one individual. For example, one of your parents might note that their child really likes the new mathematics curriculum and their new teacher. You also might find artifacts that suggest something less desirable is taking place in the school. For example, in schools that have challenges with School Climate, we often find that the hallways are very dirty, graffiti-covered, and littered. In addition, some schools hold focus group discussions and take copious notes on what those willing to come in and discuss had to say.

Other evidence you might find could be more quantitative in nature. You might actually count how many students are still in the hallway after the bell rings. You might measure how many minutes it takes the tardy students to get to their classes. Such a simple number can hold great power. For example, if your classes typically have to deal with interruptions for the first five minutes of class, do the math on what this takes away from your instructional time. Five minutes a class for six class periods equates to 30 minutes a day. Thirty minutes a day equates to 2.5 hours a week, 10 hours a month, and 90 hours of instructional time a year lost to disruptions. By measuring what is taking place in your school, you begin to move toward a system of data-driven thinking.

Either type of data you collect (qualitative, quantitative, or both), can be used as process, formative, or summative evidence needed to document what is good or not so good about your educational and instructional efforts. When collected at the beginning of the process, this data can serve as what is called a *baseline* or *pretest measurement.* This baseline measurement can be used to compare later progress measurements to document whether positive change is occurring. And as Chapter 1 suggests, oftentimes in order to get the late majority onboard with the change process, you will need evidence that shows them that the change is working.

No Running, Just Walking

To do this investigative walk-through exercise, you must walk, not run. This is why it is called a *walk-through.* If you run and don't take the time to make clear observations, you will find that you don't end up with a sufficient supply of random notes in your rubric. Or if you don't take the time to walk and make astute observations, you might find that all you document is of a simple nature and falls short of accurately addressing your deeper strengths and concerns. Another side note to consider is that we recommend this walk-through be conducted by many of your stakeholders. Oftentimes these walk-through forms are specifically targeted at principals. However, as you probably know deep down inside, we all have biases, and these biases often play tricks on us. These biases often trick our minds into seeing what we want to see. But when you have many people in the building complete the form, you are able to get a more robust and broader assessment of what your strengths and concerns truly are from numerous perspectives. Mrs. White is correct in her approach; that is, to consider what others are thinking. If you are responsible for managing the teachers or students in your school, it can be very beneficial to you in your management efforts to know what they are thinking.

So how do you gather such evidence from the stakeholders you want to help you with this activity? First and foremost, we recommend allowing the walk-through rubric to be completed anonymously. When individuals are asked to complete a form that can identify them, they often will shape their answers to adjust for a social acceptance bias. When we complete forms that identify us, we often avoid truly saying how we feel. So make sure your rubrics can be submitted at a central location that allows the stakeholders to be anonymous. Also, though we have only recommended that you have your staff and faculty complete the form, you might also consider having a few parents complete it as well. Often, in our assessments of schools we find the parent perspectives to be very different than the educator perspectives. This is the same case with students. So if you really want to complete a 360-degree assessment of the 4Cs, you might invite parents and students to complete the form. But please don't just pick the parents and students that fall into what some might refer to as the "coalition of the willing."

During a training session in the Midwest where we shared and discussed the results of a study with schools, we learned how such "coalition of the willing" approaches to data collection can be quite misleading. After giving a PowerPoint presentation on the data, the leadership team from one school, who were all seated at the same table, all raised their hands with great fervor. They wanted to share that they thought that our data was not accurate and did not gauge what students were really thinking. When asked to explain why they felt this way, they replied, "We completed a focus group with students last week and asked them many of the same questions you used to assess School Climate, and their answers were the complete opposite of your data." We asked how many and which students they had in the focus group. They stated they had more than 20 students take part and that these students were the "homeroom captains." Upon looking around the room to see how the other School Leadership Teams (SLTs) were now reacting to this questioning of the data, it was evident that they were beginning to see how our approach to collecting data was a little less biased than that of the group who had objected.

Why were the two findings different? The differing answers were due to comparing survey data that was collected on hundreds of students from many different performance levels, social groups, and cliques to data collected from a handful of students who volunteered to be homeroom captains; the latter tend to be good students who care a bit more than the not-so-satisfied students. They were comparing the opinions of some of their best students to the opinions of the whole student body. Which do you think is more accurate or less biased?

This is a completely true story. We share this story to highlight how you need to be careful when collecting data so that you do not make assumptions that are not supported or wrongly supported. In our quantitative statistical world this is referred to respectively as Type I and Type II error. We must be careful not to base our decisions on data that lead us to assume something is true when it is not (Type I error) or to assume that something is not true when it is (Type II error). And no matter whether you are wading into this uncharted or undercharted world of data-driven thinking by doing a first-level analysis of the 4Cs or diving deep into assessing the seven dimensions that drive the 4Cs, you must make sure you provide the opportunity for a broad spectrum of participants to complete the surveys or rubrics anonymously. You also must give them time, especially with the MDed 4Cs Walk-Through Rubric (Figure 4.4), to walk and not run. You must give them time to observe, reflect, and identify the many factors contributing or detracting from your success.

In addition to the needs for anonymity, for utilizing a representative sample of stakeholders, and for allowing time to collect the information, you also want to address the subject of bias just a bit more. Often, when we serve as investigators or evaluators, we are assigned a time to visit schools to collect data. In some schools we visit, it is as if they didn't even get the memo that we were coming. At the other end of the spectrum, we often visit schools that knew we were coming and have prepped their staff, students, and faculty for our arrival. At times, in these schools it seems as if the school is operating on a completely different routine than normal. The school is spotless, and the janitors and maintenance crews are asking us if the place looks shipshape. The faculty is all on their best behavior, and the students we administer the surveys to even slip from time to time and ask,

Figure 4.4   MDed 4Cs Walk-Through Rubric

Curriculum	Observable Evidence +/–	Community	Observable Evidence +/–
Strengths • Each team utilizes common lessons • There is a scope and sequence for each teacher • There is an after-school tutorial • Each class has ample materials	• Lesson plans • District provided and utilized scope and sequence • Noted an average of 20 students attending after-school tutorials • Materials available for all students	Strengths • Principal or AP greets students and parents when students dropped off at school • Newsletter sent home to parents in hard copy and e-mail offering service opportunities in school • Attempts made to bring parents to schools for programs performed by students	• Five days of viewing morning routines • Seen and read newsletters • Phone logs, information in newsletter and specific art program announcements
Concerns • There appears to be little differentiation within the curriculum • Most of class time is involved in lecture and feedback • Lack of instructional support before school and during lunch	• Few examples provided when asked of teams • Observations of various classes. Also feedback from meeting with teams • Lack of tutorials throughout the school	Concerns • Very few community volunteers • Opening-of-year breakfast had less then 30% of parents in attendance—down from 70% three years ago	• Data from parents' volunteer book • Data provided by BLT

Climate	Observable Evidence +/-	Character	Observable Evidence +/-
Strengths • Consistent rules and practices are posted in each classroom regarding behavior in class/school-wide • Most stakeholders seem friendly toward each other	• Visible in each classroom and throughout school • Observed in halls during the beginning of the day	Strengths • Morning announcement focusing on the importance of good character • Character traits posted in classrooms • Assembly to celebrate good character	• Morning announcements heard every day • Visible effort to post traits throughout the school • Monthly assembly

Climate	Observable Evidence +/–	Character	Observable Evidence +/–
Concerns • There are some stakeholders who speak inappropriately to others and their peers • Some kids standing alone before school (observed over several days)	• Heard loud yelling throughout the school day. Office referrals and complaints from parents about teachers • Observational data	Concerns • Little opportunity for students to serve in school and community • Behavioral problems are increasing in the school	• We have no active service clubs or activities • Inappropriate language heard; data concerning office referrals and suspensions

"My teacher told me not to ask you, but if I disagree with how they want us to answer should I be honest on the survey?" We appreciate the fact that these schools take the survey and the goals of the grant seriously, but the rhetorical question we must ask is, "Do you think we will collect accurate and honest information if the schools have told all of the students what we are there to study?" The obvious answer is *no.* So we suggest that on the week you designate to collect this information, keep in mind that you want to study and observe what your school is normally like. This is why we suggest approaching this effort in the role of detective, archeologist, or scientist. Try to collect the data based upon your normal routines and procedures. Try to look at it through a new lens.

This process of including many stakeholders can greatly enhance your efforts to develop buy-in and a shared leadership approach. This process provides the evidence needed to have fruitful discussions. We have found that the 4Cs are a unifying framework in that almost all of the educators we have worked with agree that all of the 4Cs are important to success in schools. The 4Cs of systemic improvement are four areas that educators can buy into and rarely argue against. They provide a unifying framework able to encompass practices such as Response to Intervention (RTI), Positive Behavior Interventions and Supports (PBIS), and Professional Learning Communities (PLC)— practices that often focus on the 4Cs. This process allows many of your stakeholders to feel that they actually have a voice in the school and in the decision-making process. When students, parents, and educators feel that they have a voice, they are more likely to buy in to the change process that emanates from data-driven thinking efforts. While the 3Rs (rigor, relevance, and relationships) provide the framework for conceptualizing what is important in the classroom, the 4Cs do the same for schools and classrooms.

Lessening the Aggravation of Aggregation

In the statistical world, when we merge different data files into one file in hopes of being able to summarize information, it is called *aggregating data*. Aggregating educational data can be quite cumbersome. However, for school level purposes, we have designed a slightly less aggravating approach. Let's first look at why we need to aggregate the data. We aggregate data because if we only look at one part of the system without considering its connection or relationship to other parts, we once again fall into a systematic approach rather than a systemic approach. If we only look at how one variable or dimension impacts another variable, we often end up with what we referred to earlier as "corn-fusing" research. We want you to look at the seven dimensions, as well as the 4Cs, together, and consider whether the gears are connecting and properly working. Compiling a bunch of information or evidence from a great number of different stakeholders on numerous variables can become a little aggravating, but it is worth the effort. Connecting the dots is essential.

As a good detective knows (or at least those detectives on TV who always solve the crime), one clue is a great place to start, but it typically is the tip of the iceberg that leads to the discovery of many other clues. Just as far too many individuals sit in prison today convicted on one piece of evidence that other clues would have negated, we must be careful not to put too much credence on one piece of evidence and allow our mission to be determined by it. As a good archeologist knows, when you find remnants of pottery and eating utensils, it often means that a village was located at the site. But a good archeologist also knows that by digging slowly through the site, we can find even more evidence to explain the customs, rituals, and way of life of those who lived there.

If you want to be a leader like Mrs. White, Dr. Miwae, or, ideally, somewhere in between, and you want to enhance your shared leadership efforts with data that can guide and document your success, you must aggregate the data you find. You must organize your data in a fashion that allows you to compare and contrast. Many educators might think "data-driven education" or "data-driven decision making" are just the buzzwords of the day. Many think that making data-driven decisions is a cold and heartless approach to making decisions concerning real individuals who have feelings. In some instances, this has definitely been the case. But data-driven decision making is not just about making a data-driven decision; it's about making informed decisions. And making an informed decision, using evidence to inform your intuition and heart, can more often lead to the right decision. In order to make the right decision through data-driven thinking efforts, you must consider the totality of the data, information, and body of evidence before making such decisions. And as you can see from our dimensions and 4Cs, we developed these factors and categories based on sound research that does consider the real people you work with and serve. We want you to consider the perspectives and opinions of all stakeholders and try to come up with solutions that can help. The point of Multi-Dimensional Education is not to produce statistics. We have enough of those already. The point is to find and use statistics, data, and other evidence to facilitate solutions.

We suggest that you begin to aggregate your data by creating a list of the findings from all of the rubrics for each of the 4Cs based upon your strengths and concerns and the observable evidence. We suggest typing these lists up so that they can be shared with the stakeholders for discussion purposes, possibly in a multimedia or Power-Point presentation. If you have time after completing the aggregation of this data, you might also go through each of the 4Cs findings and begin to subcategorize them by the seven dimensions. Also, if you have decided to go deeper into gathering data around the 4Cs as described in Chapter 3, you can add this evidence to the report at this time. If you do this, you will then be able to see how much of what you do and see in relation to the 4Cs areas can also be addressed by focusing on the seven dimensions.

So taking the time to aggregate the data or information in order to prepare for discussion of the findings is the next step once all of your stakeholders have completed their walk-through. Once again, this is where shared leadership can gain momentum. By allowing others beyond the leadership or administration team to be a part of this effort, you are allowing others to feel more empowered; you are also adding a component to your data-driven thinking efforts that provides a transparent and equitable assessment. By having a wide array of stakeholders work on the aggregation in the way we have described, it becomes a learning process and a productive experience. It starts the Courageous Conversations that need to follow.

Courageous Conversation Challenge

In Chapters 5 through 8 we will go much deeper into the 4Cs to provide you with the knowledge and assistance you need to further conceptualize, assess, and implement your efforts around those areas.

But before we discuss each of the 4Cs in more detail, let's address what the next step is after you have collected and aggregated your information or data. As stories in our chapters have illustrated, there are many different ways that schools approach and address the use of data. Some fear it, while others ignore it. Some dismiss it, while others fret about it. And some collect it, consider it, and use it to guide and inform their efforts. And some of those who do use it bring a team together (if not all stakeholders) to embrace it and discuss what really needs to happen in order to accomplish what some call true, long-lasting, systemic change. These discussions are what one principal referred to as "Come to Jesus" talks. Others might use derogatory terms to describe the discussions. We like to call them *Courageous Conversations*, because just as it takes a great amount of courage and coercing to get a troubled family or couple to the counselor or therapist, often when such mental health sessions are effective the family leaves feeling much better after the discussion. This is because they have put all of the facts on the table and have had a fair discussion about what is good and what needs to change. This is what we ask educators to do.

A courageous conversation is not a time for finger-pointing or accusation. It should not be a time when individuals are singled out. To do so is often futile and unproductive. Plus, from the systems theory perspective, we know that it is rarely ever one individual, part of the system, or factor that is holding a system back from increasing synergy and output. Courageous Conversations, when shaped around the 4Cs and the seven dimensions, are intended to take a systemic look at what is happening in a school. So if your rubrics and assessments are anonymous and collected from a wide array of stakeholders, and if the conversation is focused around each of the 4Cs, your school should be able to have a discussion that is honest, accurate, and less threatening (personally and professionally).

A great coach would never blame one player for losing a game and instead would focus on the importance of playing as a team; similarly, this discussion is intended to help the stakeholders in your building find consensus and come together. This conversation is focused on approaching this effort with shared leadership, strategic systemic insights, and specific target planning to address the areas and dimensions that decades of research and practice have shown definitively to lead to success. Just as we encouraged you to have all stakeholders take a week to collect evidence around the MDed 4Cs Walk-Through Rubric, we also encourage you to have all stakeholders participate in these conversations. If your challenges or concerns are abundant, you might first have this discussion with your staff and faculty to address the concerns and develop a systemic targeted plan to fix the gears. And from the first meeting, you can look to hold other meetings to address the issues and efforts with parents and students.

At this first meeting after completing data aggregation, we strongly encourage you to have as many educators and staff present as possible. By presenting the strengths, concerns, and evidence, and then as a team developing plans to capitalize on your strengths and remedy your concerns, there is a greater chance for a groundswell of adopters to get on board if all are in attendance. If we only bring a few select individuals (the coalition of the willing), we might increase the "us versus them" mentality we often see in divided schools. When we don't invite all to the table, those not invited often feel insulted and end up hearing and passing on an increasingly distorted synopsis of the meeting.

We believe that these meetings are eye-opening experiences for educators, and have seen this to be the case. The dimensional data as well as the 4Cs walk-through data often provide insights to educators and staff that are applicable to the school and their classrooms, offices, and cafeterias. Though in our experiences in education we have met some individuals we would have preferred had chosen a different career, a large majority of the educators we meet are the most caring and dedicated people you will find. They entered the profession to make a difference. At these meetings, those passionate spirits come out. In these Courageous Conversations, we see educators' eyes that were dull and defeated suddenly develop a glimmer of hope that there just might be a chance to recover their motivation for entering this calling. Finding the courage to have these conversations without data is slightly crazy, in our opinion. If you do not have evidence to back up the concerns you want to discuss, you are just asking for a fight. If you do not have a plan to fix and focus on that which needs to be fixed in order to improve your system, you are going up that notorious creek without a paddle. This is why we strongly suggest structuring your courageous conversation around seven dimensions and the 4Cs: there is ample research demonstrating their efficacy.

We suggest collecting the data to document what is done well and what needs to be fixed. Remember, when you collect data multidimensionally, you will normally find data that is cause for celebration. And you must take time to celebrate your successes often. But you will also possibly find data that might demand some serious conversation and work. When you do, this also is a teachable moment. Often, these conversations can produce one of those "aha" moments where the light clicks on, and suddenly the team that could not win a game all season comes out of the locker room bound and determined to win.

In the following chapters, we will provide more detail on each of the 4Cs and introduce several other rubrics and organizing tools. Please remember, the extent to which you quantify this process is up to you. What we want you to do, quantitatively or qualitatively, is direct your focus to the seven dimensions of indicators and the 4Cs of systemic improvement.

Next Steps

1. Put some time into studying the dimensions and considering what data you have on the dimensions that can be used in assessing the 4Cs.

2. Begin organizing a group of stakeholders to serve as your shared leadership committee for collecting the information based on the MDed 4Cs Walk-Through Rubric.

3. Designate a week to have your stakeholders collect information using the MDed 4Cs Walk-Through Rubrics, and hold a short meeting prior to the exercise to explain the logic behind the effort.

4. Organize a time to hold your Courageous Conversations.

5

The C of Curriculum

Once again we find ourselves in the fictional school district of Vinigan Grove. Let's face it, this district has some challenges. Here, we find two English Language Arts middle school teachers using the same curriculum in different classrooms in the same school. Two years previously, the state mandated a new curriculum to ensure a strict focus for providing high-quality English Language Arts instruction. For Grades 4 through 12, literacy now focuses more specifically on student aptitude in reading, writing, listening, speaking, viewing, and presenting, both within the English Language Arts curriculum and across all content areas.

In Classroom One, we find a teacher who is very knowledgeable about the new curriculum. He has gone through numerous training programs. He understands how the curriculum is tied to the standards. He understands what aspects of the curriculum align with the state's achievement test. He follows the district standards pacing guide and uses the worksheets and lessons from the curriculum text on a daily basis. He follows each lesson of the curriculum very closely and delivers the material in a professional way. His class is very organized and regimented. He has a schedule laid out for the year and sticks to it. He tries his best to make sure every student understands the content before moving on to the next lessons, but, to his dismay, there are a number of students in each of his classes that are falling behind. Unfortunately, the curriculum text provides a limited number of additional lessons and instructional strategies for those who did not grasp the milestones with the lesson plans, assignments, and worksheets provided; also, the curriculum timeline requires that he covers the allotted chapters and assignments before the end of the grading period.

(Continued)

(Continued)

Although he wishes he could help the students who lag behind, he feels he must stay on track and not vary from the curriculum guidelines. He knows he is responsible for the content, and the content must be covered.

In Classroom Two, we find a teacher who is also very knowledgeable of the new curriculum. She attended the same training programs. She also understands how the curriculum is tied to the standards and how the curriculum is intended to help students grasp the content to be assessed by the state's achievement test. This teacher follows the district standards pacing guide and also uses many of the curriculum's worksheets and lessons on a daily basis. But unlike the Classroom One teacher, she does not feel constrained by the timeline. She is confident that she can accomplish all of the curriculum demands by the end of grading period while moving at a pace that allows her to address all of the differentiated learning challenges in her classes. To do this, she puts extra effort into making sure the way she teaches is engaging. She creatively plans for ways to stay on schedule and keep the students engaged in the standards and curriculum. She teaches every day with great enthusiasm. She puts a great amount of effort into getting to know each of her students personally so that she can understand more about them. She also puts extra effort into building a deeper knowledge of the subject matter, and finds other resources to help her teach the material to students with different learning styles. She has recruited several parents who routinely come in to help support students better. She is able to structure the class so that cooperative learning techniques are integrated with direct instruction. She also has developed her own formative assessments to help her better gauge throughout the grading period if her students are mastering the subject materials and are ready for various assessments. She uses these formative assessments as a means to reteach content that students may not have initially grasped. And she is available before school, at lunch, and after school to help students needing extra assistance.

Addressing Curriculum

Both of the educators in this story are good teachers. They just approach teaching the curriculum differently. Curriculum is often the first of the 4Cs we discuss because in education today, curriculum is the primary area of educator accountability. Given the wide array of curricula in use, our focus is on Curriculum Expectations: delivery, instruction, and effectiveness. We focus on gathering data that can inform teachers what they are doing well and how they can improve.

Teachers have a profound impact on the academic achievement of students; this impact is very much attributed to the implementation of curriculum (Rowan, Chiang, & Miller, 1997; Sanders & Horn, 1998). The curriculum represents the totality of the material to be learned and, one hopes, mastered. Yet how do we determine what should be

taught and assessed within the curriculum? Ralph Tyler's 1949 mas-
terpiece, *Basic Principles of Curriculum and Instruction,* outlined four
principles that should guide educators in the consideration of what
and how to deliver the curriculum:

1. What educational purposes should the school seek to attain?

2. What educational experiences can be provided that are likely to
   attain these purposes?

3. How can these educational experiences be effectively organized?

4. How can we determine whether these purposes are being
   attained?

This does not mean everyone will learn and become proficient in
the same manner on every subject we teach. Some students will prefer
the arts over the sciences or vice versa. No matter what one teaches,
we believe the curriculum should be delivered with the following
considerations in mind: (1) *educational rigor,* (2) *instructional creativity,*
(3) *academic support,* and (4) *differentiated effectiveness.* Let us consider
how each of these impact on the delivery of a sound curriculum.

Finding the PERKA and Research Support

When we think broadly about curriculum, we use the acronym
PERKA to capture many of the things discussed in the story about the
two different teachers:

Pedagogy that is engaging!

   Enthusiasm about the subject matter!

      Relationships with our students!

         Knowledge about the subject matter!

            Assessment that guides learning and instruction!

Pedagogy That Is Engaging!

As we consider pedagogy that is engaging for all students, we
begin by examining the current conditions under which we are
being asked to teach. We are operating in a standards-based instructional system that tends to dictate the kind of instruction we can do.
Much of the standards-based instructional approach is rooted in

behaviorism or focused primarily on teacher-centered instruction (Posner, 2003). Therefore, to some extent teachers are often forced to take a more direct instructional approach that may limit creativity and the use of constructivist and collaborative approaches such as discovery learning and project-based learning. And while direct instruction holds great potential for teaching subjects such as reading and math effectively, it does not always provide the further-reaching holistic impacts of a more multi-dimensional comprehensive approach to school improvement. The dictates of standards tend to put us into a pedagogical trap (Feiman-Nemser, 2001) wherein we are forced to do more direct instruction whether we want to or not. In addition, the voluminous number of standards, which can read like a highly technical engineering manual, creates an additional challenge. Many teachers admit behind closed doors that there are so many standards that they have not even read all of them. Where, then, does this leave the teacher who is following the standards-based approach mandated by the administration and wants to be careful not to do anything that would jeopardize his job?

Regardless of the standards, it is hard to argue against the need for pedagogy to be engaging. We must find innovative ways to teach that still allow us to meet standards. Indeed, looking to the options we have in the way of instructional strategies can be invigorating because there really are some excellent resources that provide for different ways to deliver content to students and thus enhance our ability to meet those standards. Take, for example, a synectics model, in which we take an abstract idea and connect it to the student's prior knowledge (Joyce, Weil, & Calhoun, 2003). Synectics relates to how we connect subject material to the students' existing blueprints or schema of the subject. One of the most interesting synectics lessons we have seen was developed by an eighth-grade history teacher under one of the Teaching American History grants we are evaluating.

We observed this educator teaching about the legislative branch of the United States government. The teacher started with the basic premise that the Senate and House of Representatives are like a refrigerator. They work together, but there are more parts working on things in the cool side (the House of Representatives), and there are fewer but larger things working together in the Senate (the frozen side). The teacher went on to make a number of connections between the refrigerator and the House and Senate. Part of the homework assignment that evening was for the students to go home and make their own synectics that would explain this relationship between the

House and the Senate. They were also instructed to use several pages of the text and incorporate a number of key ideas. Synectics is obviously not the only option out there. Different methods of instruction provide us with a chance to engage students differently and create variety in the classroom, which can be engaging for the learning of the whole class and also engaging for the teacher.

It is also important for students to have multiple ways to access the curriculum. This really comes down to amount of exposure and whether or not we are providing other possible ways for students to be exposed to the content and skills we are asking them to master. Recently we had a graduate student who really understood this exposure issue and was convinced that students' fluency rates would increase dramatically if she were able to get them to spend more time at home reading with their parents. This student undertook an action research (McIntire, 2008) study to look at the improvement of literacy rates for students who read with their parents for several hours a week in either English or Spanish. While the study did not find significant differences between the literacy rates when controlling for amount of time spent reading, it did find significant rate increases between matched students who were reading with their parents and students who were not doing so. While the quantitative findings were not strong, they were supportive of the hypothesis; more important, they meant a lot to the teacher, who also found benefits reported from the students, as far as spending time with their parents and having the parents involved in the learning process. This was just another access point and a way to get the student (a teacher in this case) working to improve her curriculum delivery.

With pedagogy, we often find that what we are doing is not working. Good teachers know how to differentiate teaching strategies when they are not working for all students in the class (Gregory & Chapman, 2002). This differentiation is no easy task (Tomlinson, 2003) and requires an adequate amount of professional development to attempt the work. The fact is that teaching involves a fair amount of trial and error. Most teachers can remember a time when they prepared a lesson on some important topic they were going to teach. You might have actually spent a lot of time working on a creative way to teach the lesson, and you had some really great student engagement pieces that fit into the lesson. You were sure this lesson was going to be successful and students were really going to appreciate the lesson and learn. Do you know where this is going? Right. The lesson was a complete failure. It was nothing like what you had hoped or expected it to be; in fact, the entire experience was really the opposite of what you expected it to be. After an experience like this, you have to pause and learn something from the experience. What caused this to not work out as you had envisioned? You have to take away from the experience some lessons learned and some thoughts about how to do it better next time. This is the trial and error involved in teaching. Most are not going to hit the ball out of the park every time. Very few do. Even more important, teachers that are trying to grow are willing to take risks. They are willing to try something new to see if it has a greater result then something they have done in the past. Experimenting with rigor, creativity, and differentiated instruction can build pedagogy that is engaging.

Enthusiasm About the Subject Matter!

Enthusiasm about the subject matter is also important; we have seen that enthusiasm, as well as the lack thereof, can be contagious. When we begin to address the area of generating enthusiasm about the curriculum, we have to think seriously about the importance of what we teach. The teacher must consider the curriculum of each given day to be the most important thing for the student to learn in that discipline that day. One way to help the student understand the importance of the curriculum is to provide a relevancy that links what they are learning in that given day and class to something more important to the student. You know that we have to sell the importance of what is being learned in our classroom, especially with older students. Guy Kawasaki, one of the original Apple employees, in his book *Selling the Dream* (1991), explains that to some extent, no matter what our profession, we are all in sales. Whether we are selling ourselves, selling a product, selling a story, or selling the reasons why what we are talking about is important, we are all in sales. Even if we are not feeling up to it on a given day, a lesson has a better chance of reaching our audience if we can sell them on its importance. This often takes enthusiasm.

Relationships With Our Students!

We must also consider what the relationship is that our students see between us and them. Do they see us as a friend or mentor? Do they see us as supportive? Are we teaching and modeling for our students what it means to be scholars? Are we asking them to become scholars? Is it the learning and relationship that is most important, or the grade? Ask these questions to a student, and you are likely to get entirely different answers than you would get from the teacher. Grades take priority over learning for many students in many cases within our current model of education. If we talk about being scholars with our students, we have to talk about the idea of learning for the sake of learning and not learning just to make sure we get a grade. We have to be intentional in addressing this mindset and try to get our students thinking more about becoming learners and honing the skills and behaviors of a lifelong learner. The other thing we have to do is *model*. If we want our students to be lifelong learners, then how are we modeling such a behavior to allow for students to see what it looks like? As the chapters on Community, Climate, and Character will expand upon, the relationships we have with our students and their parents or guardians hold great potential for maximizing our effectiveness.

Knowledge About the Subject Matter!

Educators have to know their subject matter and own the subject matter. The importance of inadequate subject matter expertise cannot be overstated as a factor contributing to poor student performance (Darling-Hammond, 2000). Beyond the documented issues of teachers not being prepared, you have to be realistic about how this might impact your teachers as well as your students. Several times, we have been in conversations with teachers about their mastery of the subject matter. In one particularly heartwrenching incident, a graduate student approached one of us and broke down crying. She explained that she felt like she was about a week ahead of her mathematics class and really did not know the content the way she needed to know it. This was an especially fragile situation. She did not want to go to her principal both out of concern over losing her job and out of embarrassment. Fortunately, we were able to connect her with a content subject mentor who helped her plan and get ahead of the students. But this cannot be done in all schools. Serious conversations are essential for getting teachers up to speed on content.

Frequently, educators are assigned to teach subjects they are not experienced in or prepared to teach. In such cases, we need to recognize that knowing the subject material is good, but acknowledging one's limitations and then practicing good pedagogy with enthusiasm can often do the trick. A good teacher can often teach any subject if they approach it from the perspective that they will learn the subject with the students. Often an honest teacher who admits they have not taught the subject matter before but that they are excited to start can still be successful. Such challenges often force educators or remind them that it is not always about being "the sage on the stage" but instead "the guide on the side." And when we allow students to construct their knowledge, we suddenly realize the strength of learning theories and practices such as constructivism and discovery or invitational learning. So having some foundational knowledge about teaching any subject matter can help as well.

Assessment That Guides Learning and Instruction!

The A in our PERKA acronym stands for assessment. In this case we are not talking about tests taken at the end of the year or summative assessment, but are referring to process and formative assessment—what Rick Stiggins (2007) calls *assessment for learning.* We are suggesting that you create an environment in the classroom in which students and educators learn from assessment results, and with these results learn together what the students need to learn or what skills they still need to master. Formative assessment is a valuable reteaching tool and motivator to help students understand what they are expected to accomplish and how to get there. The research of Paul Black and Dylan William (1998) provides strong evidence that formative assessment is a key component to student mastery of standards and improvement in academic achievement. It allows teachers to understand better what needs to be adjusted in the curriculum to meet the standards and also allows students to understand their own progress toward meeting their learning goals. Formative assessment can clue us in as to how teaching styles work with specific students in our classroom (differentiated instruction). We believe there is much work to be done in this area to get teachers to an adequate formative assessment capacity so that they can use data to guide their own practice and student learning. In essence, "If we want schools to produce more powerful learning on the part of students, we have to offer more powerful learning opportunities for teachers" (Feiman-Nemser, 2001, pp. 1013–1014). But it is not enough to expect teachers to take to formative assessment if they have gaps in their own training. We may need to address this through professional development in order to get teachers up to speed on quality assessment practices that can positively affect student learning. Process assessment measuring how well one is teaching can be helpful as well.

PERKA helps us look at a number of areas within the curriculum that are key to successful teaching and student learning. These areas of engaging pedagogy, enthusiasm for learning, relationships with students, knowledge of content areas, and assessment that guides learning and instruction are closely interwoven in everything teachers do. It is difficult to exclude any of these aspects as we endeavor toward professional excellence in our calling as teachers. Curriculum is pivotal, and to some extent it tends to be what schools focus on the most, but the Multi-Dimensional Education dimensions can empower our curriculum by informing our pursuits toward improving the delivery of curriculum through PERKA.

Dimensional Connection to Curriculum

As we stated previously, Leadership Potential is a primary dimension that informs all of the 4Cs. Within the C of Curriculum, however, the other primary dimension is Curriculum Expectations. Within the Curriculum Expectations dimension, we address the instructional side of curriculum and how instruction and lessons are being received. Instructional creativity is a key indicator that looks at how the students are being affected by the instruction taking place in the classroom. Another indicator is

how academic support is provided. It is essential for educators to feel that the school has supports in place for students that extend beyond their own instructional efforts. Last, we must consider educational rigor and whether or not we are holding students to high enough expectations and then providing the support and instruction needed for them to be successful. As Vygotsky's Zone of Proximal Development tells us, you must try to find, for every student, the happy medium between not too easy and not too hard.

Curriculum, like the other Cs, has a strong connection to all of the dimensions, as they work together and play off of each other to provide an optimal experience for all stakeholders. The dimensions of Faculty Fidelity and Leadership Potential are often viewed as dimensions relating to the adults within the school who have the ability to greatly impact the curriculum. Leadership Potential itself and the vision for the school can make the intentional focus on the curriculum a primary consideration. Faculty Fidelity, specifically whether or not faculty feel supported and have some level of job satisfaction, relates closely to how the curriculum will be delivered and the kinds of professional development educators can count on receiving.

The dimensions of Developmental Perspectives and Educational Attitudes are the two dimensions involving student behavior, work ethic, and motivation. We often attribute the success or failure of the curriculum to deficits in these areas. As explained in Chapter 8 on Character, you must address these and also understand how motivation and student habits will greatly impact the success or failure of any curriculum you attempt to deliver.

School Climate, as related to curriculum, also translates into classroom climate. We must consider how to develop a classroom climate in which students know our expectations and feel they are in an environment where they can succeed. Yet unless you pay attention to some of the basic needs of students, such as safety, your curriculum is likely to be rendered ineffective, and you might not readily understand the reason. Consider the example of a student who seems to have a chronic problem with falling asleep in class. One's initial thought about the student might be that he is lazy and doesn't care about the curriculum we are trying to teach. The classroom has a good climate and we are delivering the curriculum with a high level of rigor and creativity, and other students are clearly engaged. This student, however, is completely unengaged, and his behavior is not conducive to a positive classroom climate. What we may come to learn, though, is that the student is staying up almost every night caring for his niece while his teenage sister and father go to work. Here is a 13-year-old middle school student providing child care and dealing with the stress and frustrations of parenthood. He comes to class completely exhausted and sleep-deprived. Sometimes we need to go beyond the visible to know what is going on.

This brings many of the climate, educational attitude, and development perspectives into play and provides us with a deeper understanding of why the curriculum might not be working for this student. It causes us to look at the bigger systemic factors, which in this case are the community, specifically the parent and family circumstances. This is also where the Community Engagement dimension comes in. In many cases, a student's inability to understand the curriculum might have very little to do with the curriculum. There may be factors that are really beyond our control, but that does not give us license to do nothing. Rather, we must find ways to connect to the community and better understand the students' perceptions and limitations in order to help students in their efforts to master the curriculum.

The focus on the curriculum, like any of the 4Cs, must be intentional and must consider how it is impacted by the seven dimensions. In some schools, certain dimensions may prove more important to the success of the curriculum. As you will find in starting down a path using the seven dimensions and the 4Cs, you will have your own story to tell, which will highlight the specific strengths and concerns of your organization. To help you better understand what this process might look like with a specific school, in the next few pages we have provided an example of our work within one school and how they took seven steps (explained in Chapter 3) to improving the delivery of the curriculum.

Seven Steps to Systemic Improvement in Curriculum

This was a high-achieving school with a rather affluent parent base and a high-achieving student population. The leadership was motivated to make improvements and the teachers, by and large, were on board with changes that made sense and seemed to be in the best interest of the students. This context is important, because at this school they had a great number of early adopters and very few laggards. It was an ideal environment, and thus is a good example with which to begin. We realize this is not always the case. Pushback against change from faculty is an unknown variable that can rob us of the time and energy needed to make beneficial changes. In the example we provide, we will go through the data-driven thinking process that enabled this school to systemically improve its curriculum delivery, based upon the seven steps we outlined in Chapter 3. Please use this example to help shape your efforts around the C of Curriculum.

STEP 1: Asking the Right Questions

This school began by asking several questions about the curriculum they were delivering:

Question 1: Are we holding our students to high enough expectations for learning?

Question 2: How is the instruction at the school being perceived by the students and the parents?

Question 3: Are we offering enough extra support for low-achieving and high-achieving students?

Question 4: Are we teaching in a creative manner that engages students to learn?

These questions were developed by the building leadership team in order to guide the observations needed to complete the MDed 4Cs Walk-Through Rubric as well as the C of Curriculum Rubric (see the completed example in Figure 5.1 and the blank copy for your use in the Appendix). This school also used their bucket list of dimensional data to complement their qualitative observations and conversations. In other words, they took a mixed methods approach to begin

Figure 5.1　Example: C of Curriculum Rubric

THE C OF CURRICULUM RUBRIC	
Strengths (+) and Concerns (−)	*Observable Evidence (+/−)*
Dimension 1: Community Engagement	
+ Parental involvement − Too much parent involvement	+ Highly engaged and influential parent base and community
Dimension 2: Curriculum Expectations	
+ Have high level of technology in classrooms + Excellent textbooks and resources for teachers − We do not have any well-defined programs for struggling students − We do not have any accelerated programs for high achievers	+ We notice technology being used in every classroom + We have evidence of teachers being trained on SMART Boards and the use of technology − A lack of student engagement is observable in many of the middle school classes − We notice a lot of direct instruction taking place even with technology use, but not sure if this is bad thing
Dimension 3: Developmental Perspectives	
+ We have very few referrals for cheating	+ Students appear to treat each other with respect, very few problems in the hallways − We have had more complaints this year about stealing in the middle school − There seems to be some bullying issues on the playground in 4th and 5th grade
Dimension 4: Educational Attitudes	
+ Parents believe their students to be very highly motivated + We have some very smart and highly motivated students who really like the school − There are issues of entitlement with students and parents; this puts strain on teachers and administrators	+ The new activities coordinator has done a great job of bringing about school spirit, which seems to improve student liking of what is happening at school − Grades seem to tell us that for many students there is a lack of motivation as they move into higher grades and middle school

THE C OF CURRICULUM RUBRIC	
Strengths (+) and Concerns (–)	Observable Evidence (+/–)
Dimension 5: Faculty Fidelity	
+ A very proactive faculty at the school and a strong sense of wanting to improve what we do – Many of the teachers feel overworked and, while they want to improve, are resistant to devoting much more time	+ There is a good level of collegiality at the school, and teachers collaborate and work together + Grade level teams and departments meet regularly and are productive in discussing issues and finding solutions – We really don't have any evidence of mentoring for our new teachers . . . I think we need this
Dimension 6: Leadership Potential	
+ Very qualified leadership team + The leadership team is visible and out in the classrooms, also takes time to get to know students – We have a new evaluation process, but it really doesn't provide me with a lot of insights on how to improve	+ We see the principals and headmaster out in the halls during class and at breaks + Faculty meetings are productive and actually most times we discuss ways to make the school a better place – There is no evidence of school goals posted or anything relating to the mission of the school
Dimension 7: School Climate	
+ School is a very positive place and inviting . . . we have a great campus – The carpool lane is a little concerning to me sometimes, as it doesn't seem to be managed in a very safe manner	+ School is clean and well kept + Bathrooms are great and students actually use them – There is some teasing going on in the middle school and we have students that don't seem to be a part of any group and not making connections . . . kinda sad

their Multi-Dimensional Education data-driven efforts. You will want to sit down with your team or faculties and develop questions specific to your school.

STEP 2: Collect and Organize the Data

The leadership team's members and faculty completed the 4Cs-related rubrics over a week-long period. These included the MDed 4Cs Walk-Through Rubric introduced in Chapter 4 (and available in the Appendix) as well as the specific rubrics we have provided for each of the 4Cs (for example, Figure 5.1 for the curriculum rubric). In addition, they had some students and parents complete the walk-through rubrics. They also administered the Multi-Dimensional

Assessment (MDA) provided in the Appendix, which allowed them easily to populate their bucket list on the seven dimensions. They also considered the benchmark scores and results of the tests given at the end of the year.

The example in Figure 5.1 was collected anonymously from one of the teachers; we took the liberty of typing it up. The leadership team took the collective reports for the teachers who completed the curriculum walk-through rubrics as well as the data from the MDA on Curriculum Engagement. They then developed a PowerPoint presentation with the data specific to curriculum delivery; the presentation was delivered at a beginning-of-the-year faculty meeting. This was somewhat easy for this leadership team to accomplish because they were finishing up accreditation and they already had much of this data in the format used by the team conducting the review.

STEP 3: Discuss and Reflect on the Data

The meeting for discussion and reflection was held during a "buy-back day"; instead of having professional development they chose to discuss this data using the following agenda:

- 8:00–9:00 a.m.: Leadership team presentation of the data
- 9:00–9:15 a.m.: Break
- 9:15–11:45 a.m.: Grade level teams break up to review data (Each 4C discussed for half hour)
- 11:45 a.m.–12:30 p.m.: LUNCH
- 12:30–2:00 p.m.: Grade level teams report out
- 2:00–2:15 p.m.: Break
- 2:15–3:45 p.m.: Grade level teams create goals and submit to leadership team

After the presentation of the data to the entire faculty, the teams broke into grade level groups to discuss the data presented and utilized the Strengths and Concerns pages provided in the Appendix. After each grade level team had a chance to go through the strengths and concerns, they reported their findings to the entire faculty; these were recorded on large paper by the leadership team. After the reporting out activity, grade level teams were sent back with a set of the Goal and Planning templates (see Figure 5.2). The highlights of concerns identified for The C of Curriculum were that

- students are not engaged to the level teachers want them to be engaged,

- teachers feel they are not equipped to meet all student needs, and students appear not to feel as though their needs are being met to the extent they could be, and
- teachers and students do not feel that there are enough extra support structures for struggling students.

STEP 4: Set Goals and Target Planning

After collecting the concerns and the grade level goals from the faculty, the leadership team took that information back and went through a SMART (specific, measurable, attainable, realistic, and timely) goal-setting process around each of the 4Cs. Once the goals were created, they were distributed and discussed at the next faculty meeting. Figure 5.2 provides an example of what the team developed from the bucket list and stakeholder rubric observations, and what was supported by the faculty.

STEP 5: Implement

The timeline and the tasks described in the Curriculum Goal Setting and Planning Chart provide clear direction for what needs to be done for implementation of the strategies selected to address the objectives and the overall goal. The strategies are addressed, and the professional development component is noted in the case of differentiated instruction. The task area provides details regarding who is responsible, thus providing a level of accountability. This might lead to other considerations in future meetings on how progress on the objectives is reported. In the case of the objective of improving instructional creativity, there are clearly delineated tasks for administration to facilitate the professional development offerings; times of year when professional development will take place are noted, as are the number of days allocated for the training. In this case, the school had the opportunity to participate in an instructional audit with another consulting group, and the leadership team explored possible consultants before making a selection. The audit on instruction is really a nice addition to the data you are collecting and can help you in assessing the impact of professional development on the objective.

STEP 6: Monitor and Fine Tune

The monitoring is done using a number of different resources that already exist and are easily accessible. In this case, it was easy to identify the pieces they would need for monitoring. Some schools may

Figure 5.2 Curriculum Goal Setting and Planning Chart

Curriculum Goal: By spring of 2010, strategies will be implemented to improve the overall curriculum implementation in the school as reported by students, parents, and teachers. The measure for improvement is the curriculum expectations scale. The current score is a 3.75 mean score and the desired score is a 4.0 mean score.

Objective	Strategies	Professional Development	Resources	Timeline	Tasks	Monitoring
1. Increase academic support in middle school mathematics	• Before- and after-school tutoring for middle school pre-algebra students		• Math teacher extra duty stipends	• Department identifies students in October • Before- and after-school tutoring begins in November, runs two-three days a week through spring finals (June)	• Math teacher extra duty stipends created by leadership team by October • Middle school math department develops a calendar and assigns teachers for tutoring • Middle school math team selects students	• Student attendance • Tracking grades on tests and quizzes of selected students • Tracking benchmark scores of selected students
2. Improve instructional creativity	• Have teachers trained on differentiation	• Have teachers trained on differentiation • Optional workshops for teachers at conferences made available	• Differentiation audit provided by consultant and results presented at November training	• Training on November Thanksgiving release day • Follow-up training in January on two of the half days during finals	• Leadership team to develop consultant contract	• Midyear differentiation audit conducted (March) • Teacher report out at faculty meetings on implementation of differentiation strategies. Teacher evaluations provide for observance of differentiation strategies

need to develop monitoring tools; this needs to be another task and timeline consideration. It is likely that, as you work through these kinds of goals and planning activities, you will find that the monitoring tools already exist. The key here is to start by looking at what you already have before you create new instruments, which can take a lot of time and might not be necessary. To get you started, however, the resources in the Appendix should be quite sufficient.

STEP 7: Evaluate and Communicate the Outcome

This last step is not accounted for in the worksheets, but the leadership team made it a point to review the objectives and goals set in planning at almost every faculty meeting. They selected one of the 4Cs to review at each meeting and requested a progress update from the grade level teams. The newsletter in November had a section on the school's goals for the year and also discussed the professional development in which the teachers would be participating. At the end of the school year, the goals were reviewed and the school again participated in the MDA, which allowed them to determine whether or not they had reached a 4.0 in the areas of instructional creativity and academic support. Fortunately, they did achieve these increases and had a reason to celebrate those successes. Teachers felt empowered not only because the scores went up, but also because the process for goal setting and implementation had been very intentional and targeted specifically those concerns they noted at the beginning of the school year. They felt empowered because they had a voice!

Additional Strategies and Measures for Addressing the C of Curriculum

Finally, we need to acknowledge that not all students will master the curriculum on the same timeline. Regardless of the pedagogical skills of the teacher, development is a gradual and quite personal process. Everyone is different. Some subjects are simply more difficult for certain students, and some students struggle with learning difficulties or developmental delays. Anyone who has worked with primary school students understands that the early language experience of students can impact their ability to develop reading skills. The same occurs at any educational level. Some students will master the curriculum quickly, and some will master the curriculum in an allotted time. Students who are struggling must seek additional *academic support*.

There are still others who will need additional time to master a set curriculum or make progress within it, regardless of the modes of instruction and presentation.

There are many ways you can provide academic support for struggling students and teachers in need of support. First, let's consider how the results identified through assessing students to determine their strengths and areas of concern can be utilized in a variety of approaches to assist our students:

1. Tutorials before and after school. Many teachers arrive at school early or stay late after school. Assuming a student has a way home, individual or group tutorials can be quite helpful for individual students. Remember, sometimes a child just needs some additional time or some additional review to achieve mastery.

2. Allocate time within the class to work with individual students. This can occur during an assignment or near the end of the class when homework has been assigned and students are given a chance to work.

3. Occasionally, schools assign teachers or other adults to assist students either in the class or as part of a pull-out program. This can be quite beneficial for the child if the teacher or tutor has good diagnostic skills combined with patience and a supportive attitude.

4. Peer tutoring is an excellent strategy to utilize the skills of other students in the class or school.

5. In elementary schools, teachers sometime group students. This needs to be done carefully to ensure that students do not "look down" on a particular group. Students can gain from smaller groups and concentrated and supportive instruction.

It is important for students to understand that there are multiple forms of academic support within a school. This requires that the faculty commit to making all possible efforts to ensure student success. We will not always succeed, but our attitude, combined with our relationships with students, can make a difference.

Once we have identified strategies to help the students, we must also adopt strategies to help the teachers. As our colleague Jennifer Jackson, an instructional coach and consultant who has worked on a number of our research projects, explains, "It is often not the case that teachers do not know what they are doing. Often they just need to be rejuvenated." Jennifer has helped a number of school systems adopt a process for providing support to new and not-so-new teachers to help them understand the power behind what PERKA represents. In short, the affordable coaching system Jennifer recommends is for a school to identify its two best teachers. The administration then creates a schedule and secures substitutes in order to allow these two teachers to spend a day a week with other faculty who either have requested their company or who have been identified by the school's leadership as needing such rejuvenation. Through a process of team teaching during the day, the designated teachers in the building can model for others how **P**edagogy can be more engaging, **E**nthusiasm about the subject matter is priceless, **R**elationships with our students is essential, and sharing your **K**nowledge about the subject matter can lead to better **A**ssessment that guides learning and instruction!

There are a number of other measures available to us when we consider Curriculum Expectations and the many different components important to the curriculum. Curriculum audits are conducted by a number of organizations such as Learning Point Associates and DataWorks. These audits provide an interactive way for leadership and faculty to collect data on the teaching, curriculum, and assessment taking place at the school. They provide both an outsider's view and an insider's reflection on what is taking place and the quality of teaching, curriculum, and assessment. Classroom observations by leadership teams and by peers are a valuable way to collect data on teaching. There are many resources for teacher observations; many of them are easily found online. The important consideration in selecting an observation tool is its suitability to the purpose of the observation. For example, if you just want to look at how the teacher interacts with students, then you need an observation tool that will capture that information. Also, ground rules will need to be communicated to teachers as to what the observation means and how the data will be used. Remember that you are getting personal when you enter into another teacher's domain (classroom). It is important to be clear on why you are observing and how the data will be used after the observation. If you are not going to share the data and use it in some kind of improvement process, then we suggest not bothering with the observation.

Last, there are a number of teacher evaluation measures produced by Educational Testing Service and Pearson Publishing. In the Appendix, we have provided you with a teacher evaluation for students and peers to complete to aid your teachers in their own reflections. You can also select certain questions from the MDA to use for teacher improvement efforts. It is quite possible not to use such evaluations for purposes of accountability and simply to focus on applicability. States such as Tennessee have been using value-added teacher evaluation measures for some time. The education policy changes that are currently being made lead us to believe that teacher evaluations will be a reality of the future. We have followed many of the policies and funding requirements of the Race to the Top program, and it is clear that future and even current funding will require some form of teacher evaluation that can be linked to student performance. We won't spend much time unpacking what this will look like (we can only guess), but we do see it as a likelihood in the near future. There is no shortage of evaluations, audits, and instruments related to better gauging the effectiveness of the curriculum and how it is taught at your school. It is a matter of going through the steps we outlined and identifying data you might need to collect in order to plan and set goals.

The C of Curriculum holds great promise for improving your efforts, and the seven dimensions can provide a great amount of insight as to what needs to be capitalized on or fixed to make such improvement.

Next Steps

1. Think about how the teachers in your school are reflective of PERKA and what you are doing as an educator to bring these ideas into the classroom.

2. Think about how you provide formative assessment and whether or not you think your assessment is helping both you and your students.

3. Consider how you might begin to introduce a teacher evaluation process and how it might be received by other teachers. (Walk slowly.)

6

The C of Community

In our experience working in education, we have encountered schools that understand why parents should get more involved and have figured out how to do so. At the same time, we have worked with a number of schools that are still struggling with this promising 4Cs area. The following is a true story of one school that allowed a "dozen bad eggs" to delay the kind of continuous improvement efforts that the C of Community makes possible.

After providing the school with a Multi-Dimensional Education report that documented their stakeholders' perceptions of the school's seven dimensions, we were asked to come in to consult and to provide a data-driven educator training session. One of the dimensions that this specific school was struggling with was Community Engagement. They were an elementary school, so we expected to see the Student Service to the Community score a bit low. We were concerned, however, when we noticed their Parent Involvement and Interpersonal Community Engagement scores averaging a 2.5–2.7 out of 5. Before the training, we asked the principal about these concerns. She said that she thought the parents were very involved. Around 30% of parents attended a parent-teacher conference each year. A few parents were very active in leading the Parent-Teacher Organization (PTO), which normally had 10 to 20 parents at its quarterly meetings. In addition, plays and other events were well attended. When we asked if the parents were involved in working with the kids and teachers on academics, she did not have an immediate answer. Instead she asked, "What do you mean?" She then began to explain how most of the parents who volunteered at school normally came in to help with filing or decorations. She told us that occasionally invited parents would

(Continued)

(Continued)

also come in to read books to their child's class. And then she said something that somewhat took us by surprise. She said, "But we don't encourage parents to come to school to help with academics. In fact, we try not to have parents here during the school day."

From our experience, elementary schools are a place where you frequently see parents involved. As parents, we remember being much more welcomed by the educators and our kids when they were in elementary grades. But this school had a rule that no parents were allowed to visit during school hours, and that any type of after-school activities would have to be reviewed and approved due to lack of resources to keep the school open longer hours. We asked the principal why she had this rule. She explained that beyond budget issues, she had a "dozen bad eggs" consisting of 11 parents and one grandfather who were not legally allowed to be either near their child or children in general. Due to child custody or sexual predator reasons, these parents could not come into the school. Therefore, in order to make sure this did not happen, she made a rule not to allow any parents, beyond the few they approved and invited, to enter the school during the day. She also explained that she left it up to the teachers to decide if they want to communicate or work with parents.

This school has more than 350 students. As at most schools, the child's educational success is critically important to most parents. Yet instead of addressing the specific "dozen bad eggs"—putting their pictures in a file to check at the front desk or creating a policy that all parents must show a valid driver's license upon entering the school—they issued a blanket policy. As a result, 338 other sets of parents were prohibited from being part of their children's school day. It was on that day we decided to share with the educators, in addition to our normal training, a bit more research that shows how for a very minimal cost, you have the resources to change your school's performance, and that this resource is just a phone call, letter, or e-mail away. It was on that day that we spoke for the parents that were being locked out (literally) of their child's education.

The Community Conundrum: Connecting Pedagogy, Parents, and the Public

A lot has changed from the decades when we were kids. For example, as a child, how much time did you spend outside playing after school? We can remember endless stories of after-school adventures from our youth that our parents probably never even knew about and are thankful for not knowing. But today, would you let your kids play outside without supervision? When we ask this question to educators, many answer with a very loud "No!" It is a loud *No* because, for some, our communities do not feel as safe as we or our parents perceived them to be back in the day. But not only have our communities changed; so have the neighborhoods and households of the average student. For example, how many neighbors did you know growing up? Now by "knowing" neighbors, we are not suggesting you had to live in Mayberry where everyone was friends, but how many neighbor's names or occupations did you know? Compare that to how many neighbors you or your kids know today? Most of us can recall the name of nearly every family who lived on our street during childhood. Yet very few today can even produce the names of more than a handful of their neighbors. This is even more worrisome when we consider that many of our students also don't have a parent waiting for them at home after school. What percentage of your friends growing up had two parents in the home, compared to the percentage of our students today who have two parents in the home? And how many of those parents now work full time? Much has changed in regard to community and the home life of the youth of today.

Epstein (1995) argues that school, family, and community are important "spheres of influence" on children's development and that a child's educational development is enhanced when these three environments work collaboratively toward the same goals. As mentioned earlier, many of the foundational learning and developmental theories and philosophies you were given as a pre-service teacher focus on these same spheres of influence. Vygotsky, Piaget, Erikson, Kohlberg, Dewey, and many others stressed the importance of the larger community's impact on developing the whole child and helping them accomplish a higher level of learning. Numerous literature reviews (for example, Mitchell, 2008) and meta-analyses (for example, Fan & Chen, 2001) clearly demonstrate the relationship between parent involvement and a student's success in the test of life as well as a life of tests.

Though much of what we are about to discuss falls under the moniker of Community Engagement, in this chapter we want to start by focusing more heavily on the parental involvement aspect of Community Engagement. You can have nearly every company in your town saying they support your efforts and sponsoring your programs, but without the sponsorship and, more specifically, the involvement of parents, you will probably not achieve success. In many circumstances, business sponsorship is not focused on truly addressing the academic achievement for which we are held accountable. This type of sponsorship often only allows us to collect some much-needed funds from organizations that hope such efforts might lead the students or parents back to their business. In fewer instances, business sponsorship may result in opportunities for students to visit the business on a Career Day or listen to a guest speaker from the business. The secret to building greater community support and truly using community resources to benefit our education efforts is first to convince parents to get more involved. And research suggests that the most effective way to get parents involved is not to make efforts at the school level but to rely more on the personal relationships developed between individual educators and the parents.

So what role do parents currently play in education in your school or schools? Think about what percentage of your parents currently take an active role in the education of the students in your school. We know that in our households the roles we perform for our children include taxi driver, homework lifeline, personal athletic trainer, chef, financier, and life coach, to mention a few. And like us, a few parents also want to be active in the school and partner with teachers to help our children learn and flourish. As parents, we want to know from our children's teachers how we can help them help our children do well. Yet many parents avoid such efforts because quite often such altruistic parents often only get a couple of credits for Bulletin Boarding 101. Many parents avoid being a part of the school's or teachers' efforts because they have had bad experiences with the school, either as a student or when their older children attended the school. Other parents feel underqualified to help their child with subject areas such as mathematics because "the new math is confusing" to them, or they don't know if their help will actually benefit the child or just confuse them more (not to mention the embarrassment experienced by a parent not able to help their child with content written for kids). Regardless of the reason, many of us who are parents go from counting every step as we walk our child into their kindergarten class and picking them up at the sound of the last bell to never setting a foot in our child's high school. Somewhere along the way we either lose our will as parents to be a part of our kid's educational success, or something else is driving us away.

Research suggests that there is more than one reason why parents don't take part, but such research also makes it safe to say that the blame can be spread among parents, students, and educators. There are numerous stakeholders who have a role in what happens in the education of a child. But it would appear that as soon as their kids are old enough to fend for themselves, many parents no longer rush to meet them at the end of the school day. The passion, concern, and worry we had for our "little girl" having a good day at school slowly fades away, and the need to monitor becomes just another part of our daily routine.

Yet, have you ever noticed how these same parents, many of whom could benefit by meeting or communicating with educators regularly, are able to find time to spend hours at sporting events or watching television? They can find time for working out regularly or going to church several times a week, but they can't find the time to focus on the education essential to their child's future. They'll go out for pizza once a week with their kids, but can't sacrifice an hour once a month to go to a PTO meeting or find time to help Johnny with his math homework. Those of us who are parents know all too well that it is the hardest job we will ever have and that life rarely prepares us or educates us on what we need to do to be successful parents. So maybe one of the reasons many parents are not taking part in their child's education is due to just not realizing the importance of this role.

Or maybe it is because, as research suggests, the schools (or more importantly, the teachers) aren't inviting them. It could also be that the teachers don't really want to know the parents. More than a few teachers have told us that they try to not get parents involved because there are normally a few parents that they do not want to deal with on a daily or weekly basis. Most educators have dealt with these types of parents before, and many have learned that even when we try to limit our contact with them, the ones we try to avoid still somehow find the time and avenues to provide us with their wisdom.

The bottom line is that educators need help in helping students learn. And much of the time, the person or persons who care most about the student's success—the parents—are not being used effectively. In reality, the parent or parents are often the secret behind why our good students excel, and with a little more effort, more parents could become the same kind of catalyst, helping the less proficient students in our classrooms to excel as well. If we can find effective strategies to get these parents more engaged, we will experience greater academic success and career satisfaction. If we can get the parents more involved with our efforts in the classroom and school, we will get the rest of community more involved.

Parents want the best for their children. And the meta-analysis by Fan and Chen demonstrates that parent aspirations for their children's education are a significant reason why the children achieve academically. Parents know deep down that if their children can get a good K 12 education, then they can get a good college education and have a greater chance to achieve success in life. Therefore, educators need to figure out how best to get these concerned and caring parents working with us and not against us. Many need to figure out how to add school and learning to the list of weekly family activities.

Research on Community

There is so much research on the benefits of getting the community and parents more involved in education that this chapter could easily become a book. If you don't believe us after this short summation on the research behind Community Engagement, we urge you to enter the words "parent involvement education" into your favorite Internet search engine or go the library and check out one of the many books on the topic. Much of what you will find will reflect the following research.

According to researchers Karen Smith Conway and Andrew Houtenville (*Science Daily*, 2008), in order to experience the same achievement results gained by parent involvement, schools would have to increase per student spending by more than $1,000. For the school with a dozen bad eggs this would equate to more than $350,000 in resources. Research suggests that there is a significant, positive relationship between parent involvement and student educational experiences, including improved academic outcomes (Barton & Coley, 2007; Henderson & Mapp, 2002). The literature explains that parent and community involvement activities associated with student learning have a greater effect on academic achievement than do general forms of involvement (Henderson & Mapp, 2002). More specifically, parental involvement has an even greater impact when the involvement revolves more around specific academic needs such as mathematics (Sheldon & Epstein, 2005). Such increased parental involvement has an impact on secondary students (Tonn, 2005) and an even greater impact, in some circumstances, on elementary students (Horvat, Weininger, & Lareau, 2003; McNeal, 1999).

Research also shows us that greater parental involvement and helping parents (or guardians) better understand the social-emotional learning and socialization challenges their children encounter can greatly assist our efforts to get students more engaged as well as reduce behaviors that create barriers to effective instruction and learning (Spoth, Randall, & Shin, 2008). As Boethel (2003) explains, "Relationships are the foundation of parent involvement in schools" (p. 71). The No Child Left Behind legislation and Title I requirements reflect the research demonstrating the promise that community and parent involvement hold. This is why getting parents and the community more involved is a required part of each of these title efforts.

Unfortunately, neither of those policies provided the guidance schools needed to overcome the challenges that stem from the many logistical and personal reasons that keep parents and educators from being more engaged. The lack of guidance and the overemphasis on achievement had the effect of keeping these policies from actually helping many schools to accomplish this promising C of systemic change. As Rochelle Nichols-Solomon states,

> As a strategy for change—lumped in with such reforms as high standards . . . and performance assessment—parent involvement stands out as a simple step. But profound parent involvement means shared leadership—and that means sharing knowledge, responsibility, and most difficult of all, power. (2000, p. 20)

The Dimensional Connection to Community

If you are going to adopt a new systemic model for your school, the C of Community can be a key factor in your success. If you are going to improve or replace a model that has not brought about increases in academic achievement to the level our lawmakers expect, it is important to start from the ground up to develop and implement a new way to get parents and the community more involved (i.e., second-order change). Many schools need to set new expectations for parents, students, and educators in relation to community-based shared leadership. Though teachers hold the most promise for getting parents to become major players in the success of their children's educational experience, Community Engagement must be embraced and demanded to the highest possible extent by the administration and leadership teams. And if existing staff does not want to be a part of such change, we must find evidence that might convince them to join the effort. Such evidence can come from thinking about the seven dimensions and how they connect to Community.

The Primary Dimensions to the C of Community

As we explained in Chapter 4, each of the 4Cs has one or more primary dimensions that can provide the information and data needed to drive our thinking process. Along with Leadership Potential, Community Engagement is the obvious other primary dimension related to this C of Community. When we work with schools, our

Multi-Dimensional Assessment's dimension of Community Engagement measures factors such as parent involvement, service to community, and interpersonal community engagement. We assess these factors because we have found that knowing the perceptions of your stakeholders relates to how active your school is in the community. How active your parents are in the education process and to what extent your students are connected to their neighborhoods can provide us with important insights. We also measure or triangulate the perspectives from the insights of students, parents, and educators to see where their views might differ. What we typically find in schools with a low level of Community Engagement (see Figure 6.1) is that there is a discrepancy among the stakeholders' perceptions. Therefore, a reason to measure such dimensions is to make it possible to get all stakeholders on the same page, with more positive perceptions of the dimensions.

We have discussed why it is important to get parents involved, but empowering the C of Community does not just concern parents. It also involves getting the community truly active in your schools, and getting your schools active in the community. Year after year, many school systems see school bonds shot down at election time. For numerous personal reasons, some residents of our communities vote against adequately funding the education we all know to be essential to creating a better society. It is astonishing to us that less than 3% of our federal spending goes to education. Yet if we are not collaborating with our community, how will the residents who vote

Figure 6.1 Triangulating Measures of Community Engagement

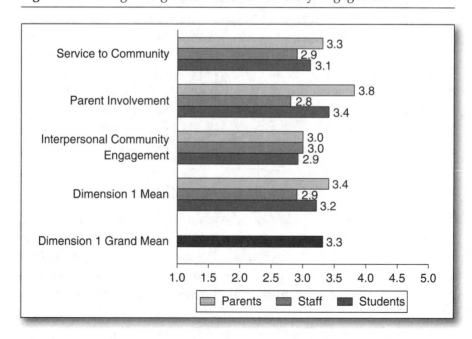

No see that we are trying to do good for the kids as well as the community? We need to get our kids and community connecting through efforts such as civic engagement and service learning. Service learning holds much more promise than simply forcing a senior to complete two hours of volunteering during the latter stages of moral development. Too often, instead of helping them at an early age to feel the life-changing chill that runs through your spine when you help someone in need of assistance, we force them to perform manual labor while they rue the hours lost that could have been spent texting and tweeting or on MySpace or Facebook. Too often, efforts that could be beneficial to our students and the community are implemented too little and too late. We must start early with such efforts and find a way to make them more meaningful for all. To do this, we must measure our present state of Community Engagement in hopes of determining what is working and what needs to improve.

Other Dimensional Connections to the C of Community

From the research on the contributions of parent involvement to academic achievement, it is apparent that the dimension of Curriculum Expectations is also tied to the C of Community. As we have learned, higher-level learning is heavily dependent upon the greater community. If a child lives in a neighborhood where they do not know many neighbors or feel that they have few places to turn to for support (Interpersonal Community Engagement), and possibly their single parent is working full time and not able to provide the support they need, who do they have to turn to other than you and your colleagues? When you are able to positively influence the concept of community for students, they feel that they belong more. In theory, a better or more connected community provides more positive role models to turn to. And when you have more positive role models influencing your students, instilling in them the importance of a good education enhances the chances for improvement in schools.

This concept of a positive community connects to developmental perspectives and educational attitudes as well. The community has a role in shaping and reinforcing one's self-concept, conduct, and character. It should come as no surprise that the majority of our prison's inmates come from challenged communities where not enough positive role models exist. Without a caring community, many of these individuals were not able to grasp the concept of compassion for others. In shaping the personality of our students, the community also helps define their view of the importance of education. One of the biggest problems kids have with school is that they are often bored and do not see the purpose of being there. They do not understand or remember that education is the key to prospering in society. Maybe they have not been given a dream of a career or calling. Maybe they live in a depressed and challenged area where even though they understand that education is the key to helping one's family move beyond the worries of poverty, they do not believe they can break the cycle of life by overcoming the learned helplessness. Unfortunately, this belief often becomes a self-fulfilling prophecy. But by working with parents and community members to fine-tune your message and goals, you can find ways to improve their attitudes toward education.

Along with the improvement in learning environment, character, and attitudes that can be brought about by greater Community Engagement, the educators in a school can also contribute to success by focusing on community. Realizing the full promise of the community depends upon the Faculty Fidelity and Leadership Potential required to develop the relationships related more specifically to academic success. Building trust with students and parents, communicating effectively to determine all stakeholders' needs and goals, and developing a shared mission and vision is essential to this C for systemic change. When we are able to get the dimensional gears moving the C of Community forward, we can generate a school climate that is productive, safe, and supportive.

Seven Steps to Systemic Improvement in Community

To get started in understanding what this process might look like, let's revisit the school with the "dozen bad eggs." The example we provide will go through the data-driven thinking process of how this school *tried* to achieve systemic improvement in community based upon the seven steps we outlined in Chapter 3.

STEP 1: Ask the Right Questions

After working with the school, we urged them to consider asking several questions related to Community Engagement:

Question 1: Are we engaging our parents in a way that they can help us academically?

Question 2: What activities are we doing to get them more involved?

Question 3: Are we communicating effectively to the parents and community how they can best help us?

Question 4: What strategies or avenues can we take to improve what we do, from the office to the classroom?

These questions were developed by the Building Leadership Team (BLT) in order to guide the observations needed to complete the C of Community Walk-Through Rubric. In this example, we will see that this school set aside the quantitative data to dig a little deeper into the issue of community. After exploring the Multi-Dimensional Assessment data we had provided, the faculty wanted to know more about how people really feel. In reality, they did not like or completely accept what the quantitative results told them. So instead they used the rubrics provided in the Appendix to inform their efforts. As explained in Chapter 4, they basically completed a thematic analysis of their observations and conversations to further inform their data-driven thinking.

STEP 2: Collect and Organize the Data

The BLT members and faculty participated in a process of completing the 4Cs Walk-Through Rubric as well as the rubrics developed for each of the 4Cs. In addition, they had some students and parents complete the rubrics. Figure 6.2 provides an example of the C of Community Rubric compiled by the BLT to summarize what the stakeholders identified.

The BLT took the rubrics completed by the stakeholders and set out to find the common and recurring themes. They were looking for strengths and also for concerns that needed to be addressed. They wanted to pay close attention to any worrisome insights reported that might identify a severe problem being experienced by individual stakeholders. Remember, sometimes the anomalies (something that stands out) and outliers are where the most alarming findings can be found. Although this took a bit of commitment and time on the part of the BLT, the process was quite a learning experience. As they reviewed each of the completed rubrics and listed the strengths and concerns that fell under the 4Cs and seven dimensions, they began to discover and discuss many things they had not realized. An exercise that originally seemed like a cumbersome task turned out to lead to one of the most productive meetings they had experienced in years. Within in a few hours, they suddenly started seeing where their problems were, and they were able to develop a PowerPoint presentation with the qualitative data that they would share with their faculty.

Figure 6.2　Example: C of Community Rubric

THE C OF COMMUNITY	
Strengths (+) and Concerns (–)	*Observable Evidence (+/–)*
Dimension 1: Community Engagement	
+ Recruited parents for playground restoration – We do not have enough parents volunteering – We do little to encourage parents to come to our school in any capacity	+ Community donated money for improvements in library – We have not been able to attract members of our community for volunteering
Dimension 2: Curriculum Expectations	
+ We have rigorous Curriculum Expectations – Some students are unable to work at the same pace as others, and we do not account for these differences. We do not provide much tutoring or more time to succeed	+ Some teachers are taking advantage of technology and pedagogical approaches to teach the curriculum – We have too many teachers who do not use various means to deliver the curriculum
Dimension 3: Developmental Perspectives	
+ Most students are compliant in their behavior – We still have some stakeholders who are struggling to develop practices of kindness, respect, and responsibility toward others	+ We emphasize the importance of being caring to others in our school – We do not provide opportunities to develop compassion toward others in our school – Some students struggle with behavioral issues
Dimension 4: Educational Attitudes	
+ Most of our students come to school ready to learn and have a good work ethic – We have students who are struggling to complete work in the school and at home – Based on several surveys, we have students who report they are not motivated to do well	+ Many of our students are connected to a club or to various athletic opportunities – We do not have clubs during the day that most students could join
Dimension 5: Faculty Fidelity	
+ We have an experienced faculty who for the most part work well together – Teachers report they do not trust other teachers on their team	+ Teachers report that they are satisfied with their job and workplace environment – Our transfer requests have increased substantially over the last three years

THE C OF COMMUNITY	
Strengths (+) and Concerns (−)	*Observable Evidence (+/−)*
Dimension 6: Leadership Potential	
+ Teachers have reported that they understand the mission of the school and feel we are working toward fulfilling the mission + Surveys show that the parents are satisfied with the leadership of the administrative staff − There are not enough leadership opportunities for all stakeholders in the school	+ Some recent surveys and observations show that the principal and VP are approachable − Teachers have complained that they do not see the administrators in the school − Some stakeholders feel that the BLT should involve more stakeholders who rotate off the team
Dimension 7: School Climate	
+ The school is clean − Students state that they do not have good relationships with their teachers − Some students seem isolated from their peers	+ The school is orderly and runs well − Some young teachers have reported that they feel isolated in the school − Incidents of bullying behavior increased

STEP 3: Discuss and Reflect on the Data

With the thematic analysis of community in hand, they set aside three hours of their next professional development day to focus mainly on community and getting parents more involved. First, the BLT presented data that was identified on the MDed 4Cs Walk-Through Rubric. This gave a basic breakdown of the strengths and concerns related to the 4Cs. Then they focused on the insights gathered on the C of Community Rubric. After the presentation, the faculty was divided into grade level groups to discuss the data presented, using the Strengths and Concerns pages provided in the Appendix. For this exercise, the BLT had made copies of all of the rubrics for each group to look through as they considered the summary provided in the presentation. Each grade level team had a chance to go through the strengths and concerns before they reported out to the entire faculty on strengths and concerns that resonated most with them. These were recorded by the BLT on easels around the room. After the reports, the grade-level teams were then charged with creating a set of the goals for the planning templates (see Figure 6.3 for an example of a completed template and the Appendix for a blank copy for your use).

The main concerns identified with regard to the C of Community were that

- parents do not feel welcome in the school and state that the teachers rarely communicate with them,
- teachers feel they do not have enough time to deal with parents, and
- the community engagement activities rarely attract enough parents or families because they are not held at times convenient for parents who work.

The strengths were that

- the leadership team is doing a good job getting businesses and individuals to contribute to fundraising activities, and
- the students like the events being held and like to have their parents come to the school.

STEP 4: Set Goals and Target Planning

After collecting the grade-level feedback and goals, the leadership team asked the faculty, "Do we need to change anything? And if so, what needs to change and how should we go about it?" These two simple questions led to what we call a courageous conversation. Some of the teachers were a little insulted that they were now somewhat expected to be accountable for parent involvement when the principal was the one who had set the no visitation policy and had told them previously that it was up to the teachers to decide if they wanted to be involved with the parents. Others said they would love it if the school adopted a new policy. One teacher stated that at her last school she was required to send home a monthly list of the homework expectations of the students and to suggest ways that the parent could help their child. Some of the teachers who were not accustomed to involving parents did not appreciate this suggestion. Meanwhile, as the faculty expressed their differing thoughts, the BLT was debating what the best next course of action would be.

Although they did not know it at the time, they were on the verge of deciding whether they were going to implement first-order change by adding a few new efforts to their existing structure, or going to attempt second-order change and transform their whole system for community and parent involvement. In reality, the dimensional data and their achievement scores were showing they had numerous challenges. For the most part, their achievement scores were rather static. Something needed to change. But, as a few faculty members suggested, perhaps the new mathematics curricula and stepped-up reading efforts would produce the needed change. As the conversation continued, it became apparent that the faculty was not in agreement on whether or not they wanted to work with parents more closely. As a result, they could not agree that day on goals or planning. The principal had to decide if she was going to change her policies and expectations. Figure 6.3 provides an example of what the leaders developed and shared with the faculty.

STEP 5: Implement

The timeline and the tasks described in the Community Goal Setting and Planning Chart in Figure 6.3 shows what the principal and her leadership team decided to do. Instead of going against the grain and trying to implement a new process (which research has shown time and time again if done correctly can contribute to increased achievement), they decided to stick with their existing system for the time being and just add a few new efforts to increase parent participation. The strategies and efforts that this school chose to embrace are addressed in Figure 6.3. There are also task areas noting who is responsible for providing some level of accountability, which might lead to other considerations in later meetings to discuss progress toward the objectives. In the case of the objective of improving parent involvement, the administration has clearly delineated tasks to facilitate the new efforts and even times of year noted as to when the efforts will take place and the number of days allocated for the effort. Unfortunately, the additional efforts would turn out to be a perfect example of how change can be derailed when leadership only approaches it from a first-order change perspective.

STEP 6: Monitor and Fine-Tune

The monitoring of this school's efforts in the C of Community was completed using a number of different resources, but relied primarily on records of parent attendance at school events and on the use of the walk-through rubrics. It is very important to monitor the progress of new efforts because you must determine if what you decided to do is working. In the case of this school, it was easy to see they would need to monitor closely. The decision to only add a few new efforts after taking the time to have a courageous conversation left some of the faculty very disappointed. These were the faculty members who wanted to change how they operated and engaged

Figure 6.3 Community Goal Setting and Planning Chart

Community Goal: By spring of 2010, strategies will be implemented to improve community involvement in the school as reported by students, parents, and teachers. The measure(s) for achievement of this goal are: Increasing the opportunity for parents to volunteer in multiple ways in the school & increasing opportunities for service by the community within our school environment. Current data shows that 10% of our parents presently volunteer within the school environment; the desired score is 20% of our parents volunteering by end of the year.

Objective(s)	Strategies	Professional Development	Resources	Timeline	Tasks	Monitoring
1. Increase parent participation as tutors before, during, and after school.	• Include in newsletter, first PTA handout, e-mail blasts concerning our tutoring needs	• Parents who wish to become tutors will have three chances to come to school to receive training	• Teachers will provide materials that students need additional work on mastering	• Initial training of tutors will begin in October. Once the training is completed, tutors will be offered assignments based on their schedule and time commitment	• Tutors will work with individuals or small groups of students in the back of classrooms or in the library work area. Other areas will be scheduled as needed	• Tutors will be signed in and out in the office. Monthly reports will be compiled and shared with BLT and with faculty. Thank-you notes will be mailed quarterly
2. Increase opportunity for parents and students to volunteer after school and on weekends to work to beautify the school grounds.	• Individuals with "green thumbs" will be sought via e-mail blasts, PTA hand-outs, and phone tree for interested individuals	• Lead volunteers will help the rest of us develop landscaping skills that we might be able to use in our homes	• School will provide plants, shrubs, and trees as needed for planting as well as ground cover	• Requests for help will be made beginning in early October and will continue throughout the year	• Several parents have agreed to supervise the work along with several of the teaching staff	• We will monitor participants and celebrate the improvement in our school grounds via-e-mail blasts

parents and community. The staff and faculty not disappointed were those who were not convinced such work was needed or would be effective. They did not want to put in the extra effort needed; the administration was inclined to think the same. This was a rather strange decision to us, given that they had a sign outside on their school that stated they were a "School of Excellence." The result was a staff that was waiting anxiously to see if the change efforts had any effects. The results were reminiscent of the old saying that goes, "If you continue to do the same old thing, you will continue to get the same old results." Their test scores actually dropped, however, and no longer were they the highest-achieving school in the district.

Some schools that take this effort more seriously may need to develop better monitoring tools or feedback loops. Developing them needs to be another task and timeline consideration. It is likely, though, that as you work through these kinds of goals and planning activities you will find that the needed monitoring tools already exist.

STEP 7: Evaluate and Communicate the Outcome

When the rubrics were completed again, the news was even worse. Parents were becoming increasingly disappointed in the school, and many are at this time searching for other schools to send their children to. Since the test scores were not good, however, the principal and leadership team announced they would be putting more effort toward improving parent involvement. But they also decided to hold off on assessing these activities and their impact until they were able to get a new system in place. Beyond considering the disappointing test scores, this last step has not taken place. To their credit, since seeing last year's test scores, they have gone above and beyond what they had initially discussed. They have read a great amount of literature on strategies to improve. They have now developed a parents' organization that meets monthly, and the organization is successfully recruiting more parents. This organization is now focusing on parent involvement related to academics. They have more teachers who communicate regularly with parents and collaborate with the parent organization. And they are building a community within the school where parents feel much more welcome. They have even recently sent home surveys to the parents to try and determine better how parents feel about the school, and parents are now allowed in the school during daytime hours. You might wonder why we use a somewhat unsuccessful example of change to highlight for you the seven steps needed to actually make systemic change. The answer is easy: We often learn our greatest lessons from our mistakes or failures. And we have learned just as much from leaders who are afraid to adopt the new systems needed for change as we have from the incredible leaders who are not afraid of anything. The fear of failure can sometimes be even stronger than the will to succeed.

Additional Strategies for Addressing the C of Community

When we think about developing or improving Community Engagement, we must move beyond the models many schools still use today, such as canned food drives, mandatory service learning, and once-a-year Earth Day cleanups of school grounds or the surrounding neighborhoods. Many schools still have a fairly antiquated system for involving parents and communities. Our invitations and communication often consist mainly of routine parent-teacher conferences or the dreaded call that the student has done something wrong. Many schools take a reactive rather than proactive approach in setting expectations for a parent's role in educating our youth. Many schools seem more often to explain to parents what is going wrong rather than working with them from the beginning of the school year to help their children meet or exceed the academic and social expectations. To us, the latter holds more common sense.

As Epstein explained, there are three spheres of influence (school, family, and community) that are enhanced when they work collaboratively toward the same goals. Epstein also suggested that these spheres work together through activities with six types of parental involvement:

1. Parenting: assisting parents in child-rearing skills

2. Communicating: school-parent communication

3. Volunteering: involving parents in school volunteer opportunities

4. Learning: involving parents in home-based learning

5. Decision making: involving parents in school decision-making

6. Collaborating: involving parents in school-community collaborations

We will use these six types to offer strategies for increasing the power of community and parental involvement in your systemic change process. Please keep in mind that increasing achievement for your school typically rests heavily on getting the underachieving students to make gains, and not necessarily on helping your highly proficient students do better. And though you might not get all of your parents on board, the more parents of less proficient students we can help get more involved, the higher the probability that we will see significant increases in test scores. As we often say, "Some will, some won't. So what?" What this is intended to mean is that of course some parents *won't* be open to being more involved; *So what?* At least you know that you tried. But the power rests in the fact that *some will.* And research suggests that by getting a larger percentage to say *Yes,* you will see greater gains.

Parenting

Though to some the thought of assisting parents in developing child-rearing skills might seem beyond what we are expected to do as educators, the fact remains that many parents need help in this area. From offering basic family support programs that assist families with health and nutrition to offering suggestions for home conditions that support learning at each grade level, you can, if you approach these issues correctly, connect with parents in a very personal and supportive way. One strategy we suggest to schools is to consider establishing a College Club. Such a club can be developed for elementary, middle, and high schools. As research we cited earlier has found, a major predictor of achievement is high aspirations on the part of parents for their children to succeed. The problem is that not all parents have gone to college or possibly even graduated from high school. Some do not know what needs to take place at each grade level to accomplish their child's dream to go to a trade school, community college, four-year college or university as a pathway to success. By creating a College Club, we are developing an effort that actually is of interest to parents and educators. In the club meetings, we can help parents grasp what is important for their child to master at each grade level. We can help them help their children embrace a dream: to be able to afford and accomplish the goal of attending college. And if we can get more parents interested in getting their child ready for college and careers, then we are also developing the partners we need to make our classroom experiences more effective and enjoyable. Given that Title I is moving in this direction, it would seem to be quite possible to find monies to develop such an initiative in your school and district.

Communicating

As the teacher at the "dozen bad eggs" school suggested, sending home weekly or monthly communication (via all-call systems, e-mail, web sites, or snail mail) to parents as to how their child did on past assignments and what to expect to see for the next month, and how they can help, holds great promise for getting more assignments completed on time and correctly. By opening up lines of communication that work for all parents no matter what their work schedule, you can reduce the communication barriers that often arise when you rely upon the student to communicate what you or other teachers want. Educators who practice this approach know that there will always be a few parents who are not responsible or interested in communicating, but most appreciate the chance to be a part of their child's educational process. Such an approach can create a team between the parents and educators to keep better track of the students' progress.

Volunteering

Epstein uses the term *parent volunteer.* We prefer *parent partner* because it avoids some of the somewhat negative connotations of being a volunteer in a school. But whichever term you use, this is a great way to get parents more involved. Today, especially in view of the current economy, some parents are at home and have more time to volunteer than others. Many of these parents are more than willing to assist with getting the other parents connected (for example, by developing a telephone tree), managing after-school workshops and tutoring sessions, or possibly developing a survey to identify parent talents, available times to help, and aspirations of their child. Once again, we should set aside the old model, in which parents mostly donate time to decorate bulletin boards or catch up on filing tasks, and focus on efforts linked to student achievement. Let's find efforts that parents want to partner with you to accomplish.

Learning (at Home)

Many parents want to help the child's learning continue at home, but some feel under-qualified to accomplish this task. Somewhat as with the first three types of parental involvement, this type requires us to share information that helps parents understand the expectations for homework and skills required for students in all subjects at each grade level. This can be accomplished by creating a regular schedule of homework that requires students to discuss and interact with their families regarding what they are learning in class. Such a process can include family participation in setting student goals each year and in planning for college or work. If the workshops organized include assistance on teaching parents how to tutor correctly, we can help parents feel more comfortable with helping kids with subjects on which parents might not feel adequately informed, such as math or science.

Decision Making

This is often reflected in efforts such as Parent-Teacher Association (PTA), Parent-Teacher Organization (PTO), advisory councils, or committees. Most of you have these types of structures already in place. The challenge is that many schools are experiencing lower levels of participation. Another challenge is determining to what extent you want to give up the power in making such decisions related to your school. This is why it takes six steps to get parents involved, not just this one. You have to get them feeling that a relationship exists in order to get them more involved and attuned to goals you hold in common.

Collaborating (With Community)

Much of what you are trying to teach in the classroom can be complemented by the cultural, recreational, and social efforts taking place in your communities. And though you might not be able to afford the time and resources to hold a field trip every week to provide a discovery learning opportunity for the students, you could, however, provide more information on such resources in the community, such as calendars of events. There are many grade-level appropriate volunteer activities in the community that could complement your curriculum. You just need to identify and organize such opportunities and make them available, if not assigned, to student and their parents.

Woulda, Coulda, Shoulda

We have worked with and for many principals who have given up trying to hold community events due to low attendance. Often, they need to consider whether or not the event they thought would be good was actually of interest to the parents or community and was held at a time when they could attend. We know many teachers who have expressed frustration with trying to get parents involved and running into disappointment when only the same handful show up for special tutoring sessions. One friend, Dan Stark, who teaches fifth grade math in an inner city high minority school district, typically has about 25% of his parents show up for evening meetings in which he works one-on-one with parents and students to help the parent help their children with their challenges. Typically, 25% of his class meets or exceeds expectations on proficiency tests. And guess what? The 25% that pass are most often the kids of the parents who take part in the extra meetings. He has learned over the years that it takes more than just offering evening tutoring sessions, because some of these parents have other responsibilities to manage (for example, a second job or younger children). This teacher has taken the next step and put much of what he offers in these sessions online for all parents to access.

We have research to guide us in what we need to do. We have technology that is making it easier to meet these needs. What many need now is data and evidence to show what they need to do, and the commitment to actually put this systemic change in process. If you can dedicate the next year to developing what works at each grade level for each teacher, you will have this part of the system in place, and it will contribute to years of success. Typically, most district offices cannot spend an additional $1,000 a year per student, which is the level of expenditure needed to produce the same level of success that parental involvement brings. Typically, a fundraiser will not come close to raising this much money either. The C of Community is one of the 4Cs that can help you achieve meaningful and lasting second-order systemic change. Using the seven dimensions to inform your community efforts is a start to accomplishing such change.

Next Steps

1. Gather a baseline assessment on your C of Community to get started on documenting and identifying what you need to change or build upon.

2. Bring together a Building Leadership Team that is inclusive of staff, faculty, parents, and students (when possible) to discuss what you want to consider in relation to the C of Community.

3. Organize your meeting times for the year to focus more on using the Multi-Dimensional Education data you will collect to better inform your discussions and the decisions you make.

4. Complete more research on successful strategies used to get parents more involved.

7

The C of Climate

Imagine that you have just moved to a new town and are seeking your first teaching position. You are most interested in working with middle school students and have applied for language arts positions at several "highly impacted" schools. You have scheduled two job interviews over the next two days.

The first job interview is for a seventh-grade Language Arts/Social Studies position at Central Middle School. After parking and walking toward a side entrance, you notice a lot of paper and trash lying on the grounds. The school looks dirty. You walk freely into the school with no staff addressing you as the students are changing classes. They are running and yelling in the halls. You hear profanity in the hallways as you walk toward the office. While in transit, you hear the tardy bell, yet many students are still in the hallway. You notice that one adult is urging the students, with a bullhorn, to clear the halls and get to class. From the sounds of the bullhorn echoing through the hallway, it takes five additional minutes after the tardy bell has rung to clear the halls.

As you near the principal's office, you notice that teachers in the classrooms are raising their voices to "encourage" the students to sit down and get ready to begin the lesson. As you walk into the office, no receptionist or staff member addresses you. You notice that there are other adults, whom you assume to be parents, also standing around not being assisted. You stand for five minutes at the counter before someone asks, "What do you need?"

You explain why you are in the school. The secretary tells you to sit down and someone will be with you shortly. Ten minutes later the principal walks out and greets you. She is the only one interviewing you. You are told that 70% of the

(Continued)

(Continued)

students receive free or reduced-price lunches, and that poverty contributes to their unruly behavior. You are also told that most of the teachers are new to the school and that you can make a "real difference" there. As part of the interview, you walk around the school with the principal. You notice that many of the students are not paying attention in class. Some are even sleeping. At the end of the interview, you are told, "The job is yours if you want it." You thank the principal and leave the building as classes are being dismissed. You are pushed and jostled several times as you walk out of the building and head toward your car.

The next day you have a job interview for an eighth-grade Language Arts/ Social Studies position at North Middle School. The interview is scheduled during the first period of the day. You arrive early and begin walking toward the main entrance. You notice that the grounds are quite clean. Several students and adults speak to you as you walk into the school. The building is clean. As you enter the building, you notice that children are heading toward their classrooms. The students seem happy. They are laughing and talking but are not disturbing others.

Adults are in the halls talking to the students. Student work is posted along the hallway. A brief bell rings with an accompanying announcement that everyone has one minute to get to their "advisories." Within 45 seconds, the halls are clear and, as you walk down the hallway and peer into the classrooms, teachers and students are talking to each other as they are sitting down at their tables and desks. You walk into the main office and are greeted by the receptionist. Other adults (whom you later recognize as classroom volunteers during your tour around the school) are talking with the office assistants. You state that you are there for a job interview. As you are shown where to sit, you are asked if you would like a cup of coffee. You notice that in the office everyone, students and adults alike, are greeted with kindness and respect. Immediately after morning announcements, the principal comes out to greet you. She invites you back to her office for the formal interview and introduces you to the other office personnel as you walk back. The interview is comfortable but professional. There are four people, the principal and three teachers, interviewing you. You are told the strengths and concerns of the building. You are told that this school has a balanced staff of beginning, mid-level, and senior staff; turnover is rare.

You are also told that approximately 70% of the children qualify for free or reduced-price lunches but that "at our school, economic poverty does not translate to academic, social, and moral poverty." The principal and interview committee walk you around the building. You notice that the teachers are engaged with their students and the students are engaged with their teachers. It is clear that learning is occurring in the classrooms; you are told that the school exceeds the established district and state expectations in all areas. The principal also brags about the physical education, art, and vocational aspects of the school that "are not tested but are equally as important as the tested areas." In one self-contained autistic classroom, students from one of the elective classes are working with the special needs students. You are very impressed at how the cafeteria workers greet and talk with the students. You are told that half of the cafeteria workers and several of the school aides and assistants started out as parents who volunteered in the school and subsequently sought employment here. Upon completing the interview, the principal states that you are the last person to be interviewed for the position. She will talk with the team and let you know something at the end of the day. At 4:00 that afternoon, you receive a phone call. You have been offered the position.

You now have two job offers. Which job would you take?

Why North Middle Is What We All Deserve

Let us return our focus to North Middle School. The environment was clean. This sends a clear message that no matter what things are like in the home or community, faculty and students will work together to ensure that learning and teaching take place in a clean building. Students were talking among themselves and with teachers. The school appeared to be a friendly place with positive *relationships* between all stakeholders. Expectations of proper behavior were modeled and posted in the hallways. Students seemed to follow directions and required only polite reminders (for example, one minute to get to their advisories). The adults seemed friendly toward you and others. There was a sense that all stakeholders *liked* being in the school. Kindness and respect were evident throughout the building. There was a vision that economic poverty does not translate to social or intellectual poverty. The students and adults seemed *connected* to the school and truly enjoyed being there. You noticed that the students and teachers were working hard to succeed. Overall there was a *positive school culture*. We believe that this is possible in *all* schools and that *all* educators are entitled to work in such conditions.

It would be interesting if the above story of the two differing schools within the same district were a rare occurrence. Unfortunately, it is not. Both schools have the same demographics. They are just a short distance from each other, drawing students from the same general area. Both schools have nearly the same number of students and adults in the building, but the climate—the culture of the schools—is radically different from one to the other. One school simply exists, while the other flourishes. One school teaches. The other educates. One school is concerned about control. The other is concerned about the social and intellectual development of both the students and the adults in the building. One school is a model for the development of a positive school climate. The other lacks a positive school climate.

For North Middle School, the ongoing development of a caring, civil school climate for the students and adults in the building is not simply something that is just thought about or discussed. Rather, it is the foundation of all they want to accomplish and is something they work to do.

Building a positive climate is not just another item on your plate. It is the plate on which everything else sits. It is for this reason that climate represents one of our 4Cs for systemic change and is connected to the other seven dimensions in the ways we will explain later in the chapter. We believe that all educators, students, and parents deserve a school like North Middle, and we know that it is possible to turn any school around to become like North Middle.

Research Support for the Development of a Positive Climate

In Chapter Two we noted how meta-analyses (Anderson, 1982; Borger et al., 1985; Dusewicz & Beyer, 1988) and Marzano's (2003) insights identified practices that facilitate climate development. Among these practices were leadership, teacher-student relationships, a safe and orderly environment, parent involvement, motivation to learn, and a positive physical environment. We maintain, and will argue in this section, that a plethora of research indicates how essential a good climate is for the promotion of excellence in all aspects of the school environment, including academic achievement. The Chicago Annenberg Research Project (Lee, Smith, Perry, & Smylie, 1999) provides an insightful study regarding the importance of a supportive climate for academic achievement. The researchers utilized citywide survey data and achievement test scores of sixth- and eighth-grade students in Chicago to determine the impact educational push (rigor) and social support had on increasing the academic achievement of students. Educational push or rigor is defined as an "experience of a strong emphasis on academic success and conformity to specific standards of achievement" (p. 2). Social support is defined as "personal relations that students have with people in and out of school, including teachers, parents, and other students who may help them do well in school" (p. 2). The authors of the Annenberg study recognized that social support can come from various sources.

Support may come from parents encouraging their children to work hard in school; from teachers providing individual care, attention, and help to students; from students encouraging each other to do well in school; and even from neighbors and community leaders offering support and assistance to students. Academic push or rigor can also come from various sources. It can come from principals' expectations for teachers to move through the curriculum and work to promote particular student outcomes. It can come from teachers' expectations for students to learn. Push may be exerted through the amount of homework teachers assign; the numbers, types, and difficulty of courses students are required to take; the amount of class time devoted to instruction; and the level of challenge of academic work (p. 10).

For the Chicago Annenberg Research Project, the academic measure or assessment came from student scores on the reading and mathematics portions of the 1997 Iowa Test of Basic Skills (ITBS). Data on schools' academic push and students' social support came from the Consortium on Chicago School Research 1997 surveys of sixth- and eighth-grade students and teachers in the Chicago Public Schools. These survey data were available from 28,318 sixth- and eighth-grade students and over 5,000 teachers in 304 Chicago elementary and middle schools. The study found that in schools where academic push was low, reading achievement rose on an average of 0.57 Grade Equivalents (GE) (5.7 months) and math achievement raised 0.90 GEs (9 months) over a year of schooling. In schools where academic push was high, reading achievement increased an average of 1.37 GEs (1 year, 3.7 months) and math achievement increased an average of 1.64 GEs (1 year, 6.4 months) over the same year.

These are very impressive results. In reading and math, the average achievement gain was significantly higher, with high push schools showing more than one year of expected or yearly growth. Clearly academic push matters. But consider what happened when high academic push is combined with high social support. The study showed that students who attend schools with high levels of academic push and who also report high levels of social support made the greatest gains in reading achievement: 1.82 GEs (1 year, 8.2 months). The math gains were even greater: 2.39, or 2 years, 3.9 months! What can we learn from this study? We must have social support and strong academic push within our schools. It is not one or the other alone, but social support and academic push in combination that makes the greatest difference in student achievement. This is a key insight that is recognized within the Seven Dimensions and the 4Cs of Climate, Community, Curriculum, and Character. The dimensions and the 4Cs are all interrelated, and we must work on each of the 4Cs to achieve our highest goals. In essence, the rigor or push of the curriculum (Dimension 2) will require the social support of all stakeholders (Dimensions 1, 3, 4, 5, 6, and 7) to assist students in reaching performance excellence in their efforts.

We maintain that an essential first step in building a positive school climate is the development of a positive connection between all stakeholders (Battistich, Schaps, & Wilson, 2004; Battistich, Solomon, Watson, & Schaps, 1997; Osterman, 2000). We can frame this by striving to develop school connectedness or attachment between all stakeholders within the school. Robert Blum (2005) describes school connection as the "belief by students that adults in the school *care about their learning and about them*" (p. 1). Blum further argues that there are consistent qualities that influence a student's positive attachment to school (p. 1):

1. Having a sense of belonging and being part of a school

2. Liking school

3. Perceiving that teachers are supportive and caring

4. Having good friends within school

5. Being engaged in their own current and future academic progress

6. Believing that discipline is fair and effective

7. Participating in extracurricular activities

A student's positive connectedness and relationships with others in school has been shown to promote psychological health (Kasen, Johnson, & Cohen, 1990; McNeely, Nonnemaker & Blum, 2002; Whitlock, 2006), to help develop a positive self-concept in students (Reynolds, Ramirez, Magrina, & Allen, 1980), to reduce bullying within a school (Peterson & Skiba, 2001), and to reduce antisocial behavior (Kuperminc, Leadbeater, Emmons, & Blatt, 1997). A school with a positive climate is one in which a consistent, predictable environment is established to encourage the flourishing of teaching and learning.

A definitive study of 2,700 students by British researcher Michael Rutter and colleagues (1979) found that a child attending a high school with good order and discipline had only a 9% chance of becoming a juvenile delinquent, whereas if the child went to a school with poor discipline the probability of delinquency increased to 48%. Student motivation essential to success in school is developed within a positive school climate (Wentzel, 1997). Positive climate impacts positively on student attendance (deJung & Duckworth, 1986; Edmonds, 1979; Purkey & Smith, 1983). A positive school climate can also help prevent school violence (Peterson & Skiba, 2001). Rutter, Maughan, Mortimore, and Ouston (1979) noted a connection between school climate and student's self-concept. Parents and other community members working with their students, as well as working with and supporting the efforts of the school in a partnership, can greatly enhance the learning of students (Patrikakou, Weissberg, Redding, & Walberg, 2005).

Additional research has shown that a focus on developing a positive climate can also have positive indirect and direct impacts on a student academic achievement (Freiberg, 1999; Rutter, 1983; Fleming, Haggerty, Catalano, Harachi, Mazza, & Druman, 2005; Brookover & Lezotte, 1979; Haynes & Comer, 1993; Stewart, 2008). Building connectedness should also involve the use of consistent practices or routines within the class and the school to ensure that the development of social skills such as basic manners, as well as respect and caring behavior toward all stakeholders, is foundational. These practices will enhance the learning environment for students as well as the adult stakeholders (Urban, 2009; Vincent, Wangaard, & Weimer, 2004). Robert Marzano (2003c), after conducting an analysis on the importance of establishing rules, procedures, and practices, concluded that rules and procedures affect not only the behavior of students but also their academic performance. This makes common sense. If a teacher has more time to teach, a student likes being a part of school and has teachers who combine social support with academic push; under these conditions, the chance that academic improvement might occur is pretty high.

Ultimately, no school will have a chance of achieving its social or academic goals unless there is leadership that works to establish a positive school climate (Edmonds, 1979; Rutter, Maughan, Mortimore, & Ouston, 1979). The relationship that the principal has with students as well as with the adult stakeholders can impact the total environment of the school and ultimately the academic success of students (Heck, Larsen, & Marcoulides, 1990). Think back to North Middle and the impression the principal made on you, the applicant. It is our belief that *principal* leadership is the catalyst for a positive or negative school climate. Researchers Susan Wynn, Lisa Carboni, and Erika Patall (2007) recently validated this observation. They reported that the key determinant for whether first- and second-year teachers choose to remain in a school and continue their career was their satisfaction with the leadership of the school and with the school climate. The research shows that a focus on the C of Climate can be helpful to you in organizing school efforts to enhance the overall success of the school.

Dimensional Connection to the C of Climate

As noted, all of the dimensions interact and influence each other. The development of a positive school climate is empowered by the seven dimensions in the following manner:

Community Engagement

As school personnel, we desire parental support for, involvement with, and insight into our efforts to build a supportive climate in which learning and living together becomes the mission of the school. However, we must acknowledge that not all parents (regardless of social status or economic means) can have a positive influence on the life of a school. This being stated, we want our parents to participate in the life of the school and to assist the school staff in developing and fostering a positive climate where all stakeholders can live and learn. We also value the work that our parents do outside of the school to model for their children a good climate in the home and, one hopes, in the neighborhood.

Curriculum Expectations

Underpinning all curriculum successes and concerns is the climate of the classroom and the school. Surely curriculum organization and delivery will be less well received and understood if the climate of the classroom, and indeed the school or community, detracts from the teaching and learning environment.

Developmental Perspectives

A good climate, shaped by developing consistent rules and routines, may help students reduce inappropriate behavior and develop the character traits (such as responsibility, perseverance, caring, and respect) that can result in increased success in all aspects of school life. Furthermore, a climate that is focused on connectedness allows the affective part of the person to flourish.

Educational Attitudes

A good climate will assist in the development of positive attitudes toward the school on the part of students, parents, and community members. Students who feel that their teachers like and value their efforts and contributions are more likely to strive for excellence than are those who feel disconnected from teachers or school. A parent who feels that the school is working with the student and the parent to help the child flourish as a student and a person is more likely to be supportive of the school. Furthermore, a positive climate built on good relationships between teachers and students encourages the educator to assist the students in working toward achieving excellence in *all* aspects of the school day.

Faculty Fidelity

Faculty members who are connected to each other and feel that their work has value generally work well together and consequently have better relationships with students, leading them to strive to succeed throughout the school day. The climate of the school and the respect we have for our peers allow us to take risks individually and as a team to meet the needs of all stakeholders. Trust and support are significant factors for all stakeholders and must be evident in the classroom and school climate.

Leadership Potential

This is once again one of the primary dimensions of the C of Climate. Strong leadership is contagious. When teachers are satisfied with and feel supported by the school leadership, they are more likely to want to remain at the school and be productive, caring, and reflective educators. By feeling they are integral to fulfilling and developing the shared mission of the school, this helps to build continuity and an expectation of growth for all stakeholders.

School Climate

This is also a primary dimension for assessing climate. When all stakeholders feel a bond to the school, they are proud to say they are involved in the school, whether as an educator, parent, or student.

Stakeholders like coming to the school and assisting in all aspects of school life. They appreciate the cleanliness of the school and the consistent expectations and routines that are a part of the life of the school. This positive school culture facilitates the academic, athletic, artistic, social, and ethical life of the school.

Seven Steps to Systemic Improvement in Climate

Assume you are a doctor conducting a physical exam on a patient; however, in this example the patient is your school, and you are utilizing all the tools available to you to provide a proper diagnosis. One of your tools is provided in the Appendix, where you will find several climate scales embedded within the sample Multi-Dimensional Assessment (MDA) that can give a quick snapshot of your school's general health regarding your climate-building efforts. You can also take advantage of climate surveys that have been previously validated by others or possibly used in your school.

If you have survey data over a period of years involving a representative sample of all stakeholder groups and using the same instrument, then you are well on your way to assessing and determining your areas of strength and concern. If you do not have such data, you should begin a baseline process to obtain good qualitative and quantitative information on your climate. For the qualitative effort, we suggest using the MDed 4Cs Walk-Through Rubric; for this C of systemic improvement, we suggest the C of Climate Rubric. You can utilize the observations and insights of all stakeholder groups to gain a broader picture that will inform you of your climate strengths or concerns and reaffirm the picture provided by the data.

This is exactly the step taken by a middle school we worked with recently. After a consideration of various data points, this school staff decided to take a comprehensive view of their climate—with a focus on getting good qualitative data. This data was to be folded into the data they had gathered via an analysis of office referrals and suspensions, their Schoolwide Positive Behavior Supports data, and the data they had gathered from several different climate surveys over the last two years. The principal felt that much of their existing data was descriptive in nature but did not accurately reflect possible negative practices or, more importantly, the positive aspects that were part of the "living school." They utilized the rubric shown in Figure 7.1 to organize their data that they would gather by walking around their school and taking notes on what they were seeing.

Figure 7.1   Example: C of Climate Rubric

THE C OF CLIMATE	
Strengths (+) and Concerns (–)	*Observable Evidence (+/–)*
Dimension 1: Community Engagement	
+ Parents were tutoring students in the school + Evidence of students working with scouting and other community groups – Some concern that the parents tutoring and volunteering in the school were always the same parents, overall representation was somewhat limited	+ Positive conversations with parents and volunteers + Teachers volunteering at after school program – Upon talking, we felt we were not doing enough to use the Internet to communicate with parents who worked jobs that make it difficult for them to come to the school
Dimension 2: Curriculum Expectations	
+ Volunteers and teachers provide support for students who are struggling in school – We are not doing enough to welcome parents into the school who may have curriculum concerns and who speak other languages or have different work schedules than our traditional school day	+ Most students appear comfortable asking for assistance – We have different ways of posting assignments on the board – Some students do not ask for assistance if they do not understand the lessons
Dimension 3: Developmental Perspectives	
+ We have eighth graders working with sixth-grade students + We appear to be polite to each other most of the time – Most issues occur during unsupervised parts of the day or when students are moving around the building	+ Service opportunities for all stakeholders are shared via the bulletin boards, morning announcements, and counselor newsletter – We do not recognize enough the good deeds that our stakeholders do in our school – Some teachers raise their voice to discipline students
Dimension 4: Educational Attitudes	
+ Most of the teachers feel all students can succeed academically and socially in the school – A few of our teachers complain that our students do not work as hard as they could	+ We create a positive climate to motivate students to learn + Most of our students work hard in school – We have noticed some students beginning to refuse to do homework and some schoolwork
Dimension 5: Faculty Fidelity	
+ For the most part, the faculty is supportive of each other	+ There is little turnover of the faculty, although we have many National Certified

(Continued)

Figure 7.1 (Continued)

THE C OF CLIMATE	
Strengths (+) and Concerns (–)	*Observable Evidence (+/–)*
+ People generally smile when they come to work – We are sometimes rude to each other in faculty meetings; i.e., talking, grading papers	teachers who could find jobs at many other schools + Students tell us that they know we believe they can be successful in the school
Dimension 6: Leadership Potential	
+ Our principal is visible in the building + Our cafeteria staff truly works hard to provide nutritional foods and encourages students to eat them – Some of the same people stay on the leadership teams of the school for many years – We do not have enough time to assist new teachers	+ Our mission is posted throughout the school + Our eighth-grade students assume leadership roles in the school—before, during, and after school – We have noticed that some of the same students are in student government, safety patrol, tutoring club, etc.
Dimension 7: School Climate	
+ Hugs are given here + Children and adults are comforted in our school – We should be more consistent in our practices and routines in the classroom and around the school. The lack of consistency sometimes confuses our students	+ We still have a 30-minute lunch break that allows two grade levels to mingle and get to know each other + We look hard for students who appear isolated and try to involve them in our activities – Our office personnel have continued to change too frequently. They do not know the students' names

The following are the seven steps taken in this school; they can also assist you in organizing your data as well as informing your efforts to enhance the climate of the building for all stakeholders.

STEP 1: Ask the Right Questions

This school had a sense of some of its strengths and concerns related to their climate-building efforts, but they needed to sharpen their tools and get clearer on their efforts. To accomplish this, they developed several questions to guide their efforts. We share these questions with you only as a beginning point to consider in assessing your school's climate. Your school's unique concerns or needs for additional information should guide your questions.

Question 1: Do I see positive relationships and a sense of connectedness and belongingness among all stakeholders within my school?

Question 2: Can I document consistent rules, procedures, and routines that are followed and supported by the great majority of the school stakeholders?

Question 3: Is this a clean, safe, and supportive environment that is conducive to teaching and learning?

STEP 2: Collect and Organize the Data

The rubric used by the school is shown in Figure 7.1; it is tied to the seven dimensions that are linked to school improvement. To clarify the process, the principal provided a brief introduction to each of the dimensions. He also shared what the School-Wide Positive Behavior Support (SWPBS) data indicated for the school as a whole. The school then used one week of "walk-around time" to gather the data and organize it in terms of the seven dimensions. Figure 7.1 is a summary of what the teachers and support staff gathered via their observations.

After completing the rubrics, the Building Leadership Team (BLT) met to compile the qualitative data from teachers at each grade level and other staff and to see if they could identify some common themes in the strengths and concerns of each stakeholder group. Afterward, they provided a report summarizing the data. The report was briefly discussed, and the staff was given the next assignment.

STEP 3: Discuss and Reflect on the Data

The staff discussed the data by grade level, with all stakeholders assigned to a grade group; that is, guidance, media, and cafeteria workers were also assigned to particular grade levels. They were given the individual rubrics from all members of the school as well as the SWPBS data as it related to their grade level. When they met again as a faculty a week later, each team had a thorough understanding of the strengths and concerns revealed by the data and was prepared to offer strategies to improve outcomes. Each grade level group gave a 10- to 15-minute PowerPoint presentation identifying their most pressing concerns and offering some strategies on how to improve the outcomes. Afterward, the BLT provided hard copies of the presentation to serve as the focus of further deliberation.

STEP 4: Set Goals and Target Planning

From the concerns collected and the suggestions for strategies that could turn the concerns into strengths, the BLT developed several strategies that the entire school would try to implement in the coming 12 months. These were shared via e-mail as well as during a faculty meeting. Based on the feedback, a final proposal was established and shared with all relevant stakeholder groups to ensure total school involvement. The following chart (Figure 7.2), containing objectives, strategies, and professional development, is representative of their goal setting and target planning.

STEP 5: Implement

It is great to have a plan. It is even better to implement the plan! This school completed its planning, then developed a guide map to direct its efforts. They felt that the lack of consistent rules and routines was allowing other issues to arise. Their goal was not to merely try to control the students, but to develop them. Therefore, after the training, consistent routines for movement in the school were established, along with consistent routines for the beginning and throughout the school day for students. Although the Assistant Principals (APs) were designated to provide an overall assessment, all of the staff and faculty were involved in implementation of the plan.

STEP 6: Monitor and Fine Tune

The APs and other staff started monitoring the efforts. The focus was on getting everyone on board and "working the plan." They worked hard to gather data that would provide evidence on how well they were doing. Two faculty meetings were scheduled to fine-tune the efforts, answer questions, and address concerns. The APs worked individually with several teachers who were struggling in their efforts.

STEP 7: Evaluate and Communicate the Outcome

At the end of the year, the efforts were evaluated in a more formal manner, and these data were shared with all stakeholders. Individuals offered various observations that confirmed their success as well as recommendations to improve their efforts in the coming year.

Figure 7.2 Climate Goal Setting and Planning Chart

Climate Goal: By *June of 2010*, strategies will be implemented to improve the climate in the school as reported by students, parents, and teachers. The measure(s) for achievement of this goal is qualitative evidence that we all are moving more consistently and in a more orderly manner in our school. Our efforts will be enhanced as we develop consistent routines on how all classrooms are beginning the day and operating throughout the day. We will also look for improvement in SWPBS data. We are also going to develop strategies to enhance the treatment of all adults by other adults within the school environment. Finally, we are going to do a more formal assessment of our school climate involving all stakeholders to identify additional concerns.

Objectives	Strategies	Professional Development	Resources	Timeline	Tasks	Monitoring
We desire to develop consistent rules and routines within all teams and throughout the school to inform all of the expectations for appropriate behavior	Work as a team to develop routines for entering the classroom and practices to ensure we (all stakeholders) are all treating each other with respect and politeness	We will have a training day in November to assist teams in developing consistency on rules and routines. We will also determine the practices we wish to practice in staff meetings	Book: *The First Six Weeks of School*	11/09–06/10	Develop, post, and practice consistent practices and routines	Reduced classroom and hallway interruptions
We desire to enhance how all adult stakeholders treat each other throughout the school environment	We are developing a series of guidelines to facilitate our efforts regarding how we learn to disagree without being disagreeable. This will be shared with all adult stakeholders	We are having a consultant who utilizes humor to emphasize the importance of civil behavior toward all	– Guidelines on proper etiquette taken from *Miss Manners*	8/09–6/10	Develop our guidelines for all stakeholders. Post these online and send home for all adult stakeholders	The C Climate Rubric Spring follow-up
Provide a greater understanding of school climate conditions by tracking our improvement efforts	We are going to use the climate assessment from the MDA for all stakeholders to determine additional strengths and concerns	We will have the assessment scored and the results will be returned to the Building Leadership Team for additional action to identify needs for professional development	TBD	9/09, with results by 6/10	Distribute MDAs to staff and students during September and send home to parents in the middle of September; have returned by end of month	Survey again in May

Additional Strategies and Measures to Address the C of Climate

Begin by focusing on these subfactors of climate:

- A positive school culture
- Stakeholders' relationships
- Stakeholders who like coming to school
- School connectedness
- Stakeholders who feel bonded to the school

Next, consider these strategies:

1. One elementary teacher we know spent the first two weeks of school developing relationships with her students and formulating the rules and routines that would govern the life of the classroom. Each student was encouraged to give input on what respect, responsibility, and caring looked like, both in the classroom and throughout the school. The students then worked to define the routines that would enable these traits to grow and develop. The teacher spent much of these two weeks practicing these established routines in an attempt to make many of their actions habitual. The time required to develop such common routines in the classroom is not wasted. Indeed, it might better enable you to better achieve your academic goals, because less time will be spent on discipline and transitions from one learning environment to another.

2. Work to develop practices and routines in the school that are consistent in all classrooms as well as in the hallways. Seek the input of all stakeholders in this effort. For example, one of the authors worked in a school that had all teachers post the homework assignments on the board closest to the front of the classroom in the left-hand corner and the classroom assignments in the right-hand corner. They also spent time at the beginning of the year in learning how to write the homework assignments in the planner to ensure that there would not be any legitimate excuses of "I didn't see the homework assignment on the board!" You may also find that there are some students or staff having difficulty fitting in to the normal functions of the school. Talk to them and reflect on your conversations. Have adults volunteer to serve as mentors to these students or adults who

are struggling. Ideally, the mentor is someone who is not teaching the child or directly supervising the adult during the present school year. This enables another caring adult to interact with the student or struggling teacher.

3. Take time at the beginning of the year to develop relationships with your students. This may sound shocking, but we believe that you are better off focusing on getting to know your students during the first week of school. This is a great time to develop classroom routines and to practice the routines to ensure that they are understood and mastered. Start a Newcomers Club for all students who transfer into your school, whether at the beginning or during the academic year. Have older students assume a leadership role in this club. Include surveys to determine the various interests of the new students. Try to match them up with other students who share the same interests. Also try to assess their academic strengths and concerns, and encourage them to seek out certain classes based on their interests. Seek to involve these new arrivals in various school clubs and sporting organizations. Remember, we want to help them develop a sense of belonging at the school as quickly as possible. A good strategy to assist in facilitating a sense of belonging and connectedness in the school is to have adults in the building sponsor clubs. Make sure that every student in the school belongs to a club, then rotate the club meeting times throughout the school year. For example, if a school has a six-period day, clubs would meet on Tuesday first period during the first week, second period during the second week, third period during the third week, and so on. A block schedule might require a different configuration, but it can still be done. Once you reach the last period of the day, you start over. This ensures that students will only miss one class a week and will only miss that class once every 6 to 8 weeks. Furthermore, it allows another adult in the school who may not teach the student to have a significant relationship with that individual.

4. Extracurricular activities are a wonderful mechanism to help build an excellent school climate as well as to emphasize the importance of sportsmanship in all sports activities. Consider providing reminders of the requirements of sportsmanship to adults and students as they enter sporting events. Consider an announcement before play begins to welcome the visitors and

remind individuals to cheer but not be abusive toward others. As a coach, make sure you model what you want your players to exhibit, and spend time on the importance of good sportsmanship and the routines that help develop it.

5. Be vigilant about the bullying that can and, in most cases, will occur in schools. Research shows that adults far too often fail to intervene, even when they know that one child is being bullied by another. Intervene! Recognize that the both the child doing the bullying and the child being bullied may need different kinds of support and assistance. Bullying that continues must be dealt with firmly and fairly. Include parents as well as other affected stakeholders when talking to the student initiating the bullying behavior. Offer support, but emphasize that the climate of the school is damaged when one student picks on another and that future events will result in increasingly serious consequences.

Climate Change

Weather is what the atmosphere is today, but climate is what the atmosphere was yesterday and will be today, tomorrow, and into the future. Before we end this chapter, we wish to offer a few additional caveats that should guide us in our actions toward all stakeholders in the building. We must care about each other. We wish to share with you how data-driven thinking does not have to be a cold, statistical approach. We want to emphasize that much of the data we want you to collect and consider is tied to how people are feeling and how you can help. Caring demands a relationship and a conscious desire to connect with the members of our school community. If we choose to care about others, then we will take time to greet and get to know our students as we encourage them to greet and get to know each other and us.

This same attitude of caring is found among educators who are building a school where there is joy in coming to school. Teachers and principals who care about and love others take the time to model, teach, and offer opportunities for students to practice and develop skills that will allow them to develop intellectually and socially. They also have Courageous Conversations to address issues and concerns with their students and peers if these are needed.

School climate matters. It matters for the students who want to feel connected to peers and to adults who care for them. It matters to the faculty and staff who labor to assist students in reaching their potential and trust that if the climate is right, they too may fulfill the goals they established for themselves when they chose to be educators. It also matters a great deal to the parents. As parents, we all want our children to become academically smarter and more competent, and we want the school faculty and staff to assist us in those goals. But we also want the school to be a *safe* place for our children to spend the majority of their waking hours five days a week, more than 180 days a year.

As discussed earlier, if we can reduce the late arrivals and disruptions that often hamper us from getting started within 5 to 10 minutes of the bell or interrupt the learning process throughout the class period, we can gain a great amount of quality instructional time.

Next Steps

1. Consider additional training and monitoring on proper steps to build relationships and compliance with practices that promote a good learning environment. Be aware of the teachers who mean well but may discipline students with a loud, threatening voice or even use bullying practices. This can cripple the climate of your school and seriously damage the educational attitudes a student brings to the learning environment.

2. Consider common practices that can be used in your school that make class time as consistent as possible across all classrooms.

3. Gather and organize all the tools that you have available to assess the climate of your school. Determine the strengths of your tools and their weaknesses.

4. Consider a one-page newsletter that goes out once a month to all stakeholders on how climate influences and interacts with each of the other six dimensions that are predictive of quality schools.

8

The C of Character

During Deb Brown's last year teaching kindergarten, a little boy named Cody showed up at her door on the first day of school. During the first week of school, Cody told her that he lived with his mom, her new boyfriend, and his two younger brothers. "I want you to know that my real dad is in prison for murder," he said.

Cody went on to explain, "Dad and his friends were trying to steal some stereo equipment. Dad's job was to hold the gun . . . but it was supposed to be empty. His friends set him up. They put real bullets in the gun. My Daddy didn't know. He didn't mean to kill anyone but it did happen. The charges were reduced to manslaughter, so my Dad won't have to stay in prison forever. But he will have to stay for a long, long time."

Deb was shocked and saddened by Cody's story. She could see into Cody's heart and feel his pain. Her heart went out to him.

In December, Cody arrived at school with exciting news. "I get to go and visit my dad over Christmas. We won't have to talk over the phone with the glass between us. I'll really get to touch my daddy!"

When Christmas break was over, Deb waited by the classroom door for Cody's return. As soon as he entered the room, Cody's smile began to grow. Deb asked Cody how his visit went.

"It was wonderful!" Cody said. "I got to go in this room with my dad. And I even got to sit on his lap! We played checkers and we wrestled. My dad got to tickle me. Do you know how long it's been since my dad tickled me?"

Cody continued, "You know, Ms. Brown, . . . on the way home in the car, I just kept thinking about my dad. I didn't say much to my mom during the drive home.

(Continued)

(Continued)

I just kept looking out of the car window and thinking. And I figured out that if my dad had been in your class, he would never have gone to prison. He would have learned about good character and he would have made better decisions with his life."

Deb's eyes began to swell with tears, but it was a good cry! "Yes, it was one of my good cries. In fact, it was one of my best cries! This young student had just discovered the bottom line on life and had reinforced for me the importance and power of teaching the character message." Deb Brown is one of those rare teachers you hope your child will have sometime during his or her educational experiences. Deb has taught 20 years in kindergarten and 11 years in Grades 4, 5, and 6, and is now the only elementary school communication teacher in the state of West Virginia. Deb has written numerous books and been honored as a Milken Award winner. Yet after 34 years of teaching, Deb still values Cody's observation as the most memorable affirmation of her life as a teacher of character in all that she does.

Exploring the Common Sense of Character

Over the past 10 to 15 years, we have noticed schools and school districts throughout the United States, Canada, and, indeed, throughout the world are starting to give character or prosocial education efforts such as character education and social-emotional learning a little more room at the table. Some have recognized that cultivating excellence in schools demands far more than a focus on curriculum. Attitudes and inclinations such as integrity (choosing not to cheat and instead persevere) and working to the best of one's abilities also play a role in academic excellence. As a result, nearly every state in the United States and most provinces in Canada have legislation or policies in place that either mandate or strongly encourage efforts that focus on the development of the whole child to be a part of the curriculum and instructional practice.

Unfortunately, to some educators, focusing on developing the whole child goes beyond what their contract requires. To some, efforts such as character education are perceived to consist of posting a few words (such as *respect* and *responsibility*) on a bulletin board or in the hallway. Character education often is believed to be a conglomerate of positive character traits or elements that are silly time consumers to be taught through direct instruction to students as plug-in programs on a daily, weekly, or monthly basis. With limited evidence of effectiveness, hundreds of companies are marketing expensive character education programs to schools struggling to stay fiscally afloat. Regrettably, to us and to many of the educators we have interviewed, this is one of the most significant shortcomings or challenges of character education today. Evidence to be discussed shortly shows that some of these programs (and, more importantly, character-based processes) do *complement* the instructional and developmental process. But to some teachers, the marketing of such programs confirms the image of character education as a temporary trend that will go away soon. Others have told us that this is the job for parents and that the schools should not be involved in the teaching of "values" to students. There are two points of view being expressed here that we want to address. The first is that prosocial education efforts such as character education are something we *do* to children. The second is that prosocial education initiatives such as character education should have no seat at the educational table—that they belong in the home. What is interesting is that *both* points of view reflect precisely the wrong view to take when focusing on developing character or the whole child within schools.

Contrary to popular belief, whole-child-focused efforts such as character education or civic engagement are *not* about just the students. Such efforts are equally, if not more, about and reliant upon the adult stakeholders in the school first becoming and providing positive role models or moral compasses for our students to learn from and follow. Prosocial efforts to develop the whole child or character should not consist primarily of activities such as naming a hallway *Respect Lane.* Unlike plants, we humans do not grow through osmosis. And, though Respect Lane might serve as a nice reminder to students and adults on how to act, we must do much more. We must do more than read to students a story with a moral message. Perhaps these approaches may be helpful or reinforce a particular idea; however, they are weak and ineffective if the adults in the school are not committed to becoming a moral and ethical force whose social and moral excellence is reflected in the life of the school. And such perspectives on, or challenges to, implementing effective whole-child-focused initiatives extend to other prosocial efforts such as social-emotional learning, civic engagement, and service learning.

Unfortunately, while conducting our research, we have had school leadership deny a place to character education within the life of their school. Some have flatly told us and their staff that character education would not be "taught" in their school. Fortunately, when we were able to talk with some of these reluctant principals and teachers and explain to them the common sense behind building character and how it helps to create a framework to increase overall school achievement, we were able to get them to try. More adults started acting as role models in the life of their students. Several principals noted that a focus on character became more important in their schools when the adults started treating each other and the students in the manner that they would want to be treated. Ironically, several of our biggest naysayers became our biggest supporters as they internalized and began to rediscover the reason why they went into teaching. They realized that character is not necessarily *taught*, but more often *caught*. And in one of the states we studied, an experimental middle and high school went from below-average achievement scores to being one of the elite in the state within four years.

For these character converts and for many of the already committed, it makes perfect common sense that if our classrooms are filled with a higher percentage of students and teachers who show respect for others, practice responsibility, show resilience, trust each other (teachers and students), practice kindness, serve others, and strive to develop moral and academic excellence (and believe us, such classrooms do exist), then we would most likely find them to be more conducive and vibrant environments for learning, with far fewer distractions. For most students, increased academic achievement and social and moral competence does not come from increasing one's IQ or mental aptitude but from acquiring a vision of success and a reason to strive for excellence in all aspects of their work, including achievement tests and assessments. And this vision comes from the adults who model, teach, practice, encourage, and expect excellence of themselves and others in the social and moral development of all within the school.

If we consider how efforts such as character education or social-emotional learning can shape the *ethos* or life of the school, we can perhaps recognize that prosocial education efforts are essential in the academic, social, and moral development of us all. Indeed, in prosocial education, so conceived, the academic, social, and moral components must work together to develop the character of all stakeholders. This is just the approach taken by Thomas Lickona and Matthew Davidson (2005) in their work *A Report to the Nation: Smart and Good High Schools*. Lickona and Davidson argue that the definition of good character requires a quest for excellence as well as the quest for ethics. Character development is therefore conceived as having *two interconnected* parts: (1) performance character and (2) moral character.

Performance character is a mastery orientation. It consists of those qualities—such as effort, diligence, perseverance, a strong work ethic, a positive attitude, ingenuity, and self-discipline—needed to realize one's potential for excellence in academics, co-curricular activities, the workplace, or any other area of endeavor. Performance character is not the same as performance. Performance is the outcome (the grade, the honor or award, the achievement), whereas performance character consists of the character strengths, such as self-discipline and putting forth one's best effort, that enable us to pursue our personal best—whether the outcome is achieved or not.

Moral character is a relational orientation. It consists of those relational qualities—such as integrity, justice, caring, and respect—needed for successful interpersonal relationships and ethical behavior. Respect includes self-respect; we have obligations to ourselves—to respect our own rights, worth, and dignity, for example—as well as to others. Moral character enables us to treat others, and ourselves, with respect and care and to act with integrity in our ethical lives (p. 18).

If we strive for the development of performance and moral character in all stakeholders then we develop an environment that is worthy of our effort as educators. In essence, we become the person our dog thinks we are!

Research on Character and Other Prosocial Education Initiatives

Regardless of one's definition or position on the role of character, moral, or social development as part of our educational efforts, as William Damon (2005) points out:

> It is an odd mark of our time that the first question people ask about character education is whether public schools should be doing it at all. The question is odd because it invites us to imagine that schooling . . . somehow could be arranged to play no role in the formation of a child's character. (p. 1)

Yet despite how one defines or views character or the development of the whole child, we all practice it to some degree by default. Those of us who teach are role models, and our actions (good or bad) as teachers are contemplated and scrutinized by our students. Classrooms and schools are moral, ethical climates, for better or worse. Students observe teachers and the greater school environment, and theoretically these observed individuals and influential environments impact character development. Within these moral climates are behaviors that children observe and contemplate adopting. Historically, the effort to increase the moral excellence of our youth started in the 1600s in America with the founding of the first public schools (McClellan, 1992, 1999); these prosocial education efforts continue, and evidence supporting a more definitive role for this kind of education within the modern American and Canadian education system continues to be documented.

A meta-analysis by Garrard and Lipsey (2007), funded by the National Institute of Mental Health and the W.T. Grant Foundation, focused on conflict resolution education (CRE) programs. This meta-analysis covered the period from 1960 to 2006 and included both published and unpublished studies. Results of this meta-analysis showed consistent declines in antisocial behavior regardless of whether the students were exposed to direct CRE skills instruction, embedded CRE curriculum, or some form of peer mediation. A meta-analysis of 38 studies of social skills training programs showed an overall moderate positive effect on student outcomes (Ang & Hughes, 2001). These studies, published between 1977 and 1999, varied in the extent of the effects shown, but on average showed positive impact on both deviant students and all students. A review of civic engagement programs reported findings from experimental and quasiexperimental studies showing that community service opportunities tied to a school curriculum promoted a number of outcomes including personal and social responsibility, work orientation, and engagement with school (Michelson, Zaff, & Hair, 2002). Research has shown that service learning can have positive effects on students and therefore schools. Dr. Shelly Billig from RMC Research (2005) provided a summary of over 50 research studies titled *The Impacts of Service-Learning on Participating Students.* She determined that service learning has positive impacts on students' academic performance, civic and citizenship practices, environmentally responsible behaviors, and social and personal growth. RMC Research, working with the Philadelphia Partnership in Character Education, utilized a multifaceted approach to the character development of students and noted that students engaged in more than 30 hours of service learning exhibit greater achievement, less tardiness, and higher average daily attendance when compared to students from matched comparison schools.

A recent randomized controlled trial of School-Wide Positive Behavior Support (SWPBS) is also worth mentioning (Horner et al., 2009). The evaluation focused primarily on the reduction of problem behavior and increase in academic achievement, and also included indicators of positive behavior as part of the risk factor score of the school safety survey, including perceived caring, perceived sensitivity to cultural differences, student bonding with school, and the quality of student–adult interactions. Other behaviors included in the same score were designed space, crowding, and level of adult supervision. Results indicated that the school culture in SWPBS schools was significantly safer and more caring than the culture in comparison schools.

One of the more extensive reviews conducted on character education was completed by the What Works Clearinghouse (WWC) and the Institute for Education Sciences (www.whatworks.ed.gov; Berkowitz, Battistich, & Bier, 2008). Eighteen studies and 13 different programs met the evidence standards of the WWC, which required that the programs be studied using one of the following research designs: randomized controlled trial, quasiexperiment, regression discontinuity, or single subject. Character education programs were reviewed to determine if impacts could be demonstrated in three domains: (1) behavior; (2) knowledge, attitudes, and values; and (3) student achievement.

In this research, the Positive Action program demonstrated positive effects on the behavior and achievement of elementary school students. Too Good for Drugs and Violence was another program reviewed that had positive effects on student knowledge, attitudes, and values. Too Good for Drugs and Violence focuses on developing personal and interpersonal skills to resist peer pressures, goal setting, decision making, bonding with others, having respect for self and others, managing emotions, effective communication, and social interactions. Too Good for Drugs is a companion program to Too Good for Violence. At the high school level, the programs are combined in one volume under the name Too Good for Drugs & Violence High School. Similarly, the Too Good for Violence program also showed potentially positive effects on behavior, knowledge, attitudes, and values. Evidence collected at the federal level on studies ending in 2005 supporting character education's effectiveness was as strong as federal-level evidence supporting the effectiveness of federally funded math curricula studies during the same time.

Current research in the field of character education, however, has been moving toward a deeper understanding of a more comprehensive process approach rather than depending on any single program (Leming, 2008). The Child Development Project illustrates this approach with their successful, comprehensive, whole-school interventions that develop the Caring School Community; these programs are designed to foster social, ethical, and intellectual development in students via the development of caring communities of learners

(Solomon, Battistich, Watson, Schaps, & Lewis, 2000). A study funded by the U. S. Department of Education (Marshall, 2006) found that when the Caring School Community approach is combined with the educational practices of Characterplus, the following outcomes were documented among participating schools:

- *Improved Discipline*—Student office referrals decreased 19%, with an overall difference between treatment and control schools of 33%.
- *Improved Achievement*—Student achievement in communication arts increased as much as 47% and in math as much as 54% after being in the program for three years.

Both common sense and research indicate that comprehensive educational efforts to develop character or the whole child show positive effects on the students and their performance, and ultimately on all the stakeholders within the school.

Dimensional Connection to the C of Character

Character development is related to the Seven Dimensions in the following ways:

Community Engagement. How is the student connected to the community? In other words, how is the child connected to the social, civic, and possibly religious organizations within the greater community? Is the child involved in Little League sports, 4-H, or scouting? Do the

adults working with our students and children represent a moral compass in the lives of these children? The same would apply to any neighborhood activities. What are the adults modeling and teaching to our children?

Curriculum Expectations. What are we doing within the school to assist students in developing a positive work attitude that will enable them to persevere on difficult assignments and strive toward excellence? How do we as adults deliver the curriculum and assist students in a developmentally appropriate manner in developing the intellectual skills needed to become reflective adults? How do we as adults work together with students in project-based learning activities to develop excellence in all we do?

Developmental Perspectives. This dimension (a primary dimension for the C of Character) focuses on measuring what we consider to be student character—how they see themselves in relation to social and ethical norms. Yet their character is shaped by the experiences they have in their homes, their communities, and within the school. Within the Developmental Perspectives dimension, we strive to have students develop the habit of serving others within the school. We model for them as we assist them in developing compassion toward others and practicing good deeds, such as kindness and respect toward others. We ask ourselves whether we develop connections to our community so that our children form habits of service, and whether we encourage both service from the school to the community and from the community back to the school.

Educational Attitudes. The formation of a child's character and the further development of the adult's character must also include assisting the child in developing a positive work ethic. A positive work ethic requires that the student and other stakeholders give their best effort and that they motivate themselves and others to master the curriculum. This must be taught, practiced, and modeled by the adults who surround the child. The development of a positive work ethic enables them to schedule, participate, and strive for excellence. Please note that striving for excellence does not mean that one will achieve it. However, one must strive in order to succeed, and this is a habit worth developing.

Faculty Fidelity. At first glance, one might ask what Faculty Fidelity would have to do with the development of character in our students. First of all, Faculty Fidelity requires a consensus on the part of the faculty that the social and moral development of their students is as important as their intellectual, artistic, athletic, and vocational development. This requires that we as a faculty are teaching and practicing what we believe. Furthermore, we further develop ourselves as moral exemplars in a school as we model for all stakeholders what we expect from them. Building these positive relationships with students is paramount to success; therefore, Faculty Fidelity is also a primary dimension to focus on when approaching the C of Character.

Leadership Potential. Developing a more holistic shared leadership approach in our schools encourages all stakeholders to contribute to the development of a climate conducive to social and moral development. By *shared leadership,* we mean to imply that Leadership Potential does not rest solely on the shoulders of principals. Can we see this in action? Yes. Think of the teachers who you consider to be the best in your school. What is it that differentiates these teachers from others? Do the best teachers model bad behavior? Do they act as if they do not care about their students? The best teachers not only know the subject matter but also know how to teach it well, with enthusiasm and a caring heart. They are able to connect with students. And like a good principal, they are able to unite educators. A character leader will recognize the importance of modeling, leading, and teaching for character development and will communicate this to all stakeholders. This is why Leadership Potential is also a primary dimension of focus for the C of Character.

School Climate. The development of positive character traits and practices in individuals will greatly enhance the development of a positive School Climate. We cannot imagine such a climate developing unless all stakeholders are working together with goodwill to ensure that the school is a place of positive relationships among all. This requires people who truly care about each other and consider the needs of others to be as important as their own needs. A positive School Climate develops when we learn to act not just on getting our needs and wants met but striving to assure that the needs and wants of all stakeholders are given equal consideration.

Seven Steps to Systemic Improvement in Character

Assume you are an anthropologist. You are seeking to understand a particular phenomenon (character development) within a school. Don't forget there are several tools in the Appendix to help you with this endeavor, including measurement tools, rubrics, and planning forms that can give a quick snapshot of your school's general health regarding its character-building efforts. You might also follow the practice of a middle school we worked with that sought to develop a comprehensive approach by constructing a large-scale analysis of their efforts in character education. They had perceived character education as being a part of the *ethos* of the school. They had surveyed all stakeholder groups utilizing evaluative assessments (not statistically valid) from the book *Evaluating Character Development* by Edward F. DeRoche (2004). In addition, they ran some focus groups with their stakeholders to determine what they were doing well and what needed improvement. As a final step, before developing plans for the upcoming school year they decided to use the MDed Multi-Dimensional Assessment. They chose to walk around the school over a 3-day period. They also invited all stakeholder groups to participate in the study. The principal realized that this would be a massive quantity of data to sort in a few weeks' time, but he wanted to see if the data from the quantitative evaluation previously done would be validated by the eyes and ears of his constituency.

STEP 1: Ask the Right Questions

Based on his initial understanding of the data, the principal and the School Leadership Team—a group representative of all stakeholders—met to consider some of the questions that would guide them as they put their eyes, ears, and minds to the task of increasing their understanding of the character of the school and community. Here are three questions that they used as a guide for those participating in the assessment:

Question 1: Do I see examples of compassion and caring on the part of all stakeholders within the school and community?

Question 2: Can I see examples of good conduct, or of misconduct, in the school and local community on the part of all the stakeholders?

Question 3: As I walk around, can I see examples of stakeholders exhibiting success-related traits such as perseverance in completion of work, respect toward others, and fairness in all school and extracurricular activities?

STEP 2: Collect and Organize the Data

The following rubric (Figure 8.1) is tied to the seven dimensions that are linked to school improvement. Each stakeholder was given a description of how the dimensions related to character. The following represents the qualitative data collected from all stakeholders by the School Leadership Team. They were interested in seeing if people noted the same strengths as well as determining if there were some concerns the school should address.

Figure 8.1   Example: C of Character Rubric

THE C OF CHARACTER	
Strengths (+) and Concerns (–)	Observable Evidence (+/–)
Dimension 1: Community Engagement	
+ For the most part, the community consists of caring adults who are involved in the lives of their students + There are ample opportunities to surround the students with adults who model and expect good character – There are concerns about sportsmanship on the part of coaches, parents, and players	+ The school informs the community of its character building efforts + Adults are modeling and expecting good character of the students within the school – Some parents and students noted that bullying exists in the school but also moves out into the neighborhood – Bullying on the school bus has been reported
Dimension 2: Curriculum Expectations	
+ Lessons on character are provided via advisor/advisee + Students are expected to do their best work and may have to do poor work over + The English teachers emphasize character in reading – How are other teachers fusing character into their lessons?	+ Traits like perseverance and diligence are valued and encouraged – A fair number of staff reported that students appeared to be using the Internet to quickly get information and were plagiarizing their work
Dimension 3: Developmental Perspectives	
+ Students are generally kind to each other, at least in the presence of other adults – Bullying has been reported by students and other stakeholders. Several adult stakeholders noted this in the walk-through	+ The importance of character modeling and development is visually present in each classroom + Our students are serving others in the school and in the community – We are serving others but not enough. We need more service opportunities and diversity in our service efforts
Dimension 4: Educational Attitudes	
+ The teachers care about the students; this helps the students care about the teachers and the work expected of them – There does appear to be pushback from parents and students when students have to re-do their work because they have turned in poor quality assignments	+ Students appear to like working together on projects and getting grades on their overall efforts + PE program works hard on the mastery of skills to give more students the chance to enjoy playing games – We should have more friendly competitions between the teams in each grade during advisor/advisee

THE C OF CHARACTER	
Strengths (+) and Concerns (–)	*Observable Evidence (+/–)*
Dimension 5: Faculty Fidelity	
+ Our faculty appear to like each other and spend time with each other before, during, and after school – Some teams appear to work together better than others	+ The faculty appear to be working together on the importance of character education in our school – We do not recognize our adults in the building and community for modeling of good character for students
Dimension 6: Leadership Potential	
+ Administrative team gives a consistent emphasis on the importance of character in school and community – We could promote the importance of character more within our community	+ Our mission is posted throughout the school + The students are encouraged by the school staff to take leadership positions – We need to work harder to diversify our leadership positions in the school for all stakeholders
Dimension 7: School Climate	
+ Our focus on caring and respect can be seen throughout the school day + Newcomers are quickly inculcated into the climate and expectations of the school – We should strive to ensure that all stakeholders who walk into the school understand the importance of respect and caring in how we address all	+ Bullying is not tolerated in the school – We may need to spend more time working with students doing the bullying to make them aware of how it hurts others. They may also need additional counseling – We have noticed that some stakeholders from the community practice poor sportsmanship during games

After compiling all of the data, Figure 8.1 was presented to the stakeholder groups as a means of furthering the discussion on the issue. Stakeholders were asked to reflect on whether the School Leadership Teams had captured the spirit of their observations, and to prepare for upcoming discussions on the data.

STEP 3: Discuss and Reflect on the Data

Meetings were held during team planning to see if the combined rubric was indicative of the strengths and concerns of the school. Each team worked together and either agreed with the compilation or made some additional notes for consideration. They also took advantage of the data generated from other assessments and school data to see if they lined up with this data. The adjusted rubrics were then returned to the School Leadership Team for consideration. Next, a newer and more comprehensive picture of the data strengths and concerns were sent to each faculty member and other stakeholder groups for additional comments via the team or other groups, such as the parental advisory group. At this point, the staff and other stakeholder group representatives were ready to determine specific strategies and establish goals.

STEP 4: Set Goals and Target Planning

Now is the time when the teams first work separately and then come together as a group to develop comprehensive and definable goals and strategies to address the concerns revealed by the data. The School Leadership Team defines goals and strategies that can be accomplished within the school year. The school staff and all interested parents held a 2-hour after-school meeting to review and finalize the recommendation. Figure 8.2 outlines specific objectives, possible strategies, and professional development opportunities identified.

STEP 5: Implement

As we have pointed out before, it is great to have a plan, but it is even better to implement the plan! This is exactly what this middle school did. Now the staff understood the goals and implementation strategies. Although this is not the complete work of the team, you can clearly see how they recognized several concerns and through the efforts of the School Leadership Team and the stakeholders, developed a workable and definable plan to address a concern (lack of service opportunities and the need to get more students involved).

STEP 6: Monitor and Fine-Tune

Now was the time to monitor and fine-tune the efforts of the school. They had determined strategies that could garner the greatest amount of knowledge, support, and participation. Everyone appeared to be onboard, attending the trainings, and beginning to implement the strategies without too many problems. The School Leadership Team and their stakeholders began to assess what was occurring. What was being heard when the School Leadership Team members met with individual stakeholders or with teams of teachers? Was the

Figure 8.2 Character Goal Setting and Planning Chart

Character Goals: By June 2010, strategies will be implemented to improve the overall service opportunities within our school to enhance our character building efforts in the school as reported by students, parents, and teachers. The measure for achievement of this goal is: *an increase of service learning activities in the school and community, with 20% more students and adult stakeholders participating in service learning opportunities.* We are also going to address a perceived rise in plagiarism that appears to be tied to the ease of accessing and using information from the Internet. We feel our students are not aware that this is cheating, and we wish to teach them appropriate ways to utilize the Internet in their research and writings.

Objective	Strategies	Professional Development	Resources	Timeline	Tasks	Monitoring
We will create additional opportunities to develop service opportunities as well as reflection time for all stakeholder groups	Stakeholders will work with the local groups such as the center for children with autism to determine opportunities for our children and adults to serve in the school as well as opportunities in the community	We will have a training day in November provided by the local Center on how our students can work to assist their students in the Center and classrooms	Center Staff Specific strategies on how we can build reflection on our work	9/09–06/10	AP will coordinate training and service opportunities Reflection journals provided in the office	Feedback on trainings and examples of student reflections
We will seek to involve all of our school stakeholders in serving others within our community	We will connect with the community, e.g., faith communities, to get the names of people who have difficulty raking their leaves in the fall. We will develop the Speed Rakers club to assist these people. This will involve our students, parents, and other interested community members	We will get a representative from the local Girl Scouts who is an expert on working with broad community organizations on building comprehensive and inclusive service opportunities	Establish a sign-up board for interested individuals. The school will solicit supplies from local businesses and stakeholders	9/09–06/10	PTA will coordinate activities	PTA will keep track of the number of businesses involved and number of activities for students
We will seek to reduce the amount of plagiarism that we have noticed coming from our students in their writing via the use of the Internet	We will offer after-school staff development on working with students on plagiarism. In particular, we will focus on the use of the Internet and the ease of plagiarism. We will develop a plan to address this with all our students through the humanities block. We will seek out videos that address plagiarism	A parent with expertise on this issue working with other schools has agreed to provide training for adult stakeholders and student government to develop strategies to address the concern	The parent volunteer for the training of staff and students. Videos to be used by staff	9/09–06/10	Principal will coordinate with a parent task force and counselor	Evidenced by office referrals and instances of plagiarism documented by teachers and staff

effort succeeding? What was needed to improve the effort? A wise individual once stated that "Anything that is of value and worth doing well is worth doing poorly." He did not mean that we should slouch to the bottom. Rather, he felt that if the action is of value and is a priority, we may not achieve perfection in our initial efforts. This is very important for leaders to understand. We will not get to excellence quickly. It takes time, reflection, and continual effort to improve. If we believe that something is of value and is worth doing, then we must give ourselves and others the right to struggle toward excellence. This is what this school was experiencing, and by their continuous monitoring and fine tuning the effort they were working toward success.

STEP 7: Evaluate and Communicate the Outcome

The School Leadership Team and other stakeholders monitored the efforts and adjusted as needed. Near the end of the term, they reported their successes back to all stakeholder groups. A celebration was held and everyone was thanked. They succeeded in the goal of increasing the service opportunities in the school and community for all stakeholders. There are many ways to report data to our stakeholders. Ideally, you are able to issue a report from the principal or Leadership Team that describes the goals that were established and what was achieved in relation to them. This was the method of this middle school. Their report indicated how the effort was implemented and fine-tuned. The next step was to build on what was learned and continue the process.

Additional Strategies to Enhance the C of Character

1. In continuing the previous section on assessment, let us begin by asking the question, "How do we know what we think we know about our character-building efforts?" In the Appendix are several scales within the Multi-Dimensional Assessment to assess stakeholder views of the school. The scales under the Developmental Perspectives dimension are specifically focused on the character domain. We recommend that you add some additional qualitative open-answer items to your assessment. Answers to these items can be solicited from the stakeholder groups within your school.

2. As noted previously, we should determine what the community feels is important for the school to do concerning the character development of its students as well as the character of the school. It is equally important for the school to understand what factors in the school and community assist or hamper efforts to develop the character of all stakeholders. This will require some effort on the part of the school staff. One strategy we learned from an administrator is to load the entire staff on the school bus and tour the neighborhoods that feed the school. Make occasional stops in neighborhoods where parents and kids are outside and take a minute to get off the bus and say "Hello." On these trips, faculty members are also asked to write down their impressions and note faith communities, social organizations, sports organizations, and businesses that could be involved or by charter committed to the character development of the students and the community at large. This list should be compiled and letters sent out for a summit on character to be held at the school. It is oftentimes quite beneficial for teachers to actually tour the areas that feed their schools. Many teachers are quite shocked to know the conditions in which many of their students live. This can only reinforce the calling educators have to assist students in their complete social, ethical, and intellectual development.

3. A good strategy to assist in helping students learn to do good is to promote compassion for others in our school. A school would need to ask, "How do we promote *compassion for others* within our school?" One of the authors worked with a school that, based on student requests and faculty leadership, chose to serve students with special needs who were in a separate building on their school grounds. With students and teachers working together, this school actually started involving the children with autism in the life of their school in innovative ways. Student surveys, discussions with focus groups, or simply asking for students to write their ideas on enhancing service opportunities within the school and broader community on a large bulletin board in a hall are all excellent ways to generate ideas to facilitate the planning, buy-in, and development process.

4. How do stakeholders feel about the *expectation, definition,* and *practice of success traits* such as respect, responsibility, caring, and integrity? As noted earlier, some of our research indicates

that if students see themselves as being, for example, responsible, and they value this attribute in themselves, there will be a correlation between this and their academic performance, regardless of their economic conditions. In other words, valuing and applying these traits within one's life has positive school outcomes.

5. Finally (and this is tied to the behavioral issues of our students), how serious a problem is *student misconduct* in our school? How do students and adults feel about the misconduct in the school? Is it acceptable? Is it a serious problem, or a minor one? What are the most serious examples of misconduct? What might we as school stakeholders do to minimize misconduct and promote positive conduct? It is very important to ask these questions. We have to discuss and analyze our misconduct data in order to determine what we need to do to mitigate the negative and promote positive conduct. From what we have noticed in our fieldwork, we have one caveat to offer: If your school is like most schools, a *limited* number of students are causing or leading most of the serious misconduct incidents in your school. It is important for school staff and students to have these numbers in order to see that the majority of the school's behavioral problems come from a limited number of students.

Character Change

Consider the following scenario: Your child, grandchild, niece, nephew, or child of a dear friend whom you love makes straight A's in school. Someone comes up to you in a local food market and notes that he saw this child's name in the local newspaper recognizing her academic excellence. You humbly accept the congratulations and remark that you are very proud of this child. A week later someone comes up to you at a local shop and states that this child is "so polite and kind toward everyone. You can always count on her to show up and assist people at the soup kitchen or at the local Habitat House." Now which compliment means the most to you: the first or the second? If you are like most people you appreciate the first compliment, but you treasure the second one. We all want our children to do well in all aspects of school life. We are proud when they do. But we are thrilled when others recognize the character of our children. Life has also taught us that you can make straight As in school but still flunk life. Reflect back on the recent debacle on Wall Street and its role in the meltdown of the economy, not just of the United States but the world. We would imagine that all of these individuals probably passed their end-of-grade assessments or their AP or IB exams. Even if they did not break the law, they clearly violated ethical practices concerning the oversight of millions of individuals' retirement and investment accounts. They had performance character (they were able to make the money they intended to), but they lacked moral character.

Next Steps

1. Consider communicating with organizations in your community to ask them to notify the school when students in your school are contributing to the betterment of the community. Thank the students for their work within the school environment. This is an excellent way to build relationships between school and community.

2. Increase your understanding of your school's character by using the rubric provided, or develop another one that can be used in walk-throughs that will either inform or support your character-building efforts. This will help you gain greater insight into the strengths and concerns of your school. You can work together with other staff and develop a composite instrument to meet your goals.

3. Make sure you examine your school's extracurricular activities if appropriate. This is part of the learning process, and we want to make sure our students are being taught and led by people who take the social, ethical, and intellectual development of students seriously.

4. Adopt a local day care center or hospital that would appreciate the assistance of your students as well as of adult stakeholders in your school.

PART III

Achievement

Whether you acquired this book on your own to better understand data-driven thinking, or the district or school you work in has adopted or is considering adopting the Multi-Dimensional Education approach to systemic change, Part III is intended to help you embrace the promise this approach has for complementing or changing the structures and processes you have in place. If you are considering such systemic change efforts, regardless of whether you are new to education or a veteran, you may need encouragement to try something new. This part of the book is intended to reassure you that the kind of systemic change we propose is valuable and worth pursuing to further focus your lens on how using meaningful data can facilitate positive change, including increased achievement. As we have stated previously, high achievement is a worthy goal, but knowing how best to improve achievement is even better. Overall improvement, however, requires that you concentrate and focus first on improving the parts that can help you achieve more.

Part I focused on identifying the dimensions of data most critical to success and how to view such data through the seven dimensions most often associated with highly effective schools. Part II focused on helping you to use the seven dimensions of data (qualitatively, quantitatively, or both) to inform and guide efforts to improve your 4Cs Framework.

Part III will further address how this systemic model, encompassing the MDed Seven Dimensions and the 4Cs, can function more efficiently when shared leadership embraces utilizing data to drive success. By readdressing systems theory and further investigating how positive systemic change comes about, this part of the book will provide confirmation and additional goal-aligned suggestions to help you develop your own model for Multi-Dimensional Education.

9

Gearing Up for Systemic Success

In early 2010, we were asked by Wicomico County Schools in Maryland to do an evaluation of their schools using our Multi-Dimensional Assessment (MDA) instrument. They were already data-driven, but they wanted more. The district made a commitment to get all schools and stakeholder groups to participate in the assessment. After the assessment, data were analyzed and formulated into reports for each school as well as a district report with a comparative analysis of data from all the schools. Next, the district scheduled a day for the principals and selected staff from each school to meet with us to receive training on their school's data and to learn about how they could act on this data by focusing on the MDed 4Cs. When we arrived for the training, we were very impressed. The individuals in charge of the data collection at the district had prepared packets for all of the attendees that included their school's data report and copies of the PowerPoint presentations we had sent ahead of time. To emphasize the importance of this meeting, Wicomico County School Superintendent John Frederickson and most of the cabinet officers and directors attended the meeting and stayed throughout the day. We spent the morning explaining the logic and theory behind the data and did several activities to explore the importance and applicability of the dimensions. The school teams were instructed not to open the shrink-wrapped school reports until after lunch. As the morning went on, you could see the curiosity and anticipation grow in the eyes of the educators as they looked at the reports wrapped in front of them, knowing that those reports held some insights into their schools based on data they had never been provided before.

(Continued)

(Continued)

After returning from lunch, it was as if we were sitting in the living room watching our kids tear off the gift wrapping one present at a time as the educators opened their individual school reports. We instructed them to take some time to go through each dimension to see how their stakeholders felt and how they might have different views. We instructed them to also look at the means tables in the reports to see how their school was perceived compared to other schools in the district. For nearly an hour, these data-driven educators were immersed in looking at the perspectives of their students, staff, and parents based on the MDed Seven Dimensions. Once they had enough time to digest the information provided, many wanted to focus on some of the concerns they had. But we also asked them to dive back into the reports and look equally at the results that should be shared and celebrated with their faculty and staff. We then spent the rest of the meeting having each school begin to formulate plans on how to share the data with their stakeholders and develop some preliminary strategies to use their strengths to improve the concerns. The reviews from the meeting were positive; the only suggestions made were that they wanted to know more about how to fix areas where they had concerns. They wanted more strategies.

After the meeting, it was decided that they would have us return to the school district in September to work with the schools one-on-one in fine-tuning strategies they were implementing, or considering implementing, for the immediate school year. In addition, a meeting was scheduled during that visit with appropriate central office personnel. During this meeting, we would work with the personnel on how they could support the efforts of the schools in implementing their plans as well as assisting each school in monitoring and assessing their efforts. Dr. Cathy Townsend, the Safe Schools Supervisor of Wicomico County, noted,

> The school and district data we received as a result of administering the MDed survey has proven to be a fantastic tool in helping our schools recognize and celebrate their successes as well as focus directly on areas in need of improvement. Great conversations, collaborative planning, and focused implementation of strategies as a result of this data have helped efforts to improve student achievement.

The main goal of this book is to share how a robust collection of seven dimensions of data involving all stakeholders can become a driving force that concentrates conversations and improvement plans on the 4Cs of Curriculum, Community, Climate, and Character. We share this chapter's introductory story to show how schools are successfully implementing our process for data-driven thinking. Based on the MDed data reports, one elementary school in the district decided that they needed to add a daily classroom meeting time to their schedule. During this time, the entire class gathers together to exchange greetings, share good news from the classroom or from the home, discuss any concerns regarding class or school issues, and go over the plan for the day. One teacher's daily classroom meeting, however, takes place at the end of the day and is used to celebrate the achievements of that school day, address any concerns, and discuss the homework and preparation needed for the next day. Within the first month of school, the staff was reporting a closer connection with their students as well as having more time during the day to address both the instructional and the social-emotional concerns of the students.

A middle school in the district noted that they were struggling to increase community and parental engagement. They have developed plans to have all faculty members make and document efforts to connect with parents and other community members. Such an effort need not take the form of a phone call to a parent; it may also involve a postcard or e-mail that highlights academic improvement on the part of the student or an improvement in a child's efforts in becoming a more caring member of the school family. The data also indicated that the staff and students did not consider their school's climate conducive to helping stakeholders flourish. The school leadership is addressing and communicating with all stakeholders concerning what needs to be done to create a more caring environment within the school.

A high school in the district utilized the MDed data to support what they had been gathering informally or through various surveys over the last year. The MDed Seven Dimensions gave this school data that further informed their perspectives. This is a school that utilizes its data and is now working intensively to identify its major concerns so that it will truly move from being a very good high school to being a great high school. Based on the authors' perspective from working with the leadership team and talking with the principal and other teachers and students, we believe that going from good to great is a very achievable goal for this school. The students and staff are passionate about what they do and now have data to better inform their efforts, celebrate their strengths, and address any concerns. All of the schools in Wicomico County had good data from various sources. The MDed assessment allowed them to compare data from all stakeholders to truly determine their strengths and concerns using a valid and reliable instrument.

What is becoming increasingly evident in schools and organizations around the country is the need to take this notion of data-driven education to the next level. There are a number of school systems and schools embracing data-driven education and reaping the rewards.

In this book we have provided a new approach to this end and have supported this new approach with time-tested research and true-to-life stories that highlight the benefits of the comprehensive systems approach that data-driven thinking can provide. We know that schools and districts that adopt such an approach are willing to roll up their sleeves and take on this endeavor, and they agree that all of the dimensions (and 4Cs) are important!

In the spring of 2010 we were asked to go to Michigan to address a gathering of educators as part of a week-long training program. We were there to discuss the seven dimensions of education we have shared with you. Included in this discussion was how the seven dimensions empower the 4Cs that lead to better stakeholder focus and planning that can improve all aspects of the school as well as the community support that enhances student achievement. We discussed each of the seven dimensions as well as the indexes of the scales we use to measure each dimension.

Next, we asked the participants individually to rank these dimensions in order from the most to the least important for enhancing the total school achievement of students. They were then to share their ideas with their tablemates to see if they could agree among themselves on an order. The exercise generated much conversation but little agreement from the tables. Indeed, many participants stated that they could not rank order the choices themselves. After ten minutes of discussion, the groups came to the understanding that they could not agree and assign a rank order. It was decided that they were all important—indeed, they were all equally important. One teacher spoke up and said with a smirk, "You knew this would happen, didn't you?" The answer was, "Yes, we did!" It happens nearly everywhere we go.

Next, we discussed the 4Cs of Climate, Community, Character, and Curriculum. We then asked them to see if they could rank order these four. "Surely four must be easier than seven to rank!" We asked them to work individually and then as a table. Once again, after fruitful discussion they could not agree on a rank order of importance. It was at this point that we congratulated and thanked them on their efforts and insights. It was then we shared with them the importance of systemic data-driven thinking and how with so many important parts to the complex system that comprises our education efforts, we must get beyond a focus on programs and systematic approaches. It was then we shared with them how the seven dimensions and the 4Cs are what research shows can improve all of our efforts. We shared with them that day how to approach education multi-dimensionally.

We hope you have come to a similar conclusion from reading the previous eight chapters. It is a difficult task (when using intellectual and practical honesty) to rank order the seven dimensions or the 4Cs. They are part of the inescapable system that makes success possible. Please look again at the gears behind the common sense of data-driven thinking in Figure 9.1. It takes all of the seven-dimensional gears working together to influence the progression of the 4Cs, which should also be working together, to bring about academic success in all areas. This gear diagram is not intended to suggest that the seven dimensions inform the 4Cs in the order of community, character, climate, and curriculum. Every school will probably have a slightly different approach and might be facing different challenges. As Chapters 5 through 8 illustrated, many times a school will decide to focus more heavily on a certain part of the 4Cs. They might have taken a somewhat triage-based approach, but none of these schools completely ignored the other three parts of the 4Cs. We cannot and should not do so in any circumstances. As we have tried to show, a linear step-by-step approach hinders the potential for real change to occur. Plus, as we have learned, each of the 4Cs is dependent upon all of the others. Climate affects the character of the school and the effectiveness of your curriculum, and climate depends upon the level and quality of Community Engagement. We are proposing a systems approach, which research shows is one of the best ways to reach your educational goals. A systems approach is essential not just for school success but for nearly any great achievement.

The same types of systems exist in business and many other facets of life. Businesses that are successful, whether large or small, are able to perfect some kind of a system for delivering the products or the services they offer. Even successful churches, nonprofit organizations, and governmental agencies operate from a systems approach. The ability to develop a successful system relies heavily on a shared vision or mission that creates a set of goals for accomplishing the vision or mission. This does not happen unintentionally. In some instances, it will happen with more intentionality than in others; as a result, one might observe a number of different levels of success. Regardless, successful systems embody the collective hope, voices, and practices needed to empower and achieve what was set out to be accomplished. What is common across the implementation of systems is that the system itself is the catalyst for change. And what we have discovered is that a successful system in education often needs a minimum of seven dimensions to drive its 4Cs to systemic improvement. It is through this system that we can truly envision what is needed for higher achievement to become a natural result of our efforts. When you embrace a Multi-Dimensional Education systems approach for your school, you will have also created a growth model that more accurately and comprehensively assesses all of your stakeholders' strengths, accomplishments, and concerns.

Change Revisited

The system as a catalyst for change must cause us to go back and rethink the two kinds of change we discussed in Chapter 2. The ideal form of change is *second-order change*, in which a school is collectively able to adopt new ways of thinking that actually manifest themselves in a new system of actions and behaviors based on new rules, insights, and premises. This is a deeper understanding of change than just

Figure 9.1   The Gears Behind Data-Driven Thinking

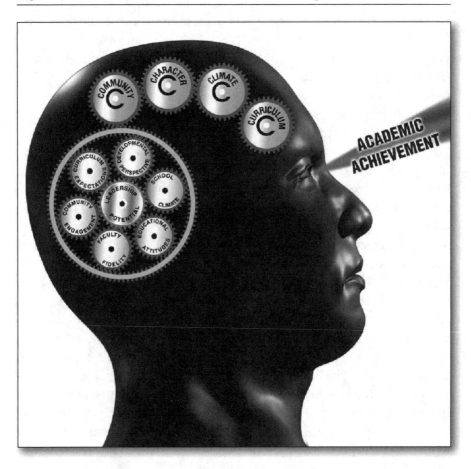

change for the sake of change, which so often is just the *first-order change* that is unable to peel the outer layers back and really get to the core of what needs fixing in the school organization.

Take a deep breath—change is hard work! This is stating the obvious; we are sure at some point in this book you have considered the amount of energy and time it will take to implement the systemic structures we propose. We know you already work hard, but what many need to consider about hard work is whether or not it is focused in an intentional manner that will bring about the change that is needed to achieve excellence. Michael Fullan is the most recognized author on change in schools. In his book *Leading in a Culture of Change,* Fullan (2001) suggests six guidelines for understanding the process of change:

1. The goal is not to innovate the most, but rather to innovate selectively with coherence.

2. It is not enough to have the best ideas. You must work through a process in which others assess and come to find collective meaning and commitment to new ways.

3. Appreciate early difficulties of trying something new—what Fullan calls the *implementation dip.* It is important to know, for example, that no matter how much preimplementation preparation one does, the first six months or so of implementation will be bumpy.

4. Redefine resistance as a potential positive force. Naysayers (laggards) sometimes have good points, and they are crucial to the politics of implementation. This doesn't mean that you listen to naysayers endlessly, but that you look for ways to address their concerns.

5. Reculturing is the name of the game. Much change is structural, and superficial. The change required rests in the culture of what people value (which is sometimes superficial) and the structures they choose to adopt in order to work more effectively together.

6. Never a checklist, always complexity. There is no step-by-step shortcut to transformation; it involves the hard day-to-day work of reculturing.

Change requires intentionality and the commitment to some kind of coherent system. A key ingredient to creating a wonderful system that produces delightful outcomes (i.e., something as wonderful as cake) is to garner enough collective involvement for innovation and new ideas able to facilitate change. Fullan's point about implementation dip is pivotal and must be taken into account due to the emphasis on instant gratification that is prevalent not only in schools but also in educational policy that desires change *now* in systems that are so broken. We have to understand implementation as a fluid activity in which we must maintain a certain level of flexibility, both structurally, in how we set out to plan change, and mentally, in how we react when change doesn't happen according to plan. Much of the change process has to do with how we respond to those unwilling to change or who are seeing things from a different perspective. Considering these different perspectives is essential to second-order change because the last thing we want is everyone agreeing to change but giving only lip service to the idea. The notion of reculturing is a key point—Fullan mentions it twice in his six points—and it really comes down to how we provide the communication and vision for our schools to get on board with the vision of change and the next steps. There is no doubt that change takes strong leadership! And by this we don't just mean the principal or superintendent, but also a shared leadership team in the school that is able proactively to get others on board and committed to the vision for change.

If you reflect on the kinds of change you are planning and the kinds of goals you are setting, there have to be moments when you wonder if what you are proposing is at all possible. We fear failure; that is part of human nature. We have all failed before, and the reality is that we want to try to avoid the feelings associated with failure. Many of us have failed, and learned from failure; in retrospect, we are better off for having failed. If we allow the fear of failure to stifle our actions, then we will not push for change, but instead continue working harder but with less intentionality by sticking to what has always worked for us, or possibly not worked as well as we would have liked, in the past. But has sticking to what has always worked really *worked?* Is the hard work we apply to our existing approaches that much different from the hard work required to adopt a new approach? Is wondering if what we are already doing will produce the results we need significantly less stressful than adopting a new way that will produce the results we want? Possibly the greatest barrier in approaching change is the fear of failure. Now is the time to wrestle with the following question: *Innovations may fail, but does that mean they were not worth attempting?* It really comes down to the question of whether we will be better off for going through a process and pushing ahead for change even if we do not completely accomplish what we set out to accomplish. For educators, a good example of this is in the expectations we set for students.

Let's say you have a student in the fifth grade who reads at a third-grade level, and you set out a plan to get the student reading at a sixth-grade level by the end of the school year. Your goal is to get the student caught up with his peers. In addition to a focused approach to help this child develop decoding skills in the classroom, you also provide some after-school reading tutorials and enlist parent support and guidance in helping the student improve and, you hope, achieve mastery at reading. You are intentional about helping the student, but at the end of the school year the student is reading at a fifth-grade level. You did not meet the goal you set out to accomplish; but one must wonder what would have happened and how would you have performed if you didn't set the goal in the first place. You may have made the maximum improvement possible with this student; without setting the goal you did, you might not have moved the reading level at all. This is the complexity of change. You are trying to accomplish goals while dealing with the reality that you may fall short of what you attempt to do. Yet you may accomplish a great deal. You must think about change differently and redefine failure.

A Principal With Principles

For the past few years, we have worked on a grant project with 10 schools in the state of Ohio. One of the schools, Gahanna-Lincoln High School, located on the northeast side of Columbus, had been working hard on using the character-based intervention program that was funded by the grant to make positive change in the school. As evaluators of the project, we annually provided the schools updates on their progress related to the seven dimensions we measure with the Multi-Dimensional Assessment (MDA). In the first two years of the grant, although they had put a respectable number of initiatives in place, Gahanna-Lincoln High School had not seen much progress on the seven dimensions. But they had devoted the first year solely to developing the ideas to put into place; as a result, the implementation efforts of the intervention began in the second year of the grant, and had only been in place a year. You could tell from the leadership team's faces at the first few annual meetings they were a little cautious about taking our data too seriously; they were just getting started. But at the end of Year Two of the grant, a change took place that they were not expecting. The principal was promoted to assistant superintendent, and the assistant principal, Dwight Carter, was promoted to principal.

Normally, when principal turnover happens and you lose a good principal, it is discouraging, but this was not the case with Principal Carter. You could tell he cared and was a dedicated and determined educator. He had served as a teacher for eight years, and had been an assistant principal in a middle school for three years before serving as assistant principal at Gahanna-Lincoln High for three additional years. He was now taking over the controls of the school, and he showed great promise. If you ever get a chance to meet Dwight, you will find that he is a very nice gentleman who has great relationships with stakeholders. He is also a principal who never stops looking for ways to improve. His office bookshelves are filled with the latest texts on leadership, and he is an avid reader of authors such as Daniel Pink. He spends his lunch hour studying his school's data, and in his top left desk drawer sits his file of annual MDA reports. He is what he refers to as "data-aware."

During the principal transition, Gahanna-Lincoln's select team of educators working on the grant intervention did not miss a beat. They were very dedicated to the project, and they never let the reports scare them away from trying to improve. It is a large school with a diverse student population. They had, and still have, their challenges. But they wanted to improve their School Climate and achievement, and they believed that a focus on getting the community more involved and building character could help. In Year Three of the grant, they doubled their efforts. They held numerous events and put extra effort into creating a more caring culture.

But at the end of Year Three, we met with them again to share our report. Once again, there was no improvement. The leadership team's look of caution had turned to confusion and cognitive dissonance. We remember that day seeing Principal Carter and a colleague sitting in the room during a break looking at the reports, dumbfounded, and wondering how the MDA scores could not have increased. We had also collected some qualitative data related to the intervention that produced comments from the school's whole faculty; these comments reflected a group that had not all bought into the change process or intervention. Though the leadership had tried, the full faculty was still not on board. They had some laggards. They were having challenges getting more parents involved. Did they give up and say, "Forget this thing called *character*"? Of course not. They tried harder. By the end of Year Four of the grant they experienced a significant improvement in School Climate, and a 50% reduction in behavior incidents and suspensions.

When we were writing this book, we went back to visit Principal Carter again to ask him what he thought of the multi-dimensional data in retrospect. On the negative side, he said that receiving the data and seeing that his school had not made the gains expected, deflated him. It also made him want to take a triage, step-by-step approach and focus on improving the more challenged parts of the school that the reports illuminated. But during our visit, we also discovered that some of Principal Carter's staff and faculty questioned whether there was not a mistake in the analysis of the reports. Some also wanted to blame it on a few chaotic events that happened the day the surveys were administered in the third year of the grant. Some of his faculty felt the reports did not reflect the reality of what was taking place in the school. Regardless, as Principal Carter stated, "Although the survey might only provide a snapshot of the school, it doesn't matter; it is still a perception that day of the organization."

When we asked him how the MDA reports helped, he explained that the reports showed where they were, what they were doing well, and what they needed to improve. With a smile, he also stated that the Leadership Potential data produced some good news. But he also said the reports showed that many students in the school felt isolated and many of them did not have friends. The reports also showed that he had not yet gotten his whole staff and faculty on board. The evidence suggested that there was a group of educators who did not want to change or put effort into developing a new system. Interestingly enough, he shared the data reports primarily with his leadership team and had not shared them with all of his staff and faculty. He also had not yet shared them with the students or parents.

Fullan's six steps are clearly at work here at Gahanna-Lincoln High School. They have great ideas and they are still diligently working, after 3 years of implementation, to find collective meaning and commitment to new ways of teaching and reaching their students. And Gahanna-Lincoln High should be proud of this effort. Of the schools receiving this grant, they were one of the hardest-working schools. Their implementation dip (for whatever reasons—possibly principal turnover), however, has continued for longer than expected. And although they had not fully confronted or included the naysayers, reculturing is making progress. What is possibly still missing from their efforts is getting beyond structural and superficial change, and finding change that all value and can accomplish. What is missing is the acceptance and use of a broader set of data and a systemic approach to improvement inclusive of all stakeholders. Principal Carter is a principal with principles, and he works hard every day on reculturing.

This example shows that change is not easy, and sometimes we do not reach our goals. Even with a great principal and a large number of dedicated and amazing faculty on the same page, in order for meaningful and effective change to take hold a completely new system that allows for data-driven innovation to be implemented freely is needed.

From Systems to Success

There are schools and school districts that are successfully using robust and informative data to drive multi-dimensional decision making. But *every* school and district needs comprehensive and meaningful data to guide their decision making. We cannot continue providing data to educators that will not assist them in understanding the various dimensions that impact all aspects of school achievement. In order to move to a system of continuous improvement in your efforts as educators, you must assess all stakeholder groups on a minimum of seven dimensions and connect this data to achievement in order to gain a robust picture of the attitudes and beliefs that guide all stakeholders and impact performance. Consider how rich this type of data or data system could be if it was put into practice. Assuming that you are gathering comprehensive data, you would know how all of your stakeholders think and feel about the leadership of the school, the school climate, the educational attitudes, and the other dimensions. With this type of data, you would then have the evidence and information that could focus and guide your efforts to enhance the educational experience of all within the school. Furthermore, the gathering, understanding, and application of this robust data would present a complete picture indicative of your efforts as educators—not just the test scores, but all you do to educate the entire student and support educators.

This moves data and statistics from the reporting status to the *informative* status that all educational stakeholders deserve. This moves data from accountability to applicability. For most educators, if they have valid and reliable evidence that reveals their successes as well as the potential concerns of their stakeholders, they are willing to not only accept the data but also to work hard to turn the concerns into strengths. What educators need from data and statistics are meaningful insights that will enable them to improve their efforts.

This is the approach Johncarlos Miller (the successful principal we discussed in Chapter 1) took with his middle school in Guilford

County, North Carolina. Johncarlos understood that he could not improve the assessed outcomes and other indicators of academic, artistic, and athletic excellence at Northeast Middle School unless all stakeholders in the school were focused, not just on the curriculum, but on the other dimensions as well. This did not mean that they did not practice educational rigor, academic support, and instructional creativity within their lessons. This did not mean that they abandoned the promising curricula that their district expected to be fully implemented. They continued the implementation process, but they also addressed all the other dimensions that would impact on their academics. This is what schools do when they truly want to achieve excellence and are willing to look at all the variables that influence the achievement of their students. Principal Miller and his staff worked hard to strengthen the climate of the school. They valued the development of the character of their students as well as themselves as educational role models. They worked hard to include members of the community in their school and to recognize the efforts of community members in assisting students outside of the traditional school day. The entire faculty took a systems approach; the result was double-digit academic gains over each of the last two years (2008–2010), reduction in office referrals and suspensions (reduction of 60% over three years), happier teachers and community members, and the development of a school climate that you would want to place your children in. They did this with nearly 60% of their students receiving free lunches and a reduction in the teaching staff due to budget cuts. This school, working with and within their community, is giving students the opportunity to achieve a bright future.

The same can be seen in the Chicago study (Chapter 7). Schools that did not emphasize academic rigor (push) or social support, both within and outside of the school, struggled in helping students achieve their academic goals. Schools that strongly emphasized academic rigor were successful in helping their students achieve more than one year's expected growth as measured on the Iowa Test of Basic Skills. But schools that emphasized academic rigor combined with social support, both inside and outside of the school, had far greater gains in academic achievement than those that emphasized academic rigor alone. In other words, a systems approach that involved academics plus social support, including social-emotional learning, made the greatest difference in the academic achievement of students. Besides research sense, this outcome makes common sense. If people feel supported and are in positive relationships with others, they are more likely to strive to achieve, not just for themselves, but also for those who support them. But common sense, as we have previously noted, is not that *common* anymore.

It seems to us, both as educators and as parents, that we should pursue a more complete view of the education of the child. We are not afraid of academic excellence. Indeed we have, for the most part, spent our lives either within or connected to public schools or universities. We value and emphasize academic excellence in all of our school- and university-age children, who range in age from 8 to 22. But we know that a single-minded focus on schooling that concentrates only on the curriculum is simply inadequate to raising the children that our families, community, and, indeed, our nation want and need. We must seek to educate the entire child; this will involve all stakeholders in the school and community working together to ensure that our children are smart and also good. It will require of schools a team-based multi-dimensional approach that will have excellence in academics as a *partial* outcome.

A Path, a Trip, a Journey

In schools, we run at a breakneck pace. We operate on an abbreviated calendar, and yet are asked to make amazing strides in a very limited time. Those who have been in the profession long enough can affirm that we have years that seem to go by quickly and we have years that seem to drag on forever. We have colleagues who make us love coming to work every day, and we have coworkers who cause us to age and make us want to stay in bed! As teachers, we experience the same thing: We have classes of students that we would like to teach another year and classes of students we wish we could replace by October. These realities, together with changing policies (be they from the district, the state, or the new federal mandates), shrinking budgets, fear of layoffs, and underfunded pension plans, are factors often outside of our control. The real challenge, then, is to put a system in place that we know provides the greatest potential for improvement. We need a system that takes into account areas of the school we can control and can demonstrate effectiveness with both the good and the difficult groups of faculty and students that make up our organization.

There is no perfect system, and there is no perfected system that will yield consistent results in education. Yet there are ways to think, plan, and act that can provide us greater insight into how to be effective. Our path will become apparent in that moment in time when we come to the realization that what we have been doing is not working or that a different path might lead to a more hopeful future. From a systems perspective, we know that the idea of *equifinality* suggests that there are many paths that can be taken to achieving similar results. The new path requires a cognitive shift from our current way of thinking. A new path asks us to pause and reconsider the old paradigm or way of thinking and to consider the potential of taking a new direction and getting others to go down this new path with us. Picking a new path means we are going to have to look through a new lens at the path we have walked before and possibly take some of what we once did on that path, but also consider what new things we will need to do in order to have a better journey down the new path.

A journey will require planning if we really want to get to our desired destination. In the Jim Carey movie *Yes Man,* there is an interesting scene in which Jim and his girlfriend just show up at the airport. They approach the ticket counter and get a ticket for whatever destination the lady at the ticket counter offers them. They end up going to Lincoln, Nebraska. It is a very spur-of-the-moment trip, which for some of us might sound very appealing and possibly even romantic. This random approach, however, is not the kind of trip we can plan for our schools or students. We would be considered negligent, to a certain extent, if our planning for improvement was so capricious. Yet many still return from conference visits with canned programs that they purchased upon walking up to a random booth in the marketplace. The trip has to be planned, and you need to try to get everyone on board for the trip with a clear understanding of where you are going and how you are going to get there.

Last, remember that it is a journey, not just a trip. The systems approach covered in this text, and the detailed components such as dimensional thinking and data-driven thinking, must be part of a larger journey that will take time. Schools do not become bad overnight, and neither do they improve overnight. We have to realize that this journey will take time and energy. There will be a number of pitfalls and challenges, as well as times to celebrate. In the end, we desire a good journey that is full of really great stories we can pass on to others, a journey along which we build lifelong relationships that bring meaning to our work and a sense of unity. A journey that allows us to reflect back on why we went into education and reinforces and documents all we have accomplished. This is a journey we can take when we begin to consider the path of data-driven systemic change and the potential it has to bring about improvement—both increased achievement and so much more.

I Want to Ride My Bicycle

One of the authors is a huge bicycle racing fan. During July, he must get his daily dose of the Tour de France, which is the most famous and most valued Grand Tour bicycle race to win and, indeed, to participate in. It captivates the attention of Europe for three weeks and is gaining an increasing audience in the United States and Canada. During the Tour, teams of riders bicycle over 2,000 miles over 20 stages or days of racing through the diverse, beautiful country of France, with some days spent in neighboring countries. Winning the Tour de France is considered by many to be the greatest victory a bike racer can obtain. Interestingly, not every participant or team member is trying to win the Tour. There are riders on each team who have specialties.

For example, several riders are lead-out riders for the sprinters at the end of a daily race. Their job is to pace the sprinter and create a draft so he can save his energy for the last 300-meter sprint to the finish line. Other riders on the Tour are there to assist and pace members of the team who have a chance to win a mountain stage of the tour—especially ones in the high mountains. Their job is to "sacrifice." These riders are not there to win but to help others win. Other team members may be experts on individual time trials and will try to win these stages for themselves but also for the team. Finally, the top three finishing times on each team are combined to make up the team time score of the day. Everyone on the team works together to help the top individuals on the team win as well as to contribute to the team goals. This effort can result in a team member winning the Tour as well as a total team victory and a podium celebration for best team at the end of the race. A bike racing team is a system. Each rider has a job to do in order to assist one team-mate or the entire team to win the overall race or a specialty stage of the Tour. There is no way for an individual to win the stages or the overall race without a strong team that takes a systems approach.

Mark Cavendish is now recognized as one of the finest sprinters in the cycling world. He has won a total of 15 stages of the Tour de France over the last three years, all during sprints which are generally designed to give the best sprinters in the world an opportunity to race each other. He would not have won the first one without a strong team dedicated to working together to succeed. That success is measured by *his* victories. By considering all the strengths of the riders on his team, plans are developed with each person doing the lead-out to work Mark through the field and prepare for his solo sprinting for the last few hundred meters. Everyone has a role to play to ensure success and they, as a system, work to do just this. Yet when you think of the Tour de France or cycling, what name comes to your mind? For those who are not avid fans, most often it is not Mark Cavendish, but instead Lance Armstrong.

The same is true in other sports and throughout life. A great quarterback needs a solid offensive line as well as receivers with good hands. A great baseball or softball pitcher needs a solid defense working behind him or her. A great basketball scorer needs a point guard who is willing to give her the ball. A great surgeon needs a good team in which everyone understands and does their job, monitoring the many different variables that can affect the surgery to ensure a positive outcome for the patient. And this does not stop in the operating room. Nurses will monitor the patient and regularly report data. Physical, occupational, or respiratory therapists might also be involved in the patient's recovery. It all requires a systemic or a multi-dimensional approach, in which people are working together to achieve excellence and successful outcomes. This is truly what shared leadership means.

This systems approach is needed to assist all stakeholders in reaching their potential, and especially if we want students to obtain academic, social, emotional, ethical, artistic, vocational, and athletic excellence. It requires a system that takes into account all the stakeholders and the multiple dimensions that impact the total life of the school. But this system requires teamwork, shared leadership, and vision. Helping students reach all of their potential is a complicated endeavor that requires a comprehensive systems approach focusing on helping educators and parents (or guardians) improve as well.

Data-Driven Dimensional Thinking

So far, we have made a strong research-based case for the importance of better assessing at least seven dimensions in education. The dimensions offer a way to think differently about and focus on the educational process that is taking place in your organization. The dimensions take the many complexities we must deal with in education and provide a way to fit them into a manageable number of different categories and, more importantly, a way to talk about them in relationship to the strengths and concerns of your organization. Thinking dimensionally requires thinking holistically and not being attached to a single end-of-the-year test score or measure of Adequate Yearly Progress (AYP), which many feel is unfairly measured or unable to be changed. We hope that by now you really understand the absurdity of looking at one test result as a measure of success. Many of you may have already been at this point when you picked up this book; by now, we hope, we continue to sing to the choir. It really is time for a new way of thinking, a new lens, and a new common sense approach. It is time for a new tune.

Dimensional data-driven thinking in and of itself is not enough. We must also be committed to collecting the evidence that can inform us about where we are on the dimensions and also provide us feedback on how the change process is or is not improving the dimensions and how we think about them. As a data-driven educator, you must use and apply this evidence to inform your efforts and focus them on the 4Cs. There are no shortcuts when it comes to being data-driven. The consequence of not taking a data-driven approach is that data will drive you by default. The summative measures of test scores and AYP are going to be the measures on which schools and teachers are held accountable; unfortunately, this is unlikely to change in the near future. A decision not to take a data-driven approach and function more holistically is, by default, a decision to await the results of the summative measures of accountability and live with the consequences, whether they be positive gains or lower, flat scores. Either way, the reality is that in the absence of a data-driven approach we will have little understanding of how those gains or losses came to be. And so we are back to the choice of whether to be reactive or proactive. Will we choose to be informed, or will we choose to let someone else inform us of our failure or success?

The story at the beginning of this chapter about priority ranking the dimensions shows us that all of the dimensions are perceived as equally important by a wide array of educators and that, in many cases, it is difficult to rank one dimension more highly than another. The dimensions also allow for a way to organize much of the data we might already be collecting. As you begin to have a discussion about your dimensional buckets, your staff or Building Leadership Team will begin to realize which buckets you have paid more attention to than others. While it might be hard to prioritize the buckets, it becomes evident as you sort data that those buckets that are full of data have been made a priority, whether intentionally or not. The dimensional buckets also offer us a way to talk about our school and improvements it needs without focusing solely on the student achievement factor.

Turning Dimensional Thinking and the 4Cs Into a Systems Approach

Increased student achievement, better students and educators, better community relations, more satisfied and effective teachers, and a better learning climate are aspects of your schools that no one is going to try to stop you from trying to bring about. These and many other things are what education stakeholders want our schools to be about and what many want our students, parents, and educators to receive. The dimensions contain many areas to which time and attention could be directed; as mentioned before; some might read about the dimensions and decide to make only a few of the dimensions the focus of the system. Doing so really needs to be regarded with some caution. The value of collecting the data from a multi-dimensional perspective and emphasis is that all of the dimensions provide place-holders for data you need to collect from stakeholders. The dimensions also encompass a broad spectrum of ideas that you eventually want to feed into the structuring framework of the 4Cs.

We have worked with schools that just looked at a few dimensions and picked what they believed to be most important at that time: a triage approach. In most cases, it was not that they felt overwhelmed by the number of dimensions or didn't understand the connection between the dimensions and the 4Cs; they simply decided, either at the building or the district level, that they only wanted to work on a few areas that appeared to be problematic in their schools. This is reactive thinking, not proactive thinking. This is systematic, not systemic. Furthermore, if you don't look at all the dimensions, you lose the benefit of how the dimensions work together to drive and improve each other. In some of our most successful schools, it has been when the school works on Faculty Fidelity dimensions and teachers are feeling more support that we really begin to see improvements in School Climate and Educational Attitudes. Even when leadership teams are able to review the results of how parents, students, and educators view their leadership, it is then that we see data pushing leadership teams to change and adapt to those perceptions and giving them a clearer sense of what they need to do to impact the other six dimensions.

Yet, as effective as the dimensions are in making schools more successful, they only reflect part of the systemic nature and focus that is encompassed and complemented by the 4Cs. The 4Cs provide a language and nomenclature for discussion of school improvement with all stakeholders. They also provide a direction or compass for a targeted approach to improvement in the four key areas. The 4Cs can easily become part of a school's mission or vision statement. For example, at Thurston Middle School in Laguna Beach, California, the school stakeholders strive for academic excellence through the development of a supportive community, promoting good character in all stakeholders, a climate conducive for optimal learning, and a curriculum that allows for the development of lifelong learners.

Simply put, the 4Cs can become the operational focus for all we do in schools as we work toward improvement. The 4Cs are a unifying structure into which we plug in the key dimensions, components, or ideas that will help the organization. The 4Cs can help to provide the vision or the essential ideas you can get others to rally behind. It is hard to overestimate the importance of the 4Cs as a unifying idea for getting all involved and speaking a common language concerning reform and continuous improvement. With the 4Cs in place, you have a way to talk about what you are doing, an ability to work toward a common vision of improvement, a way to capture many voices that want to chime in on these areas, and most importantly, a way to bring about a sense of shared leadership with a common vision.

Vision, Voice, and Shared Leadership: From the School to the Classroom

Vision embodies many of the steps you must take in your process toward school improvement. The literature on developing a strong vision is prominent in the educational research and is often given a very high priority in the discussion of turning schools around (Newmann & Wehlage, 1995; Schmoker, 1996). When you consider vision, you also have to think about whether the school's vision is dynamic or static. A dynamic vision requires that you try to bring it to life. It is a vision you communicate and share with others. A dynamic vision is really a guiding principle that you try to get everyone in the organization to buy into and understand. It is something you want to happen. A static vision may go on a few posters throughout the school and may be discussed at faculty and parent meetings, but such a vision is seldom related to genuine change. In a school with a dynamic vision, we find a number of people who can articulate the vision of the school, and the vision has a voice.

The idea of voice is closely linked to vision, and voice is really the byproduct of a well-developed, articulated, and communicated vision. Continuous improvement and reform are really not possible without creating an environment where stakeholders feel they have a voice. A recent survey of 40,000 teachers by the National Education Association had the following summary of their findings:

> The results of this survey clearly point to the necessity for the voice of educators to be included in the national debate on education reform. School improvement cannot be imposed from on

high without input from educators, but instead must have the full support of classroom teachers. The results reiterate what our members tell us: teachers have sound ideas for school improvement, and they are eager to help students succeed. Without question, collaboration is the key to successful efforts to close achievement gaps and serve underperforming schools. (2010)

Voice can be developed; vision and shared leadership working together offer the strongest potential for stakeholders to come to believe that they have a voice. Voice is not something that just happens; it is generated through the intentional direction of leaders and leadership teams that include teachers and parents. Students also need a voice, and creating an opportunity for students to feel they have a voice is an equally important aspect of improvement. Research on student voice notes the importance of creating an environment where students feel like they are participants in the improvement process (Thomson & Holdsworth, 2003; Togneri & Anderson, 2003). These school settings allow for students to be heard; what is heard from students should get affirmed by changes that take place at the school site. Collective vision and voice amount to an approach toward shared leadership. School success is dependent to a large degree on the development of school goals and the creation of a shared vision (Joyce, Wolf, & Calhoun, 1993; Rosenholtz, 1991).

This takes us back to our discussion in previous chapters of synergy and entropy, two important concepts in thinking about systems. The sum of the parts working together (*synergy*) is normally more powerful than the individual parts operating separately; this is referred to as *nonsummativity*. Synergy has to be something that comes out of our vision, voice, and shared leadership. With vision and shared leadership in place, we have two parts that are able to connect the organization to the voices of all stakeholders. It is through these vehicles that we have the highest likelihood of minimizing *entropy*, which is a measure of energy that is expended in a system but does no useful work, and which tends to decrease the organizational order of the system.

We Change Only Enough So We Do Not Have to Change

Change is not easy. It never has been. We would imagine that most, including the authors, change only enough that we do not *really* have to change. In other words, we make first-order changes. We rearrange the classroom because we read a book about physical classroom configurations and learning. We go to a four-block schedule (teaching four courses per grading period with longer class time for each class) because we think it would be a good idea to offer more time in class per instructional period—yet we might not be considering the ability of faculty and students to maintain effective time on task or whether sound research strongly suggests that a four-block is any more effective than a traditional schedule. We make changes, but these changes address specific issues and may not reflect the concerns of the stakeholders about the dimensions that really affect total school improvement.

Having a substantial impact on the learning environment for all stakeholders requires comprehensive data as well as the desire to take that data seriously and to implement changes that will turn concerns into strengths. By taking a multi-dimensional approach to assessment and implementation, you can transform your schools and make second-order changes that move us out of our present comfort zone and into the total school improvement zone. We must stop treating the symptoms of our ailment with first-order changes and begin addressing the causes of the illness. We can often revive a person who is having a heart attack, but if we do not help that person understand the lifestyle changes they need to make in diet and exercise, the probability is great that he will find himself again under emergency medical care. We need to be more proactive and preventative in our approaches; collecting the vital signs is crucial to taking a more comprehensive approach. To provide long term health for the patient requires meaningful second-order change.

Educational leaders do have choices to consider; these choices are as much ethical as they are professional. Will we continue our limited first-order change rituals focused on raising test scores or addressing another particular school concern, or will we seek to implement a multi-dimensional approach to education involving all stakeholders that holds greater potential for higher academic achievement and total school reform? Most cannot achieve their goals or raise the citizens they desire if they continue looking at school through a single lens that focuses mainly on test scores. Our research and work with schools indicates that if you focus on all the dimensions that create a good climate and environment for all stakeholders then you will more efficiently achieve your academic goals as well as many other goals that are valued by educators, parents, and community members.

The real question is whether we choose to do so. In our work with schools and school districts around the country, we have concluded that some schools and leaders will and some will not. Our approach is not for everyone. It demands true data-driven shared leadership in rethinking the life of the school and the role that education plays in the life of the child as well as other stakeholders in the school and community. It will require ruffling the feathers of many stakeholders. It is far easier to focus on test scores and take credit or make excuses for the school's success or failure as documented by the scores. If we choose to live and die by test scores, then we will continue lessening the role that schools should play in the lives of students; moreover, we will continue flattening our lives as educators and neglecting our calling as educators. Once again, this does not mean that we as authors deny the importance of academic achievement or academic excellence. We truly value this and feel it is of critical importance for the school. But it is not enough and will not result in a complete education for our students. A multi-dimensional approach, however, offers a new lens to seeing how you can enable a child to achieve all that he can achieve, both in the classroom and in the artistic, athletic, vocational, social-emotional, and ethical components of the school—and ideally in the community as well. In other words, a multi-dimensional approach is the education of the complete child and will bring about greater academic achievement and many other desired outcomes. It is the complete education experience all stakeholders deserve.

So what do you choose to do? Do you choose to ignore decades of research on effective schools that seek to educate the whole child? Do you choose to continue down the path that, for the most part, we have been walking for the last 15 years, in which a single score indicates the success or failure of your school or classrooms? Or do you choose to draw a line in the sand and take a stand: that you will be a data-driven school that makes use of multiple dimensions to make a difference in the lives and achievements of your students, parents, and educators? This will not be an easy choice to make. There is a great deal of pressure to flatten education to a single test score. Doing so is easier, but it is not better. Either intellectually or within your heart you know that a good education is not flat. It should be inflating and uplifting. It should reflect the education that you would desire for your own child.

Over the last nine chapters, we have presented an argument that there are seven dimensions that empower the 4Cs of Climate, Character, Curriculum, and Community. Neither the dimensions nor the 4Cs stand alone. They intertwine with and among each other—each influencing and being influenced by the others. This results in a dynamic and constantly changing environment and requires constant focus on the 4Cs as well as an awareness of how the dimensions influence the 4Cs. It is far easier to focus on just the curriculum and its expected outcomes than to engage in other considerations. But true leadership is not about doing what is easy; it is about doing what is right.

Next Steps

1. Reflect on your experiences with change initiatives in education. What were some of the conditions of successful change, and what were some of the conditions of unsuccessful change?

2. Think about your current organization. Do you operate under an intentional system that is really planning for the fulfillment of the purpose, mission, and vision of the organization?

3. Reflect on your organization as it relates to vision. Does your organization have shared leadership? Is there a sense of voice within the organization?

4. As a leader, write a letter to the faculty that argues for more robust collection, interpretation, and evaluation of data within your school. Consider posting it on the Internet for feedback from all stakeholders.

5. Require that all future staff development opportunities be tied to improving the concerns revealed by your data. If a provider cannot adjust her presentation to your data, then you should consider another provider.

6. As an educational leader, distinguish between the data that is merely informative and the data that could be used as instructional or might be valuable for facilitating change in your school. Next, have the faculty go through the same process. This can be done by listing and describing the seven dimensions that impact on achievement in your school. What data would they value collecting that might be placed within the dimensional model to enhance your school improvement efforts?

10

Rising Above the Standards

As we were finishing this book, we were encouraged to address the new movement regarding the common core state standards, a fast-moving reform effort taking place across the nation.

The National Governors Association (NGA), along with their partners the National Governors Association Center for Best Practices (NGA Center) and the Council of Chief State School Officers (CCSSO), has coordinated the states-led Common Core State Standards Initiative (CCSSI; http://www.corestandards.org). Yes, these are new acronyms that we should probably get used to seeing. The goal of the new common standards is to provide a clear and consistent framework across states. The standards were developed with the input of teachers, school administrators, and curriculum experts. In addition, the development of the standards included representatives from higher education, civil rights, English language learners, and students with disabilities. In the initial rounds of public feedback, there were more than 10,000 comments made about the CCSSI. Important noteworthy partners in this effort were Achieve Inc., The College Board, and ACT. The CCSSI website also notes over 50 other organizations that have endorsed the adoption of the CCSSI. The standards were supposedly developed by taking into consideration the most effective standards-based models from states across the United States and from other countries. The CCSSI was developed to provide an international set of standards that could be benchmarked regardless of where or in which state a student attends school.

The CCSSI is actually a nonprofit organization developed to provide resources and encourage all states to adopt the standards. According to its website (retrieved April 21, 2011):

> These standards define the knowledge and skills students should have within their K–12 education careers so that they will graduate high school able to succeed in entry-level, credit-bearing academic college courses and in workforce training programs. The standards
>
> - are aligned with college and work expectations;
> - are clear, understandable and consistent;
> - include rigorous content and application of knowledge through high-order skills;
> - build upon strengths and lessons of current state standards;
> - are informed by other top performing countries, so that all students are prepared to succeed in our global economy and society; and
> - are evidence-based.

Forty-eight states, two territories, and the District of Columbia signed memorandums of agreement with the NGA and CCSSO in 2009, committing to the state-led process of the CCSSI. A cursory review of the CCSSI website reveals that eight states and four territories have yet to officially adopt the CCSSI. The Common Core Standards for English Language Arts and Mathematics were released on June 2, 2010.

The impetus for the CCSSI is embedded in two main arguments:

1. The CCSSI will unify the existing state standards and provide clear comparability across states and internationally.

2. The CCSSI will help reform education and increase students' ability to compete internationally and therefore will improve the economic viability of the United States.

At present, given the existing individual state standards, comparability across states is very difficult, and even more problematic, every state has a different definition of what it means to be proficient under No Child Left Behind (NCLB). NCLB required states to adopt standards, develop assessments, and then determine cut points (basically scores) that define proficiency for adequate yearly progress (AYP). These requirements have caused many states to focus on basic content rather than on rigorous content (Harris & Herington, 2006). Add to this the fact that every state has its own set of standards, and you have a system wherein some states show great success on basic standards and other states show little or limited success on college entrance standards (Gandal & Vranek, 2001). In addition, the goal of 100% proficiency by 2014 has made NCLB an unobtainable goal and ineffective policy. The resulting system is one in which we have punished some states for adopting high standards (that have not been fully met) and rewarded other states for adopting low standards (that are easier to achieve). Add to this lack of comparability across states the difficulty of comparing these scores to international tests like Trends in International Mathematics and Science Study (TIMMS), or even the National Assessment of Educational Progress (NAEP), and what results is a real disparity wherein a state might be highly proficient on state tests but score in the lower 20th percentile on TIMMS or NAEP. A set of common core standards could certainly go a long way in aligning all states and creating a set of consistent standards, which could then be aligned to international benchmarks or at least to the NAEP.

Concerns about America's ability to compete internationally are certainly not new. As we discussed in Chapter 1, *A Nation at Risk* addressed this issue nearly 30 years ago (National Commission on Excellence in Education, 1983); yet, it continues to be at the forefront of education reform today. The fear iterated in *A Nation at Risk* was that, without a serious reform of our educational system, we would eventually be "overtaken by competitors throughout the world" (p. 1). This continues to be a major concern facing our educational system in America and is certainly an important one that needs to be addressed from the perspective of those both in K–12 and in higher education. Our economic viability as a nation is only as strong as the educational system we have in place to prepare our students for future success in the 21st century. On the website for the CCSSI, Jim Goodnight, the CEO of SAS (a powerful business analytics software and services company), gives a compelling argument for why a set of common core state standards should align our educational systems and provide us with a great platform for preparing students for the current and future workforce both within America and internationally. Goodnight states that the inconsistencies across states make it difficult to grasp how well the K–12 education is preparing students.

He further argues that without a set of consistently high standards across states we truly have no way to bring consistent quality to the public school system in America. The result is that students will continue to enter college unprepared and that college will continue to be a place of remediation toward degree attainment rather than a place to prepare students for the workforce. Goodnight's main concern is in the area of mathematics and science where we are losing ground to other countries. These same sentiments are being echoed by many of the other advocates for the CCSSI.

Adopting the Rhetoric or Accepting the Reality

If one takes the time to listen to the 15 plus videos on the CCSSI website providing support for the new common standards, one will quickly recognize the number of governors and high-level business executives speaking to the importance of the initiative for (1) our country's economic viability and (2) bringing consistency across states for academic standards. These are two very good arguments for adoption, and it does not make sense to be against high standards or against wanting our country to compete internationally at a high level. The main CCSSI arguments and what is being proposed as being the eventual impact of the CCSSI are very important to almost anyone reading this book and to most Americans. Also, with hindsight being 20/20, many of the developers who crafted NCLB might readily admit today that a CCSSI approach might have created a much more effective and generalizable approach to standards adoption across states than the model used for NCLB. The CCSSI is clearly an evolution of the policies in NCLB and, given the widespread adoption across states and strong political and corporate support, is likely to become a major component in the reauthorization of the Elementary and Secondary Education Act (ESEA), which will serve as the future overhaul of NCLB.

What is missing from the conversation about CCSSI, however, is how this initiative might serve as a meaningful reform to the American educational system. Also missing from this conversation is empirical evidence that supports the future promises made by the proponents of the CCSSI. The intent of NCLB, in principle, was really no different than the intent behind the CCSSI. NCLB pointed to the need for higher standards across states and purported that these higher standards would in some way lead to the production of students better able to compete in the global economy and would therefore increase the economic position of the United States. Here we are, more than a decade later, and if you believe what the proponents of CCSSI are saying, we appear to have made no real progress toward accomplishing those goals. Is this true? Are we really no better off than we were a decade ago or even almost 30 years ago when *A Nation at Risk* reported on the dire condition of our educational system? Whether or not we are better off is not necessarily a vital question, no matter which camp you choose to reside in. But examining whether or not standards-based learning has worked is not even being discussed in the current argument for the CCSSI as the impetus to get our educational system to where it needs to be. To us, meaningful reform in our schools relies upon so much more than adopting a new set of common core standards and goes back to many of the arguments we have made in this book regarding the problems inherent in maintaining a singular focus on student achievement and, specifically, on test scores.

Yet the adoption and future mandate of the CCSSI is likely to follow the same path as NCLB, wherein testing and accountability are aligned. At present, the CCSSI is touted as a voluntary adoption program, but there are certainly benefits for states that adopt it. For example, in applying for Race to the Top funding, states were given points for agreeing to adopt the common state standards. In addition, programs like Improving Teacher Quality are requiring applicants to address in their professional development offerings how the CCSSI will be implemented. For many states in dire need of operating funds and funds for professional development, there is really no choice but to adopt the CCSSI and thus give the state the best platform from which to compete for funding. While the adoption of CCSSI may be offered as voluntary, in reality for many states it is a very poor financial decision not to adopt it. Educational policy history would also suggest that future policy language in the CCSSI will no longer allow for voluntary participation but instead, similar to ESEA, will require mandated participation. Most likely to follow in the near future will be new tests and accountability metrics meant to hold schools accountable, thus once again rewarding some and punishing others. Accountability is certainly necessary, but what we have learned from NCLB is that accountability alone and testing in and of itself are not sufficient means for improving education.

The CCSSI in its current form or even in a different (mandated) form will continue to focus the education arena on test scores as the sole indicator of school success nationally and internationally. This in our opinion is once again a short-sighted proposition that, like NCLB, is unlikely to improve the conditions within education that indirectly relate but can greatly contribute to improved test scores. The CCSSI provides little conversation around how these new standards are going to improve the quality of teaching. Standards in and of themselves really have little bearing on how well a teacher can teach. The standards will assist in focusing the teacher on a certain area of core competencies, but they do not provide for better instruction, professional development, or even improvement of teacher training. Furthermore, the challenges of education in the areas of student discipline, teacher turnover, high school dropouts, and unsafe learning environments are not likely to be greatly affected by the effort of the CCSSI. It would appear that we are deciding to throw a slightly different blanket over many of the same issues without taking the time to thoughtfully inspect our educational system and to look at other factors that cause us to be unsuccessful. The perceived brokenness of our existing system, as the last decade has shown, is not likely to be fixed by a set of new standards. The real question is, will the CCSSI move us toward another decade of little to no improvement?

Educational reform is only as effective as the level of implementation at the school site level. What we have discussed in this book are strategies and ways to improve the learning conditions for students and instruction, while also attending to the needs of teachers and the community at large. Whether we adopt the common core state standards or not, the importance of improving the seven dimensions and the 4Cs will not change, and in fact the success of CCSSI will still be largely dependent at the local level on how we address the seven dimensions and the 4Cs. For many of us who have been in education for a long time, the CCSSI looks like the next pendulum swing taking us from state accountability to international accountability and state comparability. So what is your intuition telling you right now? Is it saying that the CCSSI will be a widespread reform able to bring us to a better place of economic dominance, higher student achievement, safer schools, more involved parents, and better schools where students actually want to go and learn? Or are you skeptical and think that this might be just another reform in a long line of reforms that have perpetuated a system toward mediocrity or worse?

Hopefully, your intuition is telling you both to hope in what the CCSSI can produce of a positive nature and to be skeptical of what it might produce of a not-so-positive nature. As you might have gathered, we believe you should ideally direct your attention to what needs to be done locally in your schools via reforms that are going to meaningfully improve the learning conditions for students and the teaching craft in your building. Improvement in learning conditions and multiple dimensions such as school climate and faculty fidelity can be accomplished regardless of the standards we are asked to adopt or mandated to implement. The CCSSI lacks empirical evidence and logic to truly support its effort, that is, a focus on the multidimensional challenges that simultaneously need to improve in order to reform our schools. The CCSSI remains an initiative focused only on the student achievement aspect of our educational system, which is short-sighted, to say the least, and lacks the ability to really improve the conditions we know are related to student achievement and successful schools in the long run.

A Final Reality Check

While putting together this last short chapter to address the CCSSI, we came across some very interesting information in the great number of videos we watched and the wide spectrum of opinion pieces we read. In closing this issue, we urge you to keep your eye on the ball. To us, the ball is not the standards we are asked to meet or the test we are asked to take but, instead, the improvement of instruction and making our schools better learning environments.

With the adoption of CCSSI, there will eventually come a new testing and accountability system. Achieve Inc. (just one of the highly invested corporate partners in this initiative) has indicated on their website a desire to provide international benchmarks for the CCSSI that would allow for international comparisons. At the present time, there are no tests within the states that we could truly say align to these new common core standards, and to do this work correctly, there will need to be such an alignment. This will cost . . . well, we are not sure what it will cost, but if it is anything similar to the cost of developing tests for NCLB, it will most likely equate to hundreds of millions of dollars. In California alone the price tag for state testing from 2007 to 2009 was $170 million (Helfand, 2005). Our country's current economic condition and the even more dire economic straits facing states and local educational agencies appear to be great roadblocks for the CCSSI.

In states such as California, there is a debate over whether the common core standards are actually lower standards than the current California standards (Stotsky & Wurman, 2010). Furthermore, since we are unlikely to have a test aligned to the CCSSI in the near future, we might continue to use the state tests, which really provide little evidence on how children are doing on the CCSSI. It's as if we are putting the horse before the cart. Yet millions of dollars have been invested into the CCSSI by corporations and nonprofit entities (that produce annual revenues in the billions). It should worry more than a few of us that the corporations and nonprofit entities funding this effort are the same corporations and entities that will profit from this initiative.

In conclusion, it makes common sense to us, even good sense, that, if we are to adopt new standards for states that are more comparable across states and international competitors, we first develop standards that do not require some states to lower their standards. We might also design tests that more accurately allow us to longitudinally track the test scores of students throughout their academic life. And once we have acceptable state standards and tests that help us gather more than cross-sectional scores that compare last year's students to this year's students, we could then move forward in adopting a more beneficial standards-based testing policy. Perhaps we could even take seriously assessing how all stakeholders feel about the dimensions that truly impact the teaching and learning environment of all within the school. Until that time comes, or in the unfortunate event that we just develop a similar NCLB design that now has common standards, we hope that smart and caring educators will rise above the standards and focus on the multi-dimensional nature of education.

Appendix

The MDed Assessment (MDA—Abbreviated Version)

Scales by Dimension

(Note: [R] means to recode as follows:
5 = 1, 4 = 2, 3 = 3, 2 = 4, and 1 = 5)

Dimension 1: Community Engagement

Parent Involvement Scale

1————————————————————————————5

(1) strongly   (2) disagree   (3) undecided   (4) agree   (5) strongly
disagree   agree

_____ 1. My parents or legal guardian is active at my school.

_____ 2. My parents or legal guardian often help me with my school work.

_____ 3. My parents or legal guardian take an interest in my school work.

_____ 4. My parents or legal guardian attend school activities regularly (examples: parent/teacher conferences, sporting events).

_____ 5. My parents or legal guardian are not active in my neighborhood or community. [R]

_____ 6. My parents or legal guardian often volunteer or do things for others in my neighborhood or community.

_____ 7. My parents or legal guardian are concerned about the well-being of my neighborhood or community.

Service to Community Scale

1————————————————————————————————————5

(1) strongly   (2) disagree   (3) undecided   (4) agree   (5) strongly
disagree   agree

_____ 1. I often volunteer or help others outside of school.

_____ 2. I rarely ever take part in activities that help others in my neighborhood or community. [R]

_____ 3. Students at this school often take part in community activities.

_____ 4. Helping others in the community is not important to students in this school. [R]

_____ 5. Students at this school are expected to donate time to helping others in the community.

NOTE: A user-friendly printable version is available at www.mdedinc. com.

Dimension 2: Curriculum Expectations

1————————————————————————————————5

(1) strongly   (2) disagree   (3) undecided   (4) agree   (5) strongly
    disagree   agree

Educational Rigor Scale

_____ 1. My teachers help me to understand what is expected in the class.

_____ 2. The teachers in my school expect me to do the best I can on my assignments.

_____ 3. The teachers in my school set clear learning goals for the classroom and expect us to accomplish them.

_____ 4. The teachers in my school provide me with assignments that are challenging.

_____ 5. The teachers in my school expect my work to be of high quality.

Instructional Creativity Scale

_____ 1. In most of my classrooms we do group work.

_____ 2. The teachers in my school challenge me to try new approaches to learning class content.

_____ 3. The teachers in my school allow for different points of view from students when teaching us new concepts.

_____ 4. The teachers in school do most of the talking, while students are expected to just listen. [R]

_____ 5. The teachers in my school use technology in the classroom.

_____ 6. The teachers in my school make an extra effort to make the subject matter interesting.

_____ 7. The teachers in my school try to get the students involved in the learning of new ideas.

NOTE: A user-friendly printable version is available at www.mdedinc.com.

Dimension 3: Developmental Perspectives

School Misconduct Scale

Please indicate which statement applies to you by marking: (1) never, (2) once or twice, (3) 3 to 5 times, (4) 6 to 9 times, or (5) 10 or more times. Work quickly and record your first impression.

1	2	3	4	5
never	once or twice	3 to 5 times	6 to 9 times	10 or more times

During the past year . . .

____ 1. How often have you broken school rules?

____ 2. How often have you cheated on an assignment or test?

____ 3. How often have you not obeyed your teachers?

____ 4. How often have you skipped school without permission?

Student Success Traits Scale

Using the following scale, please place the number that best describes your relationship to each of the words listed below.

1	2	3	4	5
I do not know what this is.	I know what this is, but I do not think about it often.	I know what this is, I think about it often, and I practice it occasionally.	I know what this is, I think about it often, and I practice it often.	I know what this is, I think about it often, and I practice it consistently.

____ 1. Honesty

____ 2. Self-discipline

____ 3. Responsibility

____ 4. Respect (for others)

____ 5. Self-respect

____ 6. Trust

____ 7. Care (for others)

____ 8. Fair

NOTE: A user-friendly printable version is available at www.mdedinc.com.

Dimension 4: Educational Attitudes

Motivation to Learn Scale

1————————————————————————5

(1) strongly   (2) disagree   (3) undecided   (4) agree   (5) strongly
    disagree   agree

_____ 1. I am motivated to do my schoolwork.

_____ 2. I am not interested in my schoolwork. [R]

_____ 3. I put in the time needed to complete my schoolwork.

_____ 4. I am often excited to complete my schoolwork.

_____ 5. I do not look forward to doing my schoolwork. [R]

Feelings for School Scale

1————————————————————————5

(1) strongly   (2) disagree   (3) undecided   (4) agree   (5) strongly
    disagree   agree

_____ 1. I participate actively in class.

_____ 2. My schoolwork is turned in on time.

_____ 3. If I do not understand something, I ask the teacher for help.

_____ 4. I pay attention in class.

_____ 5. I take the time to study outside of class.

_____ 6. If I miss class, I ask the teacher what I missed.

_____ 7. My grades are important to me.

NOTE: A user-friendly printable version is available at www.mdedinc.com.

Dimension 5: Faculty Fidelity

Teacher Trust Scale

Please indicate in the space provided the degree to which each statement applies to you by marking whether you (1) strongly disagree, (2) disagree, (3) are undecided, (4) agree, or (5) strongly agree with each statement. There are no right or wrong answers. Work quickly and record your first impression.

1————————————————————————————5

(1) strongly   (2) disagree   (3) undecided   (4) agree   (5) strongly
    disagree   agree

_____ 1. Teachers in my school often discipline students without knowing the whole story. [R]

_____ 2. The teachers in my school help me to feel safe and at ease.

_____ 3. The teachers in my school always treat me with fairness.

_____ 4. I trust the teachers in my school.

_____ 5. The teachers in my school keep their word.

_____ 6. The teachers in my school care about the students.

_____ 7. The teachers in my school are honest.

Teacher Satisfaction Scale

As you read each of the following statements, please indicate your level of agreement by marking your response in the space provided.

1————————————————————————————5

(1) strongly   (2) disagree   (3) undecided   (4) agree   (5) strongly
    disagree   agree

_____ 1. The teachers at my school are not respected for the work they do. [R]

_____ 2. The teachers at my school seem committed to their work.

_____ 3. The teachers at my school appear to get along well with each other.

_____ 4. The teachers at my school are generally positive and happy at school.

_____ 5. The teachers at my school express boredom with their work. [R]

_____ 6. The teachers at my school take pride in their teaching.

NOTE: A user-friendly printable version is available at www.mdedinc.com.

Dimension 6: Leadership Potential

Principal Trust Scale

Please indicate in the space provided the degree to which each statement applies to you by marking whether you (1) strongly disagree, (2) disagree, (3) are undecided, (4) agree, or (5) strongly agree with each statement. There are no right or wrong answers. Work quickly and record your first impression.

1————————————————————————————————5

(1) strongly   (2) disagree   (3) undecided   (4) agree   (5) strongly
     disagree   agree

_____ 1. The principal in my school often disciplines students without knowing the whole story. [R]

_____ 2. The principal in my school helps me to feel safe and at ease.

_____ 3. The principal in my school always treats me with fairness.

_____ 4. I trust the principal in my school.

_____ 5. The principal in my school keeps his or her word.

_____ 6. The principal in my school cares about the students.

_____ 7. The principal in my school is honest.

Leadership Satisfaction Scale

As you answer the following questions please understand that *administration* means principals, vice principals, assistant principals, and counselors.

1————————————————————————————————5

(1) strongly   (2) disagree   (3) undecided   (4) agree   (5) strongly
     disagree   agree

_____ 1. The principal in my school is a great example of a good leader.

_____ 2. The administration directs us toward being a great school.

_____ 3. The administration is available when needed.

_____ 4. The administration helps teachers and students carry out their roles.

_____ 5. The administration participates actively in important school activities.

_____ 6. The administration is interested in helping students succeed.

_____ 7. The administration recognizes publicly teachers who do an outstanding job.

_____ 8. The administration supports me.

NOTE: A user-friendly printable version is available at www.mdedinc.com.

Dimension 7: School Climate

MDed School Climate Scale

1————————————————————————————5

(1) strongly   (2) disagree   (3) undecided   (4) agree   (5) strongly
    disagree   agree

_____ 1. This school is a safe place to be.

_____ 2. There is mutual respect between teachers and students.

_____ 3. This school is free from bullying and harassment.

_____ 4. In this school, there is respect for the property of others.

_____ 5. In this school, classes are orderly and free of disruptions.

_____ 6. In this school, guidelines for positive student behavior are clear.

_____ 7. In this school, students are expected to follow the rules.

_____ 8. The cafeteria is a safe and pleasant place to eat.

_____ 9. You won't find vandalism at this school.

School Isolation Scale

Please indicate in the space provided the degree to which each statement applies to you by marking whether you (1) strongly disagree, (2) disagree, (3) are undecided, (4) agree, or (5) strongly agree with each statement. There are no right or wrong answers. Work quickly and record your first impression.

1————————————————————————————5

(1) strongly   (2) disagree   (3) undecided   (4) agree   (5) strongly
    disagree   agree

_____ 1. At this school, I have a good number of friends. [R]

_____ 2. I do not have a lot of friends to hang out with at this school.

_____ 3. I do not feel that anyone knows who I am at this school.

_____ 4. Other students at this school do not like me.

_____ 5. I have very few people to talk to at this school.

NOTE: A user-friendly printable version is available at www.mdedinc.com.

MDed 4Cs Walk-Through Rubric

CURRICULUM	Observable Evidence +/–	COMMUNITY	Observable Evidence +/–
Strengths		**Strengths**	
Concerns		**Concerns**	
CLIMATE	Observable Evidence +/–	CHARACTER	Observable Evidence +/–
Strengths		**Strengths**	
Concerns		**Concerns**	

NOTE: A user-friendly printable version is available at www.mdedinc.com.

THE C of _____ (Write in C here)	
Strengths (+) and Concerns (−)	*Observable Evidence (+/−)*
Dimension 1: Community Engagement	
+ + − − −	+ + − − −
Dimension 2: Curriculum Expectations	
+ + − − −	+ + − − −
Dimension 3: Developmental Perspectives	
+ + − − −	+ + − − −
Dimension 4: Educational Attitudes	
+ + − − −	+ + − − −
Dimension 5: Faculty Fidelity	
+ + − − −	+ + − − −
Dimension 6: Leadership Potential	
+ + − − −	+ + − − −
Dimension 7: School Climate	
+ + − − −	+ + − − −

NOTE: A user-friendly printable version is available at www.mdedinc.com.

Teacher Evaluation: Middle and High School

	Strongly Disagree	Disagree	Undecided	Agree	Strongly Agree
Teacher Presentation	1	2	3	4	5
The teacher was prepared and organized for class.	O	O	O	O	O
The teacher clearly explained course expectations and requirements.	O	O	O	O	O
The teacher used class time wisely.	O	O	O	O	O
The teacher was knowledgeable about the subject he or she taught.	O	O	O	O	O
The teacher was supportive.	O	O	O	O	O
The teacher showed enthusiasm when teaching.	O	O	O	O	O
The teacher was clear and easy to understand.	O	O	O	O	O
I would highly recommend this teacher to another student.	O	O	O	O	O
Overall this teacher did a good job.	O	O	O	O	O
	Strongly Disagree	Disagree	Undecided	Agree	Strongly Agree
Teacher Communication	1	2	3	4	5
The teacher provided useful feedback on how students were doing on schoolwork.	O	O	O	O	O
The teacher was available to help before or after class.	O	O	O	O	O
The teacher was helpful and responsive to students.	O	O	O	O	O
The teacher was willing to listen to student questions and opinions.	O	O	O	O	O
The teacher was concerned about the students' wellbeing.	O	O	O	O	O

(Continued)

(Continued)

	Strongly Disagree	Disagree	Undecided	Agree	Strongly Agree
Student Effort	1	2	3	4	5
I studied and put a good amount of effort into the course.	O	O	O	O	O
I was challenged by this course.	O	O	O	O	O
I was prepared for each class.	O	O	O	O	O
This course actively involved me in what I was learning.	O	O	O	O	O
My knowledge increased in this course.	O	O	O	O	O
I made progress toward achieving course goals.	O	O	O	O	O
The teacher inspired me to learn in this class.	O	O	O	O	O
	Strongly Disagree	Disagree	Undecided	Agree	Strongly Agree
Grading Effectiveness	1	2	3	4	5
The exams covered important aspects of the course.	O	O	O	O	O
Exams and assignments were clear and graded fairly.	O	O	O	O	O
The instructor made helpful comments on assignments and exams.	O	O	O	O	O
Assignments helped students in understanding course material.	O	O	O	O	O
Students were given information on how they will be graded.	O	O	O	O	O
The teacher returned exams and assignments in a timely manner.	O	O	O	O	O
Overall this course was a good learning experience.	O	O	O	O	O

	Strongly Disagree	Disagree	Undecided	Agree	Strongly Agree
Classroom Climate	1	2	3	4	5
There is mutual respect between teachers and students in this classroom.	O	O	O	O	O
This classroom is a safe place to be.	O	O	O	O	O
This classroom is free from bullying and harassment.	O	O	O	O	O
In this classroom, there is respect for the property of others.	O	O	O	O	O
This classroom is orderly and free of disruptions.	O	O	O	O	O
In this classroom, guidelines for positive student behavior are clear.	O	O	O	O	O
In this classroom, students are expected to follow the rules.	O	O	O	O	O
This classroom is a safe and pleasant place to learn.	O	O	O	O	O

What grade are you in? 6th 7th 8th 9th 10th 11th 12th

What grade do you anticipate receiving in this course? A B C D F

What are three strengths of this teacher?

_____

_____

_____

What are three ways the teacher could improve?

_____

_____

_____

NOTE: A user-friendly printable version is available at www.mdedinc.com.

Elementary Teacher Evaluation available at www.mdedinc.com.

Multi-Dimensional Data Needs Assessment (DNA)

Directions: Take a few moments to complete this data needs assessment. This is just a quick check list for your consideration of where your organization might be in its data collection efforts.

Classroom Level Data Needs Assessment

Data Type	Data Available (check box)	Data Currently Being Used (check box)	Explain How the Data Is Being Used
Student Portfolios	☐	☐	
Student Attitude Surveys	☐	☐	
Grade Level Common Assessments	☐	☐	
Student Journals	☐	☐	
Student Motivation Surveys	☐	☐	
Common Grade Level Tests	☐	☐	
Common Grade Level Quizzes	☐	☐	
Student Satisfaction Surveys	☐	☐	
Student Safety or Environmental Surveys	☐	☐	

Questions on School Site Use of Data

Question	Yes or No	Explain
Did you participate in any training this year that involved how to better use data?		
Do you participate in Professional Learning Communities and/or grade level teams where data is discussed by the group?		
Do you set goals for your students?		
Do you set professional development goals for yourself?		
Do you use data for instructional lesson planning?		

NOTE: A user-friendly printable version is available at www.mdedinc.com.

Results Analysis: Please consider the following questions about your school data.

What appear to be our strengths?

1. _____

2. _____

3. _____

4. _____

5. _____

How do the three stakeholders differ on the dimensional scores?

1. _____

2. _____

3. _____

4. _____

5. _____

What appear to be our concerns?

1. _____

2. _____

3. _____

4. _____

5. _____

How are we presently addressing our concerns?

1. _____

2. _____

3. _____

How might we address our concerns in a schoolwide focus?

1. _____

2. _____

3. _____

4. _____

5. _____

NOTE: A user-friendly printable version is available at www.mdedinc.com.

Goals and Objectives

This Goal and Objectives template has been designed to help you clarify your goal under each of the 4Cs and determine the objectives that will be needed to meet the goal. Objectives should be stated clearly and should be measurable using a scale(s) within the dimensions. Also provided are the six areas that you will need to consider in your plan for meeting the objectives you have developed.

_____ (write in C here) Goal: By _____ of 20_____,

_____

_____

_____

Objective(s)	Strategies	Professional Development	Resources	Timeline	Tasks	Monitoring
1.						
2.						
3.						
4.						

NOTE: A user-friendly printable version is available at www.mdedinc.com.

Prioritizing Objectives for the Month

It is important to address the objectives under each of our goals. This does not mean that you will address all of the objectives immediately. You must prioritize the one(s) that you feel would be achievable and make a difference. Therefore, prioritize what you will do in the next month to meet these objectives.

1st Priority: _____

2nd Priority: _____

3rd Priority: _____

4th Priority: _____

5th Priority: _____

NOTE: A user-friendly printable version is available at www.mdedinc.com.

References

Anderson, B. D. (May, 1972). *A methodological note on contextual effects studies in education.* Paper presented to the Canadian Educational Research Association. (ERIC Document Reproduction Service No. ED069806)

Anderson, C. (1982). The search for school climate: A review of the research. *Review of Educational Research, 53*(3), 368–420.

Ang, R. P., & Hughes, J. N. (2001). Differential benefits of skills training with antisocial youth based on group composition: A meta-analytic investigation. *School Psychology Review, 31,* 164–185.

Baker, E. L., Barton, P. E., Darling-Hammond, L., Haertel, E., Ladd, H. F., Linn, R. L., et al. (2010). *Problems with the use of student test scores to evaluate teachers.* Washington, DC: Economic Policy Institute.

Barton, P. E., & Coley, R. J. (2007). *The family: America's smallest school.* Princeton, NJ: Educational Testing Service.

Battistich, V., Schaps, E., & Wilson, N. (2004). Effects of an elementary school intervention on students' "connectedness" to school and social adjustment during middle school. *Journal of Primary Prevention, 24* (3), 243–262.

Battistich, V., Solomon, D., Watson, M., & Schaps, E. (1997). Caring school communities. *Educational Psychologist, 32*(3), 137–151.

Berkowitz, M., Battistich, V., & Bier, M. (2008). What works in character education: What is known and what needs to be known. In L. Nucci & D. Narvaez (Eds.), *Handbook of moral and character education* (pp. 134–157). New York: Routledge.

Berliner, D., & Biddle, B. (1995). *The manufactured crisis: Myths, fraud, and the attack on America's Public Schools.* Cambridge, MA: Perseus Books.

Bernhardt, V. L. (2003). No schools left behind. *Educational Leadership, 60*(5), 26–30.

Billig, S. (2005). Impact of service learning on participating students. Retrieved from http://www.servicelearningpartnership.org/site/docserver/SL_Impacts_Fact_Sheet_March05.doc?docID=801.

Black, P., & William, D. (1998, October). Inside the black box: Raising standards through classroom assessment. *Phi Delta Kappan, 80*(2), 139–148.

Bloom, B. S. (1976). *Human characteristics and school learning.* New York: McGraw-Hill.

Bloom, B. S. (1980). The new direction in educational research: Alterable variables. *Phi Delta Kappan, 61,* 382–385.

Blum, R. (2005). *School connectedness: Improving the lives of students.* Baltimore: Johns Hopkins Press.

Boethel, M. (2003). *Diversity: School, family, & community connections.* Austin, TX: Southwest Educational Development Laboratory.

Borger, J. B., Lo, C.-L., Oh, S. S., & Walberg, H. J. (1985). Effective schools: A quantitative synthesis of constructs. *Journal of Classroom Interaction, 20*(2), 12–17.

Bridgeland, J. M., DiIulio, J., & Burke Morison, K. (2006). *The silent epidemic: Perspectives of high school dropouts.* Washington, DC: Civic Enterprises in association with the Peter D. Hart Research Associates. Retrieved from www.gatesfoundation.org/united-states/documents/TheSilentEpidemic 3–06FINAL.pdf.

Brookover, W. B., Beady, C., Flood, P., Schweitzer, J., & Wisenbaker, J. (1979). *School social systems and student achievement.* New York: Praeger.

Brookover, W. B., & Lezotte, L. W. (1979). *Changes in school characteristics coincident with changes in student achievement* (Occasional Paper No. 17). East Lansing: Michigan State University, East Lansing Institute for Research in Teaching. (ERIC Document Reproduction Service No. ED181005)

Bryk, A. S., & Driscoll, M. E. (1988). *The school as a community: Theoretical foundations, contextual influences, and consequences for students and teachers* (Report WP 88–11–05). Chicago: The University of Chicago Benton Center for Research in Curriculum and Instruction.

Bryk, A. S., Lee, V. E., & Holland, P. B. (1993). *Catholic schools and the common good.* Cambridge, MA: Harvard University Press.

Burstein, L. (1980). The analysis of multilevel data in educational research and evaluation. In D. C. Berliner (Ed.), *Review of research in education* (Vol. 8). Washington, DC: American Educational Research Association.

Burt, C. (1963). Is intelligence distributed normally? *The British Journal of Statistical Psychology, 16*(2), 129–135.

Celio, M. B., & Harvey, J. (2005). *Buried treasure: Developing an effective management guide from mountains of educational data.* Seattle, WA: Center on Reinventing Public Education.

Comer, J. P., & Haynes, N. M. (1991). Meeting the needs of black children in public schools: A school reform challenge. In C. V. Willie, A. M. Garibaldi, & W. L. Reed (Eds.), *The education of African-Americans* (pp. 67–71). New York: Auburn House.

Corrigan, M. W., & Chapman, P. E. (2008). Trust in teachers: A motivating element to learning. *Radical Pedagogy, 9*(2). Retrieved from http://radical pedagogy.icaap.org/content/issue9_2/Corrigan_Chapman.html.

Corrigan, M. W., Grove, D., Vincent, P. F., Chapman, P. E., & Walls, R. T. (2007). The importance of multi-dimensional baseline measurements to assessment of integrated character education models. *Journal of Research in Character Education, 5*(2), 103–129.

Csikszentmihalyi, M. (1990). *Flow: The psychology of optimal experience.* New York: Harper & Row.

Damon, W. (2005). Good? bad? or none of the above? The unavoidable mandate to teach character. Education Next, 4(2), 21–27. Retrieved from http://educationnext.org/goodbadornoneoftheabove/.

Darling-Hammond, L. (2000). Teacher quality and student achievement: A review of state policy evidence. *Educational Policy Analysis Archives, 8*(1), 123–140.

Deal, T., & Peterson, K. (1990). *The principal's role in shaping school culture.* Washington, DC: U. S. Department of Education.

deJung, J., & Duckworth, K. (1986). *High school teachers and their students' attendance: Final report.* Eugene: University of Oregon Center for Education Policy and Management, College of Education. (Eric Document Reproduction Service No. ED266557)

DeRoche, E. F. (2004). *Evaluating character development: 51 tools for measuring success.* Boone, NC: Character Development Group.

Driscoll, M. (2000). *Psychology of learning for instruction.* Needham Heights, MA: Allyn & Bacon.

Drucker, P. (1954). *The practice of management.* New York: Harper & Row.

Dusewicz, R. A., & Beyer, F. S. (1988). *Dimensions of excellence scales: Survey instruments for school improvement.* Philadelphia: Research for Better Schools.

Dyer, H. S. (1972). Some thoughts about future studies. In F. Mosteller & D. P. Moynihan (Eds.), *On equality of educational opportunity.* New York: Random House.

Edmonds, R. R. (1979). Effective schools for the urban poor. *Educational Leadership, 37*(2), 15–23.

Ellis, T. I. (1988). *School climate.* Alexandria, VA: National Association of Elementary School Principals. (Eric Document Reproduction Service No. ED291154)

Epstein, J. L. (1995). School/family/community partnerships: Caring for children we share. *Phi Delta Kappan, 76,* 701–712.

Erickson, E. H. (1950). *Childhood and society.* New York: W. W. Norton.

Fan, X., & Chen, M. (2001). Parental involvement and students' academic achievement: A meta-analysis. *Educational Psychology Review, 13,* 1–22.

Feiman-Nemser, S. (2001). From preparation to practice: Designing a continuum to strengthen and sustain teaching. *Teachers College Record 103*(6), 1013–1055.

Feirstein, B., (Writer), & Spottiswoode, R. (Director). (1997). *Tomorrow never dies* [Motion picture]. United States: Metro-Goldwyn-Meyer Studios.

Feldman, J., & Tung, R. (2001, April). *Whole school reform: How schools use the data-based inquiry and decision making process.* Paper presented at the meeting of the American Educational Research Association, Seattle, WA.

Finkelstein, N. D., & Grubb, W. N. (2000). Making sense of education and training markets: Lessons from England. *American Educational Research Journal, 37*(3), 601–631.

Fleming, C. B., Haggerty, K. P., Catalano, R. F., Harachi, T. W., Mazza, J. J., & Druman, D. H. (2005). Do social and behavioral characteristics targeted by preventive interventions predict standardized test scores and grades? *Journal of School Health, 75,* 342–349.

Fletcher, J. M., Coulter, A. W., Reschly, D. J., & Vaughn, S. (2004). Alternative approaches to the definition and identification of learning disabilities: Some questions and answers. *Annals of Dyslexia, 54*(2), 304–331.

Flynn, J. R. (1999). Searching for justice: The discovery of IQ gains over time. *American Psychologist, 54*, 5–20.

Freiberg, H. J. (Ed.). (1999). *School climate: Measuring, improving, and sustaining healthy learning environments.* Philadelphia, PA: Falmer Press.

Fullan, M. (1991). *The new meaning of educational change* (2nd ed.). New York: Teachers College Press.

Fullan, M. (2001). *Leading in a culture of change.* San Francisco: Jossey-Bass.

Fullan, M., & Stiegelbaures, S. (1991). *The measuring of educational change.* New York: Teachers College Press.

Fusarelli, L. (2004). The potential impact of the No Child Left Behind Act on equity and diversity in American education. *Educational Policy, 18*(1), 71–94.

Gandal, M., & Vranek, J. (2001). Standards: Here today, here tomorrow. *Educational Leadership, 59*(1), 6–13.

Garrard, W. M., & Lipsey, M. W. (2007). Conflict resolution education and antisocial behavior in U. S. schools: A meta-analysis. *Conflict Resolution Quarterly, 25*(1), 9–38.

Gay, L. R., & Airasian, P. W. (2003). *Educational research: Competencies for analysis and applications.* Upper Saddle River, NJ: Pearson.

George, P. (2001). Implementation of data-driven decision making among principals in Florida. *Educational Leadership, 59*(1), 28–32.

Glickman, C. (2002). The courage to lead. *Educational Leadership, 59*(8), 41–44.

Government of Ontario. (2005). Unique professional support for new teachers to help boost student performance. *Canadian Journal of Educational Administration and Policy, 60.*

Gregory, G., & Chapman, C. (2002). *Differentiated instructional strategies: One size doesn't fit all.* Thousand Oaks, CA: Corwin.

Guskey, T. R. (2000). *Evaluating professional development.* Thousand Oaks, CA: Corwin.

Harris, D. N., & Herington, C. D. (2006). Accountability, standards, and the growing achievement gap: Lessons from the past half-century. *American Journal of Education, 112*(2), 209–238.

Haynes, N. M., & Comer, J. P. (1993). The Yale school development program: Process, outcomes, and policy implications. *Urban Education, 28*(2), 166–199.

Heck, R., Larsen, T. J., & Marcoulides, G. A. (1990). Instructional leadership and school achievement: Validation of a causal model. *Educational Administration Quarterly, 26*, 94–125.

Helfand, D. (2005, November 11). ETS to continue state's testing. *Los Angeles Times.* Retrieved April 22, 2011, from http://articles.latimes.com/2005/nov/11/local/me-test11.

Henderson, A. T., & Mapp, K. L. (2002). *A new wave of evidence: The impact on school, family, and community connections on student achievement.* Austin, TX: Southwest Educational Development Laboratory.

Hipp, K. A., & Huffman, J. B. (2002). *Documenting and examining practices in creating learning communities: Exemplars and non-exemplars.* Paper presented at the meeting of the American Educational Research Association, New Orleans, LA. (ERIC Document Reproduction Services No. ED468685)

Holcomb, E. L. (2004). *Getting excited about data: Combining people, passion, and proof to maximize student achievement* (2nd ed.). Thousand Oaks, CA: Corwin.

Hollenback, J. R., & Klein, H. J. (1987). Goal commitment and the goal-setting process: Problems, prospects, and proposals for future research. *Journal of Applied Psychology, 72*(2), 212–220.

Horner, R. H., Crone, D. A., & Stiller, B. (2001). The role of school psychologists in establishing positive behavior support: Collaborating in systems change at the school-wide level. *Communiqué, 29*(6), 10–12.

Horner, R., Sugai, G., Smolkowski, K., Eber, L., Nakasato, J., Todd, A., et al. (2009). Wait-list controlled effectiveness trial assessing school-wide positive behavior support in elementary schools. *Journal of Positive Behavior Interventions, 11*, 133–144.

Horvat, E. M., Weininger, E. B., & Lareau, A. (2003). From social ties to social capital: Class differences in the relations between schools and parent networks. *American Educational Research Journal, 40*(2), 319–351.

Joyce, B., Weil, M., & Calhoun, E. (2003). *Models of teaching* (7th ed.). Englewood Cliffs, NJ: Prentice-Hall.

Joyce, B., Wolf, J., & Calhoun, E. (1993). *The self-renewing school.* Alexandria, VA: Association for Supervision and Curriculum Development.

Kagan, S. (2010). *Talk less, teach more.* Retrieved from http://www.kaganon line.com/free_articles/dr_spencer_kagan/ASK32.php.

Kasen, S. N., Johnson, P. N., & Cohen, P. N. (1990). The impact of social emotional climate on student psychopathology. *Journal of Abnormal Child Psychology, 18*(2), 165–177.

Kawasaki, G. (1991). *Selling the dream.* New York: HarperCollins.

Kelley, R. C., Thornton, B., & Daugherty, R. (2005). Relationships between measures of leadership and school climate. *Education, 126*(1), 17–25.

Kuperminc, G. P., Leadbeater, B. J., Emmons, C., & Blatt, S. J. (1997). Perceived school climate and difficulties in the social adjustment of middle school students. *Applied Developmental Science, 1*, 76–88.

Lee, V., Smith, J., Perry, T., & Smylie, M. (1999). *Social support, academic press and student achievement: A view from the middle grades in Chicago.* Chicago: Chicago Annenberg Research Project.

Lehr, C. A., Johnson, D. R., Bremer, C. D., Cosio, A., & Thompson, M. (2004). *Essential tools: Increasing rates of school completion.* Minneapolis, MN: National Center on Secondary Education and Transition. Retrieved from http://www.ecs.org/html/Document.asp?chouseid=6649.

Leming, J. (2008). Research and practice in moral and character education: Loosely coupled phenomena. In L. Nucci & D. Narvaez (Eds.), *Handbook of moral and character education* (pp. 134–157). New York: Routledge.

Levin, H. M. (1970). *A new model of school effectiveness: A report on recent research on pupil achievement.* Stanford, CA: Stanford University, Stanford Center for Research and Development on Teaching. (ERIC Document Reproduction Service No. ED040252)

Lickona, T., & Davidson, M. (2005). *Smart and good high schools: Integrating excellence and ethics for success in school, work, and beyond.* Cortland, NY: Center for the 4th and 5th R's and Character Education Partnership.

Maehr, M. (1990). *The "psychological environment" of the school: A focus for school leadership* (Project report). Champaign, IL: National Center for School Leadership.

Mandinach, E. B., Honey, M., Light, D. (2006). *A theoretical framework for data-driven decision making*. Paper presented at the Annual Meeting of the American Educational Research Association, San Francisco, CA.

Marsh, H. W., & Roche, L. A. (1997). Making students' evaluations of teaching effectiveness effective: The critical issues of validity, bias, and utility. *American Psychologist, 52*(11), 1187–1197.

Marsh, J. A., Pane, J. F., & Hamilton, L. S. (2006). *Making sense of data-driven decision making*. Retrieved November 22, 2009, from http://www.rand.org/pubs/occasional_papers/2006/RAND_OP170.pdf.

Marshall, J. (2006). Results from caring community™, The Character*Plus* Way. Retrieved from http://www.characterplus.org/files/CSC_CharPlus_4_Year_ResultsPDF.

Marzano, R. J. (2003a). *Classroom management that works: Research based strategies for every teacher*. Alexandria, VA: Association for Supervision and Curriculum Development.

Marzano, R. J. (2003b). Using data: Two wrongs and a right. *Educational Leadership, 60*(5), 56–60.

Marzano, R. J. (2003c). *What works in schools: Translating research into action*. Alexandria, VA: Association for Supervision and Curriculum Development.

Marzano, R. J., Zaffron, S., Zraik, L., Robbins, S. L., & Yoon, L. (1995). A new paradigm for educational change. *Education, 116*(2), 162–173.

Mason, S. (2002). *Turning data into knowledge: Lessons from six Milwaukee public schools*. Madison, WI. : Wisconsin Center for Education Research.

Mayer, B. (2000). *The dynamics of conflict resolution: A practitioner's guide*. San Francisco: Jossey-Bass.

McClellan, B. E. (1992). *Schools and the shaping of character: Moral education in America, 1607–present*. Bloomington, IN: Educational Resources Information Center.

McClellan, B. E. (1999). *Moral education in America: Schools and the shaping of character from Colonial times to the present*. New York: Teachers College Press.

McIntire, T. (2008). *The study of a parent involved reading intervention on 3rd grade students*. (Master's thesis: Vanguard University, 2008.)

McNeal, R. B., Jr. (1999). Parental involvement as social capital: Differential effectiveness on science achievement, truancy, and dropping out. *Social Forces, 78*(1), 117–144.

McNeely, C. A., Nonnemaker, J. M., & Blum, R. W. (2002). Promoting school connectedness to school: Evidence from the National Longitudinal Study of Adolescent Health. *Journal of School Health, 72*, 138–146.

Michelson, E., Zaff, J. F., & Hair, E. C. (2002). *Civic engagement programs and youth development: A synthesis*. Washington, DC: Child Trends. Retrieved from www.childtrends.org/Files//child-Trends-2002–05–01-FFR_CivicEngagement.

Mieles, T., & Foley, E. (2005). *From data to decisions: Lessons from school districts using data warehousing*. Providence, RI: Annenberg Institute for School Reform at Brown University.

Mitchell, C. (2008). *Parent involvement in public education: A literature review*. Philadelphia: Research for Action. Retrieved from http://www.maine.gov/education/speced/tools/b8pi/reports/review.pdf.

Mood, A. M. (1970, February). *Do teachers make a difference?* Paper presented at a conference sponsored by U. S. Office of Education, Bureau of Educational Professions Development. (ERIC Document Reproduction Service No. ED040253)

National Commission on Excellence in Education. (1983). *A Nation at risk: The imperative for educational reform.* Washington, DC: U.S. Government Printing Office.

National Commission on Teaching and America's Future (2008, April). *Learning teams: Creating what's next.* Washington, DC: Author.

National Education Association. (2010, March 3). *Independent survey results confirm NEA's position: Teachers voices must be heard in ed reform debate.* New York: Author. Retrieved from http://www.nea.org/home/38340.htm.

Newmann, R. M., & Wehlage, G. G. (1995). *Successful school restructuring: A report of the public and educators by the Center on Organization and Restructuring of Schools.* Madison, WI: Center on Organization and Restructuring Schools.

Nichols-Solomon, R. (2000, September). Conquering the fear of flying. *Phi Delta Kappan, 82*(1), 19–21.

Orfield, G. (Ed.). (2004). *Dropouts in America: Confronting the graduation rate crisis.* Cambridge, MA: Harvard Education Press.

Ormrod, J. E. (2006a). *Educational psychology: Developing learners* (5th ed.). Upper Saddle River, NJ: Prentice Hall.

Ormrod, J. E. (2006b). *Essentials of educational psychology.* Columbus, OH: Pearson.

Osterman, K. F. (2000). Students' need for belonging in the school community. *Review of Educational Research, 70*(3), 323–367.

Patrikakou, E. N., Weissberg, R. P., Redding, S., & Walberg, H. J. (2005). School-family partnerships: Enhancing the academic, social, and emotional learning of children. In E. N. Patrikakou, R. P. Weissberg, S. Redding, & H. J. Walberg (Eds.), *School-family partnerships for children's success* (pp. 1–17). New York: Teachers College Press.

Peters, T., & Waterman, R. (1982). *In search of excellence.* New York: Harper & Row.

Peterson, R. L., & Skiba, R. (2001). Creating school climates that prevent school violence. *The Clearing House, 74*(3), 155–163.

Popham, W. J. (1999). Why standardized tests don't measure educational quality. *Educational Leadership, 56*(6), 8–15.

Popham, W. J. (2001). *The truth about testing: An educator's call to action.* Alexandria, VA: Association for Supervision and Curriculum Development.

Posner, G. J. (2003). *Analyzing the curriculum* (3rd ed.). New York: McGraw-Hill.

Purkey, S., & Smith, M. (1983). Effective schools: A review. *Elementary School Journal, 83* (4), 427–452.

Reynolds, W. M., Ramirez, M. P., Magrina, A., & Allen, J. E. (1980). Initial development and validation of the academic self-concept scale. *Education and Psychological Measurement, 40*(4), 1013–1016.

Rogers, E., & Singhal, A. (1996). *Diffusion of innovations* (4th ed.). New York: Free Press.

Rosenholtz, S. J. (1991). *Teacher's workplace: The social organization of school.* New York: Teachers College Press.

Rowan, B., Chiang, F., & Miller, R. J. (1997). Using research on employees' performance to study the effects of teachers on students' achievement. *Sociology of Education, 7*(10), 256–284.

Rutter, M. (1983). School effects on pupil progress: Research findings and policy implications. *Child Development, 54*, 1–29.

Rutter, M., Maughan, B., Mortimore, P., & Ouston, J. (1979). *Fifteen thousand hours: Secondary schools and their effects on children.* Cambridge, MA: Harvard University Press.

Sailor, M., Stowe, M. J., Turnbull, R., III, & Kleinhammer-Tramill, P. J. (2008). A case for adding a social-behavioral standard to standards-based education with schoolwide positive behavior support as its basis. *Remedial and Special Education, 28*(6), 366–377.

Sanders, W. L., & Horn, S. P. (1998). Research findings from the Tennessee Value-Added Assessment System (TVAAS) database: Implications for educational evaluation and research. *Journal of Personnel Evaluation in Education, 12*(3), 247–256.

Sarason, S. B. (1990). *The predictable failure of educational reform: Can we change course before it's too late?* San Francisco: Jossey-Bass.

Savin, H. (February, 2000). Effective improvement systems. *Education and Treatment of Children, 23*(1), 48–59.

Schmoker, M. (1996). *Results: The key to continuous school improvement.* Alexandria, VA: Association for Supervision and Curriculum Development.

Schmoker, M. (2001). *The results fieldbook: Practical strategies from dramatically improved schools.* Alexandria, VA: Association for Supervision and Curriculum Development.

Science Daily (2008, May 28). Parental involvement strongly impacts student achievement. Retrieved from http://www.sciencedaily.com/releases/2008/05/080527123852.htm.

Seifert, T. L. (2004). Understanding student motivation. *Educational Research, 46*(2), 137–149.

Sheldon, S. B., & Epstein, J. L. (2005). Involvement counts: Family and community partnerships and mathematics achievement. *The Journal of Educational Research, 98*(4), 196–206.

Simonton, D. K. (2001). Talent development as a multidimensional, multiplicative, and dynamic process. *Current Directions in Psychological Science, 10,* 39–42.

Skinner, B. F. (1969). *Contingencies of reinforcement.* New York: Appleton-Century-Crofts.

Snider, J. (2010, February 10). Tying teacher tenure to student scores doesn't fly. *Education Week, 29*(21), 20–21.

Solomon, D., Battistich, V., Watson, M., Schaps, E., & Lewis, C. (2000). A six-district study of educational change: Direct and mediated effects of the child development project. *Social Psychology of Education, 4*(1), 3–51.

Spoth, R., Randall, G. K., & Shin, C. (2008). Increasing school success through partnership-based family competency training: Experimental study on long-term outcomes. *School Psychology Quarterly, 23*(1), 70–89.

Stewart, E. B. (2008). School structural characteristics, student effort, peer associations, and parental involvement: The influence of school and individual-level factors on academic achievement. *Education & Urban Society, 40*(2), 179–204.

Stiggins, R. (1994). *Student-centered classroom assessment.* New York: Merrill.

Stiggins, R. J. (2007). A*n introduction to student-involved assessment for learning* (5th ed.). Upper Saddle River, NJ: Prentice-Hall.

Stotsky, S., & Wurman, Z. (2010, July). *Common core standards still don't make the grade: Why Massachusetts and California must regain control over their academic destinies.* (Pioneer Institute White Paper No. 65).

Striefer, P. (2000). School improvement: Finding the time. *National Association of Secondary School Principals, 612*(84), 66–71.

Swanson, C. B. (2004). *Who graduates? Who doesn't? A statistical portrait of public high-school graduation.* Washington, DC: The Urban Institute.

Thomson, P., & Holdsworth, R. (2003). Theorizing change in the educational 'field': Re-readings of 'student participation' projects. *International Journal of Leadership In Education, 6*(4), 371–391.

Thorndike, E. L. (1927). *Measurement of intelligence.* New York: Teachers' College, Columbia University.

Togneri, W., & Anderson, S. (2003). *Beyond islands of excellence: What districts can do to improve instruction and achievement in all schools.* Alexandria, VA: Association for Supervision and Curriculum Development.

Tomlinson, C. A. (2003). Differentiating instruction for academic diversity. In J. M. Cooper (Ed.), *Classroom teaching skills* (7th ed., pp. 149–180). Boston: Houghton Mifflin.

Tonn, J. L. (2005, June 8). Keeping in touch. *Education Week, 24*(39), 30–33.

Tyler, R. (1949). *Basic principles of curriculum and instruction.* Chicago: University of Chicago Press.

Uguroglu, M. E., & Walberh, H. J. (1979). Motivation and achievement: A quantitative synthesis. *American Education Research Journal, 16*(4), 375–389.

Urban, H. (2009). *Lessons from the classroom: 20 things good teachers do.* San Francisco: Urban Publishing.

Vincent, P. F., Wangaard, D., & Weimer, P. (2004). *Restoring school civility: Creating a caring, responsible, and productive school.* Boone, NC: Character Development Group.

Waters. T., Marzano, R., & McNulty, B. (2004). Leadership that sparks learning. *Educational Leadership, 61*(1), 48–52.

Wayman, J. C. (2005). Involving teachers in data-driven decision-making: Using computer data systems to support teacher inquiry and reflection. *Journal for Education of Students At Risk, 10*(3).

Wayman, J. C., Stringfield, S., & Yakimowski, M. (2004). *Software enabling school improvement through analysis of student data.* Baltimore: Center for Research on the Education of Students Placed at Risk, Johns Hopkins University.

Webb, N. (2002, April). *Assessment literacy in a standards-based urban education setting.* Paper presented at the annual meeting of the American Educational Research Association, New Orleans, LA.

Welhage, G. G., Rutter, R. A., Smith, G. A., Lesko, N., & Fernandez, R. R. (1989). *Reducing the risk: Schools as communities of support.* New York: The Falmer Press.

Wellman, B., & Lipton, L. (2003). *Data-driven dialogues: A facilitator's guide to collaborative inquiry.* Sherman, CT: Mira Via.

Wentzel, K. (1997). Student motivation in middle schools: The role of perceived pedagogical caring. *Journal of Educational Psychology, 89*(3), 411–419.

Wertsch, J. V. (1985). *Vygotsky and the social formation of the mind.* Cambridge, MA: Harvard University Press.

Whitlock, J. L. (2006). Youth perceptions of life in school: Contextual correlates of school connectedness in adolescence. *Applied Developmental Science, 10*(1), 13–29.

Wolf, R. (1966). The measurement of environments. In A. Anastasi (Ed.), *Testing problems in perspective.* Washington, DC: American Council on Education.

Wynn, S., Carboni, L., & Patall, E. A. (2007). Beginning teachers' perceptions of mentoring, climate, and leadership: Promoting retention through a learning communities perspective. *Leadership and Policy in Schools, 6,* 209–229.

Wynne, E. (1972). *The politics of school accountability.* Richmond, CA: McCutchan.

Yazzie-Mintz, E. (2007). *Voices of students on engagement: A report on the 2006 High School Survey of Student Engagement.* Bloomington, IN: Center for Evaluation & Education Policy, Indiana University School of Education.

Index

Figures and tables are indicated by an f or a t after the page number.

CORWIN
A SAGE Company

The Corwin logo—a raven striding across an open book—represents the union of courage and learning. Corwin is committed to improving education for all learners by publishing books and other professional development resources for those serving the field of PreK–12 education. By providing practical, hands-on materials, Corwin continues to carry out the promise of its motto: **"Helping Educators Do Their Work Better."**